1986

World Population and U.S. Policy

THE AMERICAN ASSEMBLY was established by Dwight D. Eisenhower at Columbia University in 1950. Each year it holds at least two nonpartisan meetings which give rise to authoritative books that illuminate issues of United States policy.

An affiliate of Columbia, with offices at Barnard College, the Assembly is a national, educational institution incorporated in the state of New York.

The Assembly seeks to provide information, stimulate discussion, and evoke independent conclusions on matters of vital public interest.

CONTRIBUTORS

DAVID E. BELL, Clarence J. Gamble Professor of Population Sciences and International Health, School of Public Health, Harvard University

JOHN BONGAARTS, Senior Associate, Center for Policy Studies, The Population Council

ANSLEY J. COALE, William Church Osborn Professor of Public Affairs, Princeton University

PAUL DEMENY, Director, Center for Policy Studies, The Population Council

JANE MENKEN, Professor of Sociology and Public Affairs, Princeton University

SAMUEL H. PRESTON, Professor of Sociology, University of Pennsylvania

GEORGE B. SIMMONS, Professor of Population and Health Planning, School of Public Health, University of Michigan

MICHAEL S. TEITELBAUM, Program Officer, Alfred P. Sloan Foundation

THE AMERICAN ASSEMBLY
Columbia University

World Population and U.S. Policy

The Choices Ahead

JANE MENKEN
Editor

W·W·NORTON & COMPANY
New York *London*

Published simultaneously in Canada by Penguin Books Canada Ltd.,
2801 John Street, Markham, Ontario L3R 1B4
Printed in the United States of America.

The text of this book is composed in Baskerville.
Composition and manufacturing by The Haddon Craftsmen, Inc.

First Edition

Library of Congress Cataloging-in-Publication Data

World population and U. S. policy.

At head of title: The American Assembly, Columbia University.
Includes index.
1. Population assistance, American. 2. United
States—Population policy. I. Menken, Jane A.
II. American Assembly.
HB884.5.W67 1986 363.9 86-12803

ISBN 0-393-02419-9

ISBN 0-393-30399-3 (PBK.)

W. W. Norton & Company, Inc.
500 Fifth Avenue, New York, N. Y. 10110
W. W. Norton & Company Ltd.
37 Great Russell Street, London WC1B 3NU

1 2 3 4 5 6 7 8 9 0

Contents

Preface
WILLIAM H. SULLIVAN 3

Introduction and Overview
JANE MENKEN 6

1. The World Demographic Situation
PAUL DEMENY 27

2. Are the Economic Consequences of Population Growth a Sound Basis for Population Policy?
SAMUEL H. PRESTON 67

3. Population Trends and Economic Development
ANSLEY J. COALE 96

4. The Transition in Reproductive Behavior in the Third World
JOHN BONGAARTS 105

5. Intersections: Immigration and Demographic Change and Their Impact on the United States
MICHAEL S. TEITELBAUM 133

6. Family Planning Programs
GEORGE B. SIMMONS 175

7. Population Policy: Choices for the United States
DAVID E. BELL 207

Final Report of the Seventy-first American Assembly 229

INDEX 249

World Population and U.S. Policy

Preface

WILLIAM H. SULLIVAN

In 1963, The Twenty-third American Assembly, entitled *The Population Dilemma,* issued a report calling attention to the rapid growth of population in the underdeveloped world and concluding that, unchecked, such growth would adversely affect efforts to improve economic and social conditions in the developing countries, thereby vitiating American financial and technical assistance to such efforts. The report called for significant and systematic American support for family planning and other population control measures in the Third World.

This report was widely circulated among influential opinion leaders in the United States. The background volume that emanated from the same Assembly, also entitled *The Population Dilemma,* was translated into several languages and received wide distribution in the Third World. Regional American Assemblies on this subject were held in Asia, Africa, and Latin America. In short, the Twenty-third Assembly had a wide impact upon world opinion and contributed to the concern being

---

WILLIAM H. SULLIVAN is president of The American Assembly.

felt in this country that population growth could derail development in the Third World.

That concern soon crystallized into accepted policy. By the end of the decade of the sixties, official U.S. assistance to family planning became a consistent feature of American aid programs, and the government of the United States took the lead in preaching population control to foreign audiences. Although there was initial resistance to this message in the Third World, and especially in China, the relationship between population growth and development gradually came to be accepted. In the case of China, there was a sudden epiphany on the subject in the late seventies and the institution of the world's most vigorous family planning program.

In 1984, at the United Nations Conference on Population in Mexico City, the United States delegation surprisingly announced a change in United States policy. The essence of the change was contained in the phrase "population growth is, of itself, a neutral phenomenon." This phrase represented the point of view of a number of scholars and economists (sometimes referred to as "supply side demographers") who had taken public issue with projections of population problems that they regarded as alarmist. Although the U.S. delegation in Mexico stipulated that it was still official U.S. policy to help achieve a "condition of population equilibrium," it recommended a different choice of "strategies and methods for achievement of that goal." The new choice centered on economic reforms that stress a market economy to "put a society on the road toward growth and, as an after-effect, toward slower population increase as well."

This new U.S. policy caused a major contretemps among those in this country who have been active supporters of the traditional U.S. governmental approach to international population controls. The National Academy of Sciences convened a meeting on the issue and great polemics ensued in population publications. It seemed an issue on which it was desirable to seek a national consensus about policy.

To that end The American Assembly undertook a program that began with a meeting at Arden House, in Harriman, New

York, from April 17–20, 1986. This meeting, The Seventy-first American Assembly, brought together distinguished Americans from various sectors of our society. They discussed an agenda prepared by Dr. Jane Menken of Princeton University, who acted as director of the Assembly. In preparation for their discussions, they read background papers prepared under Dr. Menken's editorial direction. At the close of their deliberations, they issued a report, which is included as an appendix to this book.

The background papers used by the participants have been compiled into the present volume, which is published as a stimulus to better informed views on this contentious issue. They attempt to determine where the facts lead in the dispute about the relationship of population growth to economic development.

Funding for this project was provided by The Ford Foundation, The Rockefeller Foundation, The Andrew W. Mellon Foundation, The William and Flora Hewlett Foundation, and The Laurel Foundation. We are grateful for their support. The opinions expressed in this volume are those of the individual authors and not necessarily those of the sponsors nor of The American Assembly, which does not take stands on the issues it presents for public discussion.

Introduction and Overview

JANE MENKEN

In 1950, about a decade before the Twenty-third American Assembly, the subject of which was "The Population Dilemma," approximately 1.7 billion people lived in the countries of the developing world. The annual growth rate in this region was over 2 percent per year for the period 1950 to 1955, as a result of a birthrate of 44.4 and a death rate of 24.2 per 1000 population. Women could expect to bear 6.2 children on average if they survived to the end of their reproductive years; under the mortality conditions of these years, a newborn could expect to live 41.1 years.

How had the situation changed by 1985, shortly before the Seventy-first American Assembly on the topic of United States

---

JANE MENKEN is professor of sociology and public affairs, and assistant director of the Office of Population Research at Princeton University. Dr. Menken's research interests and publications have included fertility and contraception and have focused on developed and less developed countries. She has been active in consulting and in the leadership of professional organizations, particularly the Population Association of America and the American Public Health Association.

international population policy? During the intervening twenty-five years, according to United Nations figures, the population of the developing world had more than doubled, growing by about 2 billion, to 3.7 billion. The annual growth rate for the period 1980–85 was still about 2 percent, although both the birth and death rates had fallen, to 31 births and 10.8 deaths per 1000 persons. Under the fertility and mortality conditions of this period, women could expect to bear 4.1 children on average, and a newborn could expect to live 57.3 years, with much of the extension of average lifetime coming from improved survival of infants and young children.

The only important similarity in the figures is in the growth rate; birthrates have fallen by about 28 percent and death rates by 55 percent, but the growth rate remains at nearly the same level. In fact, during the late 1960s the growth rate in the developing world rose as mortality declined more rapidly than fertility, so that the annual rate for the 1965–70 period was over 2.5 percent. It subsequently declined to the current level.

During the 1960s and 1970s there were many assessments of the world population situation. Some were made by alarmists who wrote of the "population explosion" or even "the population bomb" and credited population growth with responsibility for many, if not all, of the afflictions of the developing world. Others, taking a more judicious view, still concluded that rapid growth had consequences detrimental to prospects for improving conditions in much of the world. These consequences were thought sufficiently unfavorable to warrant efforts aimed at reducing fertility, and thereby slowing population increase. Indeed this has been the primary rationale for the programs that have been and are sponsored by the United States government. Voluntary family planning programs that provide services valued in and of themselves for helping people to have the number of children they want and improving the health of mothers and children are the major component of U.S. population assistance.

In 1974 in Bucharest, the United Nations sponsored an International Conference on Population. The United States urged countries to adopt policies aimed at slowing growth, primarily through family planning. The strong position taken by the United States and other Western countries in favor of antinatalist policies was attacked by many countries of the political left in the Third World, especially—although not exclusively—socialist and Marxist states. The opposition came from Algeria, India, Argentina, and even China, among others. They argued that economic development would lead "naturally" to fertility declines and that what was really needed were transfers of capital and technology. The United States subsequently maintained and actually increased its backing of family planning programs as part of development assistance. Its policy in population matters remained relatively static for many years, so much so that Paul Demeny described it in 1984 as "a field lately characterized by more than a fair share of intellectual complacency and inertia."

But the debate on population has now been reopened. U.S. support for international family planning assistance has come under concerted attack from elements of the political right, from those who are opposed to what they view as inappropriate governmental interference, and from the antiabortion movement. The intellectual support for these challenges to established U.S. policy came from writers such as Herman Kahn, Julian Simon, and Ben Wattenberg, who, while not opposed to the principle that individuals should be able to control the number of children they have if they so choose, contest the view that rapid growth had deleterious effects. One argument is that population growth is a significant and effective long-term stimulus to economic development, exerting its influence by, among other ways, increasing the tempo of innovation. It is not surprising that the population question is being reevaluated today, whether in justified reaction to the exaggerated claims of some supporters of population control, or in reaction to the challenges posed, or simply because no policy should remain in effect without periodic reexamination.

United States Population Policy

In the summer of 1984, the United Nations again sponsored an International Conference on Population, this time in Mexico City. The statement prepared for the conference by the White House Office of Policy Development represented a major shift in the official American position on the importance of world population trends and on appropriate actions the United States might take. It therefore opened the way to consideration of the questions to which this volume is addressed. Is the problem of rapid population growth as serious as has been claimed? Are the effects of continuing high fertility detrimental enough to warrant continuation of the U.S. policy of giving population control significant emphasis in its assistance plans? Or is the main concern development itself, with population only a minor side issue? What policy choices does the United States have and what directions should U.S. international population policy take?

Because the introduction of the 1984 policy statement, according to *Population and Development Review,* "marks the most notable conceptual and philosophical departure from previous U.S. population policy statements," it is here quoted nearly in full.

> For many years, the United States has supported, and helped to finance, programs of family planning, particularly in developing countries. This Administration has continued that support but has placed it within a policy context different from that of the past. It is sufficiently evident that the current exponential growth in global population cannot continue indefinitely. There is no question of the ultimate need to achieve a condition of population equilibrium. The differences that do exist concern the choice of strategies and methods for the achievement of that goal. The experience of the last two decades not only makes possible but requires a sharper focus for our population policy. It requires a more refined approach to problems which appear today in quite a different light than they did twenty years ago.
>
> First and most important, population growth is, of itself, a neutral phenomenon. It is not necessarily good or ill. It becomes an asset or a problem only in conjunction with other factors, such as economic policy, social constraints, need for manpower, and so forth. The relationship between population growth and economic development is not necessarily a negative one. More people do not necessarily mean less growth. Indeed, in the economic history of many nations, population growth has been an essential element in economic progress. . . .

Among the developing nations . . . population increase [after the Second World War] was caused by . . . tremendous expansion of health service—from simple inoculations to sophisticated surgery—[which] saved millions of lives every year. Emergency relief, facilitated by modern transport, helped millions to survive flood, famine, and drought. The sharing of technology, the teaching of agriculture and engineering, and improvements in educational standards generally, all helped to reduce mortality rates, especially infant mortality, and to lengthen life spans.

This demonstrated not poor planning or bad policy but human progress in a new era of international assistance, technological advance, and human compassion. The population boom was a challenge; it need not have been a crisis. Seen in its broader context, it required a measured, modulated response. It provoked an overreaction by some, largely because it coincided with two negative factors which, together, hindered families and nations in adapting to their changing circumstances.

The first of these factors was governmental control of economies, a development which effectively constrained economic growth. The post-war experience consistently demonstrated that, as economic decision-making was concentrated in the hands of planners and public officials, the ability of average men and women to work towards a better future was impaired, and sometimes crippled. In many cases, agriculture was devastated by government price fixing that wiped out rewards for labor. Job creation in infant industries was hampered by confiscatory taxes. Personal industry and thrift were penalized, while dependence upon the state was encouraged. Political considerations made it difficult for an economy to adjust to changes in supply and demand or to disruptions in world trade and finance. Under such circumstances, population growth changed from an asset in the development of economic potential to a peril.

One of the consequences of this "economic statism" was that it disrupted the natural mechanism for slowing population growth in problem areas. The world's more affluent nations have reached a population equilibrium without compulsion and, in most cases, even before it was government policy to achieve it. The controlling factor in these cases has been the adjustment, by individual families, of reproductive behavior to economic opportunity and aspiration. Historically, as opportunities and the standard of living rise, the birth rate falls. In many countries, economic freedom has led to economically rational behavior.

The pattern might be well under way in many nations where population growth is today a problem, if counterproductive government policies had not disrupted economic incentives, rewards, and advancement. In this regard, localized crises of population growth are, in part, evidence of too much government control and planning, rather than too little.

The second factor that turned the population boom into a crisis was confined to the western world. It was an outbreak of anti-intellectualism, which attacked science, technology, and the very concept of material progress. Joined to a commendable concern for the environment, it was more a reflection of anxiety about unsettled times and an uncertain future. In its disregard of human experience and scientific sophistication, it was not unlike other waves of cultural anxiety that have swept through western civilization during times of social stress and scientific exploration.

The combination of these two factors—counterproductive economic policies in poor and struggling nations, and a pessimism among the more advanced—led to a demographic overreaction in the 1960s and 1970s. Scientific forecasts were required to compete with unsound, extremist scenarios, and too many governments pursued population control measures without sound economic policies that create the rise in living standards historically associated with decline in fertility rates. This approach has not worked, primarily because it has focused on a symptom and neglected the underlying ailments. For the last three years, this Administration has sought to reverse that approach. We recognize that, in some cases, immediate population pressures may require short-term efforts to ameliorate them. But population control programs alone cannot substitute for the economic reforms that put a society on the road toward growth and, as an after-effect, toward slower population increase as well.

Nor can population control substitute for the rapid and responsible development of natural resources. . . .

This statement emphasizes in two ways the primary importance of development in solving population problems: it gives reduced significance to any effects of population increase on economic growth and credits economic development with generating behavioral responses leading to a voluntary lowering of fertility. The Bucharest conference sponsored by the United Nations led to the slogan "development is the best contraceptive"; the thesis of the U.S. statement before the

Mexico conference seems to be that an economic system based on the free market serves this purpose. It is interesting to note that there has been a convergence of the political left in developing countries and the right in the United States: both place emphasis on the economic system, but with preferences for different systems.

The remaining sections of the document state that the primary objective of U.S. policy will be "to encourage developing countries to adopt sound economic policies and, where appropriate, population policies consistent with respect for human dignity and family values," that "slowing population growth is not a panacea for the problems of social and economic development. . . . Population assistance is an ingredient of a comprehensive program that focuses on the root causes of development failures . . . economic development and population policies are mutually reinforcing. . . ." It continues, "The United States will *continue* its long-standing commitment to development assistance, of which population programs are a part." The statement goes on to recognize the health benefits to the mother and, especially, to babies of spacing children so that there are longer intervals between births, and to restate the basic objective of all U.S. assistance: "betterment of the human condition." It notes that "population assistance amounts to about ten percent of total development assistance." Part of this assistance is intended to help "ensure that a wide range of modern demographic technology is made available to developing countries" to help provide the kinds of demographic data that contribute to better planning within these countries.

This statement also breaks from the past in its very strong stance against abortion. Since 1974 no U.S. funds have been used to pay for abortion as a method of family planning. Under the new policy, no U.S. population assistance will go to nongovernmental organizations which "perform or actively promote abortion as a method of family planning" (regardless of the fact that no U.S. funds are used for that activity), or to nations that support abortion unless they set up "segregated accounts which cannot be used for abortion," or to the United Nations Fund for Population Activities unless it can offer "concrete assurance" that no U.S. funds will be used for abortion and that the fund supports neither abortion nor coercive family planning programs.

Examination of the many previous policy statements from any of at least the four previous administrations illustrates the sharpness of the change with respect to the relationship between development and population growth resulting from high fertility. For example:

> As improvements are made in nutrition, sanitation, and health care in developing countries, mortality rates have declined. But birth rates have remained high, creating or aggravating problems of development. It would be difficult to exaggerate the magnitude of this problem. . . . High birth rates threaten equitable development. Four major reasons for this are:
>
> - high birth rates reduce the per capita availability of scarce resources;
> - they contribute to worsening income distribution;
> - they damage maternal and child health;
> - they reduce the opportunities of women for full participation in the economic activities of their societies.
>
> Despite some recent declines in birth rates in the developing countries, hard-won gains in real GNP of about 5 percent annually during the past decade have been seriously eroded by annual population growth of 2½–3 percent. In much of Africa, where population growth averages close to 3 percent and is still rising, per capita food supplies are actually falling. . . .
>
> The resources necessary for food production and human shelter are limited in the world today. . . .
>
> Birth rates are higher among the poor and uneducated. This not only causes an immediate worsening of income distribution, but also through reduced savings, makes the long-term redistribution of wealth more difficult.
>
> The health of both mothers and children is jeopardized through the effects of early childbearing, close birth-spacing, and septic abortion. . . . Delaying the onset of childbearing and promoting child-spacing through safe, effective, and acceptable family planning methods can do much to improve maternal and child health. . . .
>
> High birth rates impact adversely on women's economic participation: it is difficult for women who are constantly pregnant to avail themselves of broader opportunities in education and employment. . . . Only as women's opportunities improve, particularly in education

and employment, and women see viable and socially acceptable alternatives to large families will they demand better family planning services. . . .

The preceding is taken from the 1980 Annual Report of the Chairman of the Development Coordination Committee, International Development Cooperation Agency. The following are excerpts from the conclusion of a U.S. Agency for International Development (USAID) Policy Paper on Population Assistance issued in September 1982, well into the second year of the Reagan administration.

Population Assistance will continue to be an essential element of U.S. development assistance. The content and direction of the U.S. program is guided by a number of factors:

—the commitment to helping LDCs [less developed countries] achieve self-sustaining economic growth;

—the belief that individuals and couples should be able to decide freely the size of their families;

—the conviction that sustained economic development and the achievement of a decent life for all LDC citizens can only occur when population growth no longer outpaces economic progress; . . .

—the belief that it is in line with U.S. strategic as well as humanitarian interests to help LDC governments achieve national economic goals. . . .

Finally, A.I.D. will stress in its programming the integration of family planning services with health and other development activities.

These statements are based on the strong belief that population growth and, in particular, high birthrates are not neutral with respect to economic development and that family planning programs can hasten the decline in fertility that has traditionally accompanied or followed improvement in social and economic conditions.

The Evidence on the Consequences of Population Growth

The Coale-Hoover Study

Much of the early scientific rationale for concluding that rapid growth is detrimental to economic development derived from the influential study, published in 1958, by Ansley Coale and Edgar Hoover of the implications of continuing high fertility in comparison to reducing fertility on the growth of per capita income. As Coale said in a 1983 review, their

> emphasis was a deliberate escape from the debate then current, and still continuing, between pessimists who saw inevitable disaster from high population growth in poor countries and optimists who saw the sources of poverty elsewhere and denied any important adverse effects of population growth. [Their] intention was to avoid black-or-white assumptions about disaster on the one hand or the absence of difficulties on the other, and to ask how much difference lower fertility would make.

The study was based on a model of the economy that made assumptions about rates of savings, the productivity of capital, and governmental policies concerning allocation of resources to industry and agriculture, education, and housing. They estimated the growth in national product and in per capita income under one assumption about mortality (that it continued to decline) and two about fertility (that it remained constant and that it fell continuously over twenty-five years to a level 50 percent lower than it had been at the start). Their findings: "After 30 years, the population with lower fertility would be only 76 percent as large as the sustained-fertility population; the per capita income with reduced fertility would be nearly 50 percent greater." In 1958 they projected the course of the population and economy of India on this basis; some twenty-five years later, the observed values were in startling agreement with their projections under the assumption that fertility did not change.

Although much of the research since then has tended to focus far more on the *causes* of population change, the consequences of rapid growth have been the subject of a number of studies. In the early 1970s, results of elaborate models that predicted the effects of rising numbers of people (exemplified by the book *Limits to Growth*) captured the public imagination. They indicated that continued population growth was at best alarming, and more likely would have fearsome consequences for the world. The World Bank devoted its *World Development*

Report, 1984 to population. The U.S. National Academy of Sciences (NAS) undertook two studies of the effects of rapid population growth; the first was released in 1971 and the second in early 1986. It seems appropriate to review the National Academy of Sciences findings briefly as background to any discussion of U.S. international policy.

Rapid Population Growth

The 1971 NAS report considered the effect of increasing population on many areas of life.

Resources. Perhaps the overriding fear expressed in the discussions of population growth in the 1960s and early 1970s was that the resource base, food included, would be outstripped by rapid increases in the numbers of people it had to support. This concern was not new; its intellectual base can be traced to the nineteenth century population debate stimulated by the Reverend Thomas Malthus. The 1971 NAS report was relatively optimistic on the issue of resources. It called food "the crisis that has not materialized" and concluded that technological progress offered promise of assuring the availability of resources at least to the end of the twentieth century and probably beyond, so long as efficient management could be achieved, but with exceptions. The committee responsible for the report believed there were regions of the world where food production was not keeping pace with population growth.

Economic Development. The effects of rapid growth seemed certain, in the committee's opinion, to "increase the number of landless, subsistence, or disadvantaged" and to raise "administrative burdens and social costs of absorbing urban arrivals." They concluded, however, that

> unprecedented and still accelerating population growth has not prevented very rapid economic advance. Population growth, though not a negligible block to development and modernization, has also not been an overriding factor. . . . It appears clear that rapid population growth in the less developed countries has been a decided obstacle

rather than an aid to economic growth and that the more rapid the rise in numbers, the greater the deterrent effects.

The influence of the Coale-Hoover study can be seen in their conclusions about improvements in income.

If the less developed regions could raise their current per capita income growth rates by one third, it would reduce their per capita income doubling time from somewhat over 25 years to 18 years. Under current circumstances this could be accomplished entirely through a fall of the average birth rate in the less developed regions from their roughly 40 per 1,000 level to 30 per 1,000, a 25 percent shift, which, in addition to its income effects, could have perhaps equally larger family-welfare effects not captured by conventional income measures.

In their judgment, adverse effects of rapid population growth were more likely to arise not because of its effects on the so-called factor inputs (land, labor, capital) but from the impact of growth on the "residual" processes that affect economic development, for example, "through significantly reduced opportunities for raising levels of education, health, and other human resource–developing programs."

To summarize, rapid population growth has neither prevented overall economic growth nor brought about widespread famine. However, rapid population growth has resulted in a slow growth of per capita incomes, per capita food production, and standards of living, while national economic growth rates are rapidly rising. Moreover, with current population growth rates, the present optimism about food production need not apply far into the future. An immediate and continuous decline in fertility would soon increase the welfare of individuals and households in all economies, and after 15 to 20 years could result in very substantial—and cumulatively rising—overall economic gains, particularly in the developing countries.

Political Consequences. The NAS committee also addressed directly other consequences feared by the population pessimists, saying that

high population density and rapid growth are blamed for many disturbing features of a changing world: urban violence, political instability, poverty, pollution, aggressive behavior, revolution, and hypernationalism. Nevertheless, empirical attempts to relate population growth to these political pathologies have been uniformly unsuccessful. There is no evidence that population growth decreases the level of political stability or increases the probability of conflict and violence and aggressive behavior.

But this conclusion followed from lack of evidence, either positive or negative. No studies existed that could provide the basis for solid conclusions.

In other ways, too, this report reflects the NAS experts' assessment of the inadequacy of the knowledge base in relevant areas. They were concerned that "although larger populations can have more effective governments, because per capita costs are reduced, the strains produced by trying to handle larger numbers with increasing demands for public services have high potential for problems" and that unbalanced numbers could also be conducive to conflict among ethnic groups in some parts of the world. They worried that a changing age structure tilted toward the very young could lead to unrest and change in respect for elderly. The potential for political debate and conflict over family planning also troubled them. Some of their other concerns, about which they could reach no definitive conclusions, were consequences for the family, the effects of rapid urbanization and substantial migration, and the difficulty of absorbing people into the labor force and the consequent underemployment or unemployment. When they considered education, they concluded that the effect of population growth would depend on how willing governments were to devote resources to education and, in turn, on the demand for education.

Abortion. This committee, in its report, faced squarely the problem of abortion. They acknowledged that when a population is growing rapidly, there may be a large number of unwanted pregnancies and frequent resort to induced abortion, particularly when the desirability and feasibility of limiting family size becomes recognized. Under these circumstances, the rate of abortion can rise markedly, bringing serious ethical, moral, and political questions to the fore. Most immediately, health planners are faced with the medical problems resulting from illegal abortions. "The need for abortion should be minimized by providing women who wish to avoid pregnancy with easy access to contraceptive materials and information," but "complete elimination of abortion is probably a distant and unobtainable goal." Encouragingly, "experience in some countries shows that the goal of decreasing induced abortion by the use of other family planning methods is feasible when accompanied by intensive education and information programs."

Recommendations. "Population growth is only one of several variables that affect the quality of life. . . . thus it would be a gross oversimplification to blame numbers of people alone for the set of problems confronting modern society." They recommended a series of policies related to inducing fertility change, including that all people have the freedom to determine family size and that there be national population-influencing policies to serve national objectives of economic development, public health and welfare, and environmental conservatism. They stressed the need for research on the diverse aspect of population change for which knowledge was (and in many cases, remains) inadequate.

The 1986 Study of the Economic Consequences of Rapid Population Growth

Some fifteen years later, early in 1986, the National Academy of Sciences released a report entitled *Population Growth and Economic Development: Policy Questions,* which was prepared by a panel of experts, almost exclusively economists. Their study took as its framework a series of nine questions about the effect of slower population growth, achieved by the reduction of fertility through a national family planning program, on various aspects of economic prosperity and development.

Resources and the Environment. Many of the early fears that population growth would lead to exhaustion of nonrenewable resources did not take into account the impetus that scarcity would have for development of adaptive strategies involving alternative resources. Slower growth "may delay the time to depletion of a particular resource, but it does not change the number of people who have access to that resource, but only their distribution over time."

The number of people alive at any one time can, however, affect the amount of a *renewable* resource, such as arable land, that is available to each person. For some resources, reduced availability lowers individual productivity (and therefore individual income). In Bangladesh, there is impressive evidence that agricultural productivity dropped as population grew rapidly in this most densely settled rural nation. Although in many cases improved technology (use of fertilizers, for example) or institutional change (such as the introduction of property rights) can counter the effects of population size, slower population growth would ease the problem, at least in the short term. Over the longer term, population growth could provide the stimulus for innovation. There are, however, dangers in relying on innovation: the resource in question could be completely depleted before adaptation could occur, and, even if existing institutions could be "fixed," the process could be difficult and costly, with the need to bear this cost itself a consequence of population growth.

The effect of population growth on the environment again depends on whether societies are willing or able to control environmental degradation. Species loss is one problem clearly related to population growth and extension of settled areas for which the likelihood of solutions or reduction in the near future seems slim; in most countries higher priority is being given to other issues. Slower population growth might allow time for protective policies to be developed.

Capital Supply, Productivity, and Per Capita Income. Coale and Hoover believed that higher ratios of capital to labor would lead to higher per capita output and, therefore, higher per capita income. Lower population growth would, under their formulation, increase the supply of capital by encouraging savings. The NAS study finds that the increase in the ratio of capital to labor would indeed be greater in a population that was growing more slowly, as contrasted with a rapidly growing one. Research in the years between 1958 and 1986 has shown, however, that the effect of capital supply on per capita income is smaller than economists had believed earlier, although still positive. The recent conclusion is that slower population growth does have a "capital deepening" effect, but the influence on per capita income is not decisive.

Innovation. One argument advanced in favor of population growth is that increases would stimulate development of new ideas and technologies. But does slower growth hamper innovation, thereby leading to lower per capita income? This was the question the NAS group posed. Its conclusion was that there were economies of scale in manufacturing, so that cities were more productive, but only up to a moderate level of city size. Since much of the developing world depends on imported technology, size or density within the country itself would have little effect on innovation. There is some evidence, however, that agricultural advances may be stimulated by increasing population density in sparsely settled regions, such as in parts of Africa, but technical progress is likely to be outweighed by reductions in productivity, particularly in densely populated areas (Bangladesh being the most commonly offered example). In sum, there is little evidence that slower growth would hamper innovation.

Human Capital. Improving education and health is part of every country's development plan. Children in large families tend to have lower education and poorer health than their peers who have fewer siblings. But this association does not mean that higher fertility necessarily *causes* poorer health and less schooling. Rather, it is possible, according to the report, that families may make a trade-off, choosing more children and therefore having less money to spend on each child. But where couples had previously not exercised deliberate reproductive choice, family planning programs that enable parents to reduce the number of unwanted children are likely to increase both level of education and the health of the children.

When considering national growth rates in relation to increases in school enrollment and levels of school expenditures, the NAS experts found that enrollment was unrelated to growth, but that faster growing populations tended to spend less per child on education. Whether education is now considered such an important goal that countries are willing to devote large portions of their national budgets to providing schooling, or whether there is simply no relationship is not known. There seems to be little relationship between population growth and government health expenditures in the few studies available for developing countries. Health programs usually are dominated by services provided in urban areas and are predominantly curative. Population growth in many countries was not thought to be a major impediment to health programs because they are structured in this way.

Income Inequality and Employment Issues. Historical studies have shown that, in the past, when populations grew more slowly, wages tended to rise, so that the incomes of workers would be higher relative to those of owners of capital than they would be if there were rapid growth. The same type of effect can follow from contemporary family planning programs. If they help poorer people to reduce their fertility, then the supply of labor will be lower and wages will rise more rapidly than otherwise, thus reducing income inequality.

The effect may be especially pronounced for women.

> In most countries, women bear most of the time, health, and energy burdens of bearing and raising children. When this burden is increased by unwanted children, there is probably a greater welfare loss for women than for men. Programs to improve contraception are thus likely to raise the welfare of women relative to men; in most societies, such a change would produce a reduction in sexual inequality.

When considering issues of employment, the NAS group distinguished between the effects of *urbanization* and the effects of national population growth. Urbanization, when caused by migration from rural areas to the cities, can be beneficial in that it gives more people access to the benefits of the modern sector of the economy, including the prospect of high wage employment, and better education and health facilities. But when urbanization is very rapid, these facilities may not grow quickly enough. The conclusion of this report is that the distribution of services, with enormous favoritism shown toward the urban areas, is at least a partial cause of the problem. "A first step toward slowing excessive urban growth would involve reducing the public sector's disproportionate subsidies for urban residents and urban-based economic activities."

There is little evidence of excessive unemployment even in rapidly growing countries. But issues related to employment are quite different in developing countries than in the United States. In the absence of welfare benefits, as one member of the NAS panel commented, "the poor cannot afford to be unemployed." The effects of rapid growth may be expected in income and underemployment, rather than no employment at all.

Do the Childbearing Decisions of One Couple Affect Society? Does having an additional child have a negative effect on the public welfare? The NAS committee discusses the possibilities in some detail and concludes that the consequences of individual childbearing decisions do provide a basis for policies directed toward family planning. This topic is taken up in much greater detail by Samuel Preston in his chapter in this volume.

In sum, both of the National Academy of Sciences reports take a much more balanced view of the role of population growth in impeding or promoting economic development than the impassioned messages offered over the last twenty years by some scientists, popular writers, and politicians on both extremes of the debate. Slowing population growth alone cannot make a poor country rich. I am reminded of a comment Etienne van de Walle made after President Lyndon Johnson remarked, in one of his speeches, that spending one dollar on reducing fertility in a population with a high birthrate was better than spending twenty dollars on general development. Professor van de Walle felt the evidence could be reformulated more accurately. He asserted instead that the twenty dollars earmarked for development would be more effective if *one* were spent on a population program.

The new studies undertaken by the National Academy of Sciences were directed explicitly to the economic consequences of population growth. They can add little to our thinking about some of the questions raised earlier concerning other societal effects of rapid versus slower increase in numbers. But there is no doubt that the population debate has again been reopened. There is also little doubt that U.S. policy in the past was influenced by voices that today are considered extremist, and were so viewed by much of the scholarly world at the time. But the questions facing the United States today must be addressed in light of current knowledge. Should U.S. policy change? If so, to what extent? And how do we avoid overreacting to the extremist positions of today? Should the policy focus on economic development programs alone? Do the benefits of family planning programs go beyond their effects on the individuals directly involved in the programs? Is that question irrelevant? Are family planning programs justifiable on humanitarian assistance grounds alone?

The Current Population Debate

In the context of this reevaluation of U.S. international population policy, it seems appropriate to take stock once again of the world population situation and consider what we know about the consequences of the rapid growth that results from high fertility and what we know about how fertility changes. It is also essential to look at the other important way in which the United States makes decisions that affect the demography of populations of other countries—immigration policy—and consider the policy options open to the United States.

Paul Demeny, in his chapter on the world demographic situation, reviews population history, emphasizing the recent past in which growth, measured both as rates and as absolute numbers, achieved levels unknown in the past, and then projects long-term prospects for the future at the global level. Since consideration of overall trends masks considerable diversity among the regions and nations of the world, he evaluates the components of population growth, fertility and mortality, for eight major regions as well as the more and less developed country groupings. The results are unambiguous: if we believe rapid growth is detrimental, the figures offer no room for complacency. The United Nations projections, labeled "high," "medium," and "low," for the year 2025, a mere forty-five years in the future from the 1985 population of 3.7 billion, are 9.1 billion, 8.2 billion, and 7.4 billion. The lowest projection is that population will at least double in less than half a century, despite the decline in the growth rate that has taken place since the early 1970s.

Samuel Preston was a member of the National Academy of Sciences panel on the economic consequences of population growth and played a major role in drafting its 1986 report. His chapter for this volume stems from and goes well beyond that earlier work. In it, he applies the apparatus of welfare economics for determining whether a policy is reasonable to some of the issues we are considering, asking whether the economic consequences of population growth provide a sound basis for population policy, and concluding that the present emphasis on family planning programs appears well justified.

Ansley Coale, shortly after the National Academy of Sciences report was issued, prepared a brief statement on what he has called the "nonrevisionist" view of the importance of population growth in relation to economic development. He accepted our invitation to include it here.

What is known about fertility change and, in particular, the role of family planning programs is reviewed in the next two chapters by John Bongaarts and George Simmons. Bongaarts focuses first on traditional patterns of fertility and their biological and social determinants, including marriage patterns, spontaneous abortion, breastfeeding, and sterility, and then describes the patterns of transition that populations typically undergo as they change from high to moderate or low fertility. Simmons takes the practical approach: what are the politics of establishing family planning programs; what do programs do;

when and where can they be effective; what are the characteristics of effective programs? It should perhaps be noted that there is a large literature on the causes of population change that is alluded to but not reviewed in any detail in this volume, primarily due to space considerations.

The final two chapters consider the policy issues facing the United States and the options available. Michael Teitelbaum offers a brief history of the mixed, sometimes unsavory, record of the United States on immigration and immigration policy and a rapid tour of the recent past in which immigration, legal and undocumented, has been hotly debated—and is still an unresolved topic. David Bell places in perspective the public policy choices for the United States by selecting two issues for discussion: what should the U.S. policy be toward rapid population growth in the Third World, and what should our policy be toward slow population growth in the industrialized countries? As fertility in the developed world has tumbled, we are reminded that slow growth, as well as negative growth, may have deleterious effects on the societies involved.

The papers in this volume cannot cover all aspects of this complex subject or all points of view. The topics have been selected to provide some brief coverage of the background for the current and ongoing debate over population and to stimulate informed discussion of the issues involved in the new population dilemma.

1

The World Demographic Situation

PAUL DEMENY

In December 1915, Walter F. Willcox, the eminent American demographer, concluded his presidential address to the American Economic Association with some comments on world population growth.

> The evidence indicates that two centuries ago the population of the earth was not far from one billion, now it is nearly or quite one billion and two thirds. . . . In any form of sentient life an increase of the individuals is evidence of adjustment and a decrease is evidence of maladjustment. Both increase of happiness and increase of numbers show a better adaptation to environment, and where numbers have increased we may infer the increase of human happiness. If this argument is sound, the increase of the earth's population in less than two centuries by about two thirds of a billion persons is the only quantitative test and proof of the progress of mankind.

PAUL DEMENY is a vice president of the Population Council, an international scientific and professional organization headquartered in New York City, and is director of the Council's Center for Policy Studies. Before joining the Council, Dr. Demeny was a member of the faculties of several U.S. universities. He has written extensively on demography and its relationship to economic development and public policy.

Since during the countless millennia of premodern human history rates of population growth on the average remained near zero, it is not surprising that Willcox was so impressed when he contemplated the accelerating tempo of demographic expansion in the two centuries then just passed. Yet, looking back from the vantage point of 1986, a population increase of two-thirds of a billion can now be attributed to the strikingly short span of time of the nine years preceding that date. This simple comparison highlights the historical uniqueness of the contemporary demographic situation, in particular its single most salient feature, the unprecedented magnitude of the global population increase that is being experienced in the second half of the twentieth century. It also suggests why rapid expansion of population size, quite naturally interpreted as a sign of progress not so long ago, is seen today by most observers as a process fraught with ambiguity and, by many of them, even as a manifestation of a societal maladjustment casting a shadow over humankind's future welfare.

Of these two topics—the contemporary demographic picture and what it means for human welfare—only the first will be addressed in the following brief account. Despite the chapter's narrow focus, the subject matter it deals with is still vast, and some cautionary words are in order. A few pages can attempt to give not more than broad contours of the contemporary demographic landscape. Yet for the purpose of many issues on which demographic phenomena have a bearing, the global population and its characteristics are elusive abstractions averaging out regional diversity: relevance requires shifting attention to specific components of the global aggregate. Considerations of national policy, in particular, must primarily draw on assessments of the demographic situation in the country in question: in such assessments, too, a closer look invariably reveals further diversity. It is also likely to show that changes in various subpopulations often move over time in directions concealed by average trends. This chapter, nevertheless, must largely dispense with attempts to discuss demographic patterns below the level of broad regional aggregates.

Whatever the size of the populations looked at, the principal means of demographic description is numerical. It is less useful to characterize a population as "small" or "large" or a growth rate as "rapid" or "slow" than it is to give a quantitative expression to such notions. But in the brief discussion that follows, numbers are necessarily kept to a minimum and, whenever opportune, are presented only in the form of graphs.

Important as are numbers and their graphical representation in characterizing demographic quantities, they should, as a rule, be taken with a grain of salt. Although our knowledge of global population phenomena has greatly improved over time, and especially since the 1950s, the accuracy of many demographic estimates leaves much to be desired. This is especially so for areas with deficient basic statistics—to wit, censuses, surveys, and vital records. A significant portion of the population of the less developed world lives in areas that can be so characterized, especially in Africa and South Asia. Frequent repetition of this warning would be tedious, however, and will be avoided in the discussion below.

Even when statistics are deficient, however, careful sifting of the available evidence and application of sophisticated methods of demographic estimation can go a long way to produce reasonably trustworthy estimates. On a worldwide basis the United Nations, and especially its Population Division, has long been a leader in preparing such estimates. Quantitative information presented in this chapter draws heavily on estimates and projections published or made available by the United Nations, in particular through the U.N.'s "1984 Assessment" of demographic trends and prospects. Long-term population projections prepared by the World Bank are also used to adumbrate possible demographic developments in the last three-quarters of the twenty-first century.

Population Growth

The first question asked about population by a curious visitor to this planet would undoubtedly be: how many are there? It is a simple question to ask, less simple to answer. There is, unfortunately, no world authority to count heads; the heads are located in some 200-odd countries and territories. Those in charge of the counting in each country apply themselves to the task at different dates, with differing competence, capacity, and diligence; and in some rare remaining instances, not at all. With this caveat, the best answer to this question, if posed in 1986, would be 4.9 billion, a figure rounded to the nearest 100 million. It would be a reasonable bet, although one not quite without risk, that the actual figure is within 2 percent of this estimate: not smaller than 4.8 and not larger than 5 billion.

Population estimates for earlier years, for example for 1970 or 1980, are likely to be slightly more accurate, since they are closer to or bracketed by actual censuses taken. As we go backward in time, reliability again weakens: first slowly, then rather rapidly. Still, for the last three centuries the broad lines of global demographic change are fairly well established:

Year	1700	1750	1800	1850	1900	1950	1980	1985
Population (millions)	679	770	954	1241	1633	2516	4450	4837

The upper diagram of Figure 1 depicts the steady upward march of these global figures. Since the curve is based on well-spaced estimates—one in every fifty years until 1900, decadal estimates between 1920 and 1950, and quinquennial estimates afterwards—the curve is smoother than reality would warrant; but adjustment for yearly variations, if that were possible, would not change the character of the curve at all. It is quite certain, for example, that there is no notch in the "true" curve, at least none after 1800; not even such major calamities as World War I and the deadly influenza pandemic that followed it broke the monotonic increase in the size of the global population. The small circles on the graph indicate points at which four successive billion marks were passed. It took all of human history until the industrial revolution to reach the size of one billion; adding the second billion took some 120 years; the third, 33 years; the fourth—between 1960 and 1974—just 14.

Successive shortening of the length of time needed to add a fixed amount to an initial stock is the characteristic property of exponential growth. But more than compound interest was at work in this process: the rate of compounding was itself increasing. This is implicit in the sequence of the figures just noted: doubling time from the first billion was 120 years, implying an average annual growth of 0.58 percent; doubling time from 2 billion was 47 years, implying annual growth at the rate of 1.47 percent. A more detailed picture of the rising rates of growth is shown in the lower left panel in Figure 1.

Here a "true" picture would exhibit a more serrated line: for example, the graph averages out the higher growth of the first decade of the twentieth century with the somewhat slower growth during the second decade. A temporary dip that does show on the graph occurs in the 1930s and the 1940s, attributable to the Great Depression and to World War II. But this dip is a minor sideshow compared to the pronounced overall upward climb of the growth rates for 250 years after 1700 and their sudden, almost discontinuous doubling at the midpoint of the twentieth century.

The single most dramatic feature of the graph, however, is the turning point that occurs in the 1965–70 quinquennium. During that time the rate of global population growth had surpassed 2 percent per annum—the exact estimate by the U.N. is 2.04 percent—and the rate of growth thereafter embarked on a downward course. Unlike earlier downturns in the time series of that index that soon proved merely temporary deviations from the upward trend, the late 1960s without doubt represent the all-time high watermark in the rate of expansion of the global population. The reasons for the certainty of this assertion are implicit in the dynamics of the proximate determinants of global growth—fertility and mortality—and will be considered below. Suffice to note here that the decline from the peak growth rate has been both steady and fairly rapid: the estimated growth rate during the period

FIGURE 1. World Population Growth: 1700–1985

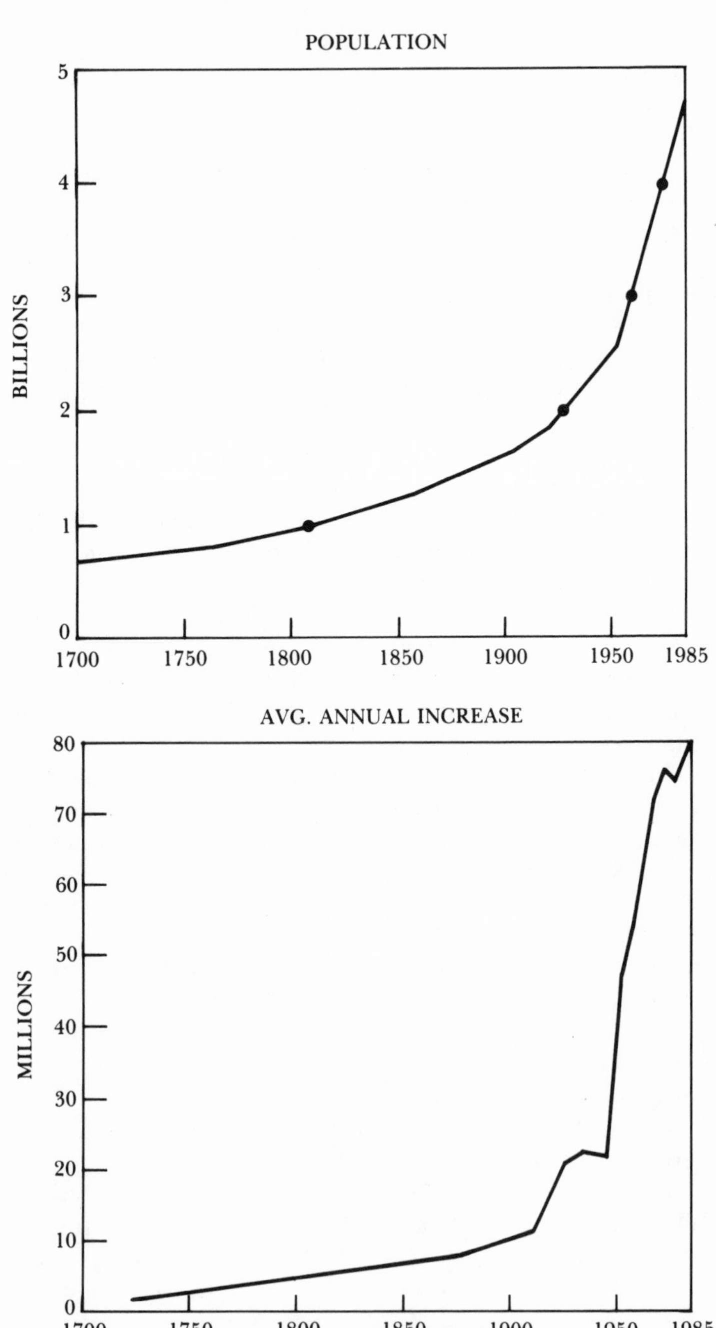

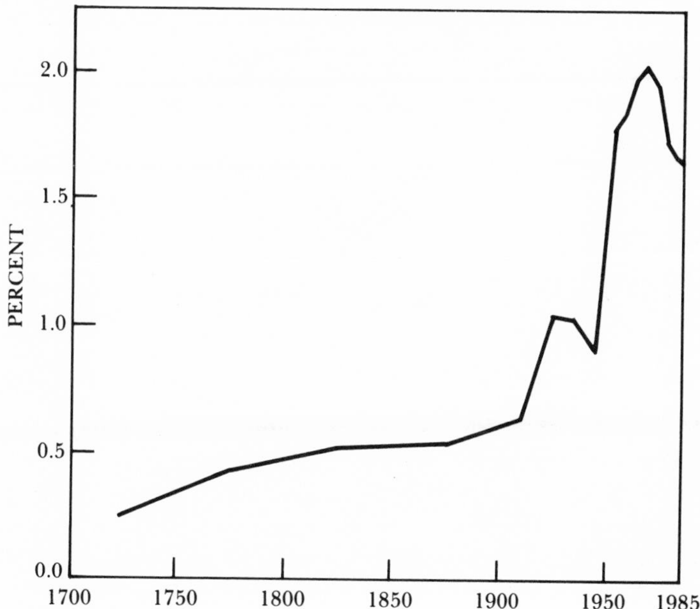

1980–85—1.67 percent—was already lower than that of the 1950–55 quinquennium that marked the beginning of the "population explosion" after World War II.

The growth rates that followed the peak attained in the late 1960s were, however, not low enough to generate a turning point in growth of the absolute number of people added to the existing global population year after year. This is shown in the lower right panel in Figure 1. The annual absolute increase of the world population was just short of 72 million in the late 1960s; a decade later it was 77.4 million, and for 1985–86 it may be estimated as 80 million—some 220,000 persons per day. The most conspicuous feature of this graph, however, is, once again, the steady acceleration of the demographic expansion over the entire period shown, especially following World War II.

What are the likely rates of global population growth beyond 1985? Addressing this question calls for consideration of population growth not as a process *sui generis,* but as the joint outcome of trends in fertility and mortality. An illuminating first look at long-term growth prospects is nevertheless afforded by Figure 2. The left side of the graph recapitulates the twentieth century segment of the upper panel in Figure 1. In the right side, beyond 1985, three "naive" projections extrapolate the historical time series, each incorporating the simple assumption that population increases at a fixed rate. The highest posited rate in these "naive" projections equals the rate estimated for 1985—that is, 1.65 percent. The other two illustrative extrapolations assume the constant rates of 1 percent (which equals the average rate of growth during the thirty-year period just before the "population explosion"—that is, between 1920 and 1950) and 0.5 percent (the average rate of growth during the nineteenth century). By the end of the twenty-first century, growth at the 1.65 percent annual rate would yield a world population of over 32 billion people, an outcome implausible on its face. The other two projections would result in a population of 15.3 billion and 8.6 billion, respectively; the assumptions generating these results imply, however, a discontinuous break from the pre-1985 growth path.

More realistic extrapolations of the past trend would mesh with earlier growth rates at the start but would envisage steady decline of the growth rate over time. Indeed, the lower left panel of Figure 1 implies such a pattern and calls attention to the fact, not obvious at a casual glance, that the global population growth curve (the upper panel of Figure 1, and the left segment of Figure 2) exhibits an inflection point located in the late 1960s. This suggests future growth that traces the familiar logistic curve—a curve resembling an elongated letter *S* tilted to the right. Each of a set of three projections prepared by the United Nations (using a methodology not based on extrapolating aggregate population figures) conforms to this pattern of growth. The projections, labeled "high," "medium," and "low," were carried up to the year 2025, yielding at that date a population of 9.1 billion, 8.2 billion, and 7.4 billion, respec-

FIGURE 2. World Population Growth: 1900–2100 (1900–85: estimates; 1985–2100: projections and extrapolations)

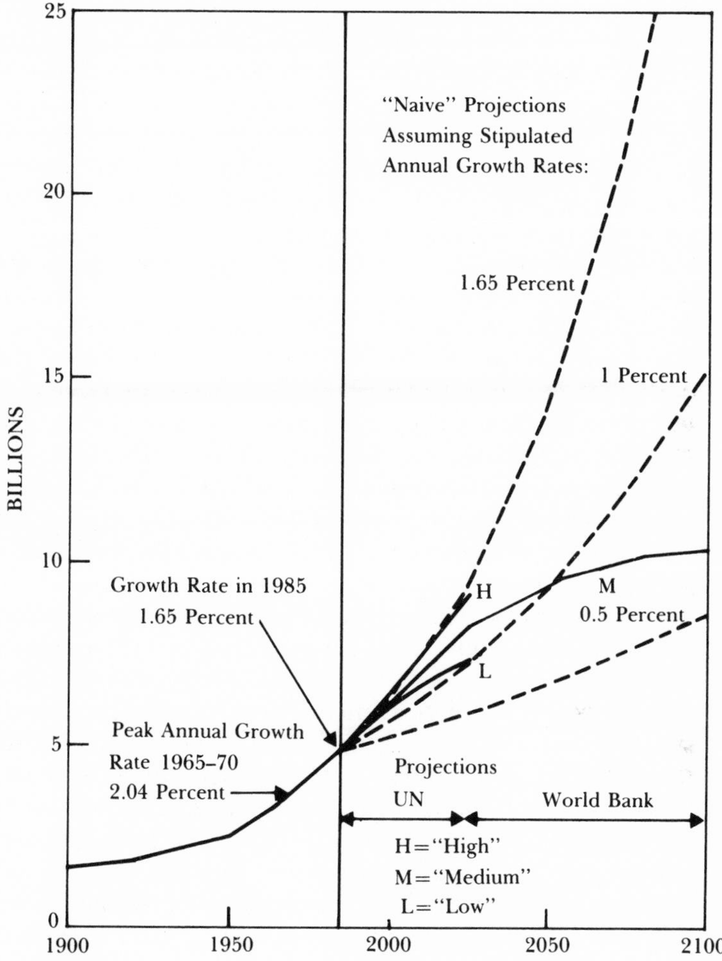

tively. Using the same methodology as the U.N. and essentially continuing the U.N. medium projection, the World Bank projected a 2100 population of 10.4 billion. Clearly, such a single long-term projection is not much more than a reflection of the particular assumptions incorporated in it: equally convincing S-curve extrapolations of the U.N.'s "low" and "high" projections to 2100 would yield a population of 8 billion and 15 billion, respectively. If the time paths leading to these figures do define the corridor within which the actual evolution of world population may lie, the range of alternative long-term demographic futures is wide, and implications of possible policy choices that may influence the path actually followed are far-reaching.

Actually, the range of possible long-term population growth trends is even wider. Behind the average trend discussed above lie subpopulations with differing observed growth paths. Some individual countries now exhibit negative rates of growth, and even on the broad regional level some areas appear to be entering a stage of incipient population decline. Thus the assumption that populations are approaching a stationary state—a state of no growth but no decline either—is contradicted even by contemporary experience. Clearly, then, negative growth rates cannot be excluded from the range of possible long-term demographic futures. Conversely, large subpopulations within the global aggregate are still experiencing accelerating growth rates, and for others a reversal of a recent decline remains a possibility. It can be confidently predicted that the growth rate eventually (and not only in some far-remote future) must decline toward zero; but predicting the time when an inflection of the growth curve will occur and the speed with which growth rates will fall afterwards and, perforce, setting an upper limit to the population size that might be attained at specified distant future dates are far more difficult.

We shall return to the question of future demographic prospects in the closing section of this chapter. To conclude consideration of population growth as a subject of interest in its own right, a look at the recent growth experience below the global level is, however, in order. Table 1 gives total population figures for 1950 and for 1985 for the world, subdivided into eight regions, and shows the implied rates of growth and absolute population increases during the intervening thirty-five years. The areas shown in the table are identified by their familiar geographic labels. "Northern America" is understood here as comprising the United States and Canada. The U.S. population represents 90 percent of this region's total. "Europe" excludes the European portion of the Soviet Union, and "Latin America" includes the Caribbean. "South Asia" comprises the vast crescent of countries from Turkey to the Philippines; the largest among these countries is India, representing about half of the area's total population in 1985. The remainder of Asia—"East Asia"—is dominated demographically by China (1,060 million in 1985) and Japan (121 million); the two countries together make up roughly 95 percent of the region's population.

The table also shows a subdivision of the world into "more developed countries" (MDCs) and "less developed countries" (LDCs). Despite its obvious flaws, this single classification does retain a considerable degree of interest as it still delineates areas that on the whole exhibit pronounced demographic as well as socioeconomic differentials. One awkward aspect of the MDC/LDC subdivision is that the very labels it employs suggest that membership in each category of countries should be shifting over time as some of the members succeed in turning themselves into "more developed countries." For example, one would expect Singapore to be included in the LDC group in 1950 but counted among the MDCs in 1985. But to be meaningful, most comparisons require a fixed membership within the two development leagues, and that is the convention followed here. Specifically, the MDC group includes Northern America, Europe, and the Soviet Union, plus Japan, Australia, and New Zealand. All other areas are classified as LDCs. So defined, less developed countries comprised 67 percent of the world population in 1950 and 76 percent in 1985.

The years 1950 and 1985, as was shown above, bracket a span of time characterized by exceptionally fast demographic growth: on the global level there has never been, nor will there ever be, another period of thirty-five years during which growth was so rapid—just short of 1.9 percent per year. To a remarkable degree the proposition applies to most broad

TABLE 1: Population Growth by World Regions, 1950–85

	Population (millions)		Population increase 1950–85	
	1950	1985	Millions per year	Average annual increase (percent)
Northern America	166	264	2.8	1.32
Europe	392	492	2.9	.65
Soviet Union	180	279	2.8	1.25
Oceania	13	25	.3	1.91
Latin America	165	405	6.9	2.57
East Asia	671	1250	16.5	1.78
South Asia	704	1568	24.7	2.29
Africa	224	555	9.5	2.59
MDCs	832	1174	9.8	.98
LDCs	1684	3663	56.5	2.22
World total	2516	4837	66.3	1.87

subregions as well. Europe is a minor exception: it grew faster in the nineteenth century, although still below 1 percent per year. The once near-empty areas of Northern America and Oceania are also exceptions: there, immigration-fueled nineteenth century growth was at times also faster than growth between 1950 and 1985. Still, the near–1 percent average annual growth of the more developed countries as a whole during 1950–1985 represents a historically very rapid rate of expansion. The same applies with even greater cogency to the absolute increase of the population. Net MDC growth during the period was 340 million, equivalent to more than the combined population of the United States and the Soviet Union in 1950. The rate of population growth steadily declined, however, for all MDCs during the period. It was 1.28 percent per year from 1950 to 1955 and 0.64 percent per year from 1980 to 1985, a 50 percent drop in three decades.

In LDCs, which as a whole more than doubled their population during the period considered, the speed of expansion was without any historical precedent. Peak LDC growth occurred in the 1965–70 quinquennium, at the annual rate of 2.53 percent. The necessity of a downturn from that height—or, in general, the inappropriateness of projecting populations at a fixed "current" growth rate—can be appreciated by contemplating the hypothetical long-term implications of such a rate. The total LDC population was 2.33 billion in 1965: sustained growth at 2.53 percent per year would bring that figure to 71 billion by the end of the twenty-first century and to 890 billion one hundred years thereafter. Indeed, by the 1980–85 period, LDC growth had declined to the estimated rate of just 2 percent, a 20 percent drop in roughly fifteen years. It should be noted, however, that because of the large weight China's population represents within LDCs, the rapid deceleration of China's population growth had a major influence on the decline of the rate of expansion. LDC growth, excluding China, was estimated as still as high as 2.33 percent per year in the period 1980–85, or only 7 percent below the peak rate fifteen years earlier.

If the marked decline in MDC growth rates noted above is prima facie evidence for rapid demographic change in the countries that make up that group, it ought not be inferred that slow change in the rate of growth (such as among LDCs, excluding China) or constancy of that rate (such as observed in a number of countries in the less developed world) is necessarily evidence for slow demographic change or for the absence of any change at all. To judge this matter correctly we must consider the forces that shape demographic growth.

The Demographic Transition

Human populations are self-renewing aggregates. They do not grow merely by adding to their existing stock: growth is the balance of accretion and decay, of births and deaths. Below the global level, population growth can also be affected by entry and exit through migration, but we shall consider here only what demographers call "natural increase," increase generated by the excess of births over deaths. When numbers of these events are related to the size of the population from which they originate, a "vital rate" is derived—a birthrate or a death rate. The difference between the two equals the rate of natural increase, or, disregarding migration, the rate of growth. Thus it may be estimated that in 1985 there were 129 million births and 49 million deaths in the world. This yields a global birthrate of 26.7, a death rate of 10.2, and a rate of natural increase of 16.5, each of these rates being expressed per 1000 population and per year. (More commonly, rates of increase are given in percentage terms: in the example just given the rate of increase is 1.65 percent.)

It is evident that arithmetically a given rate of growth can be the result of differing combinations of birth and death rates; for example, growth may be absent because high birthrates are matched by high death rates, or because both birthrates and death rates are equally low. The example is not arbitrarily chosen: much of humankind's past closely resembles the former condition while the long-term demographic future, if death rates are to be kept low, must be characterized by the latter. In between these two limiting states takes place the process called "demographic transition," a more or less protracted period during which birth and death rates move from a pretransition level of around 40 per 1000 to a post-transition level that eventually settles down in the neighborhood of perhaps 12 to 14 per 1000.

It is a well-established generalization, expected both on a priori grounds and supported by much observed historical evidence, that the onset of the decline of the death rates tends to precede the decline of the birthrates. Also, during that phase of the transition when both rates are in decline, death rates are apt to fall initially faster than birthrates. The sequence and characteristics of these two distinct but interrelated processes therefore imply a period when a widening gap is opened between birthrates and death rates; hence population growth accelerates. Later the gap is gradually narrowed and ultimately is closed as the decline of death rates runs its course while the downward trend of the birthrate becomes more pronounced, eventually attaining the same low level as the death rate.

This stylized description of the process of the demographic transition is consistent with a great variety of specific patterns of change over time. Depending on the initial—pretransition—level of the vital rates, on the duration of time that separates the onset of the decline in the death rate from that of the birthrate, and on the relative speed with which each of these measures tends toward its eventual posttransition level, periods of population growth of greatly differing length and intensity can ensue. Describing the current world demographic situation amounts to describing patterns of population change and characteristics that reflect differing current phases of the demographic transition; correctly discerning future patterns of change requires correct interpretation of the dynamics of the transition process in which various populations currently find themselves. Toward those ends, Figures 3 through 8 give a concise description of the most important indicators of the demographic state of major world regions, as well as the observed evolution of these indicators over the recent past. Figures 4 through 8 also picture possible future courses of these indicators, not as predictions of long-term trends but in order to provide reference points against which the range of plausible demographic futures can be discussed.

Although looking at changes in population growth as jointly determined by changes in birth and death rates is a substantial step toward clearer understanding, these rates, in turn, are imperfect indicators of the underlying phenomena that affect long-term growth: fertility and mortality. Changes in mortality, as was noted above, usually precede changes in fertility during the course of the demographic transition; hence, it is logical to discuss mortality trends first. It should be noted, however, that the regularity of the sequence, mortality change followed by fertility change, does not necessarily mean that the latter is caused by the former. Decline of mortality may provide some of the explanation for subsequent fertility decline, but it is more likely that both sets of changes are shaped by other factors, factors outside the domain of demography proper. Demographers are wont to explain change in population phenomena by other facets of population change. On the level of definitional identities, such "explanations" work well and can be analytically highly useful. The identity "population growth equals births less deaths" is a simple example of such definitional explanation. In similar fashion, a decline of the birthrate can be "explained" by an increased recourse to birth control, and the latter can be further traced back to other "causes" by ascertaining the changing numbers of couples using specific contraceptive methods. Beyond that, analysis might clarify the different sources from which contraceptive users obtain the necessary services, and so on. The analytic process of looking for explanations in this fashion resembles the peeling of an artichoke. Initially, successive layers of causation can be revealed in an orderly and well-fitting sequence; but eventually a core is reached where simple disentangling of the surface phenomenon from the underlying explanatory layer is no longer possible or at best leads to results that are ambiguous. The present discussion stays close to the measurable demographic surface, with only perfunctory attempts at deeper levels of explanation.

Mortality

Among humans, the chances of dying vary greatly with age. As a consequence, the death rate of a population is strongly influenced not only by the overall level of mortality but also by the age composition of the population in question. Age distributions depend on past levels of fertility and mortality. High fertility and falling mortality generate a young age distribution; in comparison, a history of low fertility makes for an age distribution in which the proportion of older persons is relatively high. Sustained low mortality, implying high probabilities of surviving to an old age, makes this aging effect more pronounced. Not surprisingly, in the contemporary world one finds great variations between world regions in the overall shape of age structures. For example, in 1985 the proportion of children under age fifteen in the population of the MDCs was 22.2 percent; the corresponding figure in the LDCs was 39.4 percent. Conversely, the proportion of the old-age population—those sixty-five years of age and older—was 11.2 percent in MDCs but only 4.2 percent in LDCs. This difference in age structure is the explanation for the fact that, despite much lower probabilities of dying at any given age among MDCs in comparison to LDCs, the overall death rates in these two groups of countries did not differ greatly: in the years 1980 to 1985 the estimates were 9.6 per 1000 population in MDCs and 10.8 per 1000 population in LDCs. Comparisons between individual countries can be even more striking. For example, in the same period the death rate in the United States was 9.1 per 1000, more than twice as high as Costa Rica's death rate of 4.2 per 1000, even though in every age group U.S. mortality was lower than mortality in Costa Rica. A realistic assessment of relative mortality levels could be done by comparing death rates age group by age group, but obviously that would be a very cumbersome procedure.

A convenient summary measure of the mortality of a population in any given year (or other specified time period) is the expectation of life at birth. This measure indicates the average number of years a group of newborn babies would live if they were subject throughout their lifetime to the mortality conditions that obtained in that year. Table 2 presents the values of this index in various world regions from 1950 to 1955 and from 1980 to 1985, along with the implied change, both in absolute and in percentage terms, during the three decades that separate these two sets of estimates. The upper panel of Figure 3 gives a more detailed picture of mortality change by presenting four quinquennial estimates separated by ten-year intervals for each area. Improvements in mortality registered in terms of expectation of life at birth can be read off this diagram as upward movements along the vertical axis. (Movement along the horizontal axis reflects changes in fertility as explained below.) Finally, the left segment of Figure 4 traces the full course of mortality change in terms of estimates of the expectation of life for successive five-year intervals between 1950 and 1985, thus facilitating consideration of plausible future changes in that index.

TABLE 2: Expectation of Life at Birth, World Regions, 1950–55 and 1980–85

	Expectation of life (years)		Change from 1950–55 to 1980–85	
	1950–55	1980–85	Years	Percent
Northern America	69.1	74.4	5.3	7.7
Europe	65.3	73.1	7.8	11.9
Soviet Union	64.1	70.9	6.8	10.6
Oceania	60.8	67.9	7.1	11.7
Latin America	51.1	64.2	13.1	25.6
East Asia	42.7	68.4	25.7	60.2
South Asia	39.9	54.9	15.0	37.6
Africa	37.8	49.4	11.6	30.7
MDCs	65.8	73.1	7.3	11.1
LDCs	41.1	57.3	16.2	39.4
World	46.0	59.5	13.5	29.4

The estimates shown in Table 2 and those represented in Figures 3 and 4 tell a story of a remarkable, and in some areas extraordinarily rapid extension of the average length of life during the decades following World War II. By the early 1980s the average level of world mortality was comparable to the level of mortality experienced by the most advanced countries during the period between World Wars I and II. The table also shows that large mortality differentials still remain between world regions, but that these differentials narrowed appreciably during the period considered. The less developed countries as a group gained more than sixteen years: this represented an average improvement of more than one-half year in the expected length of life for every calendar year. The gain for MDCs, 7.3 years, was less than half of the LDC gain. As would be expected, improvement is easier from a lower starting point than from already high levels of survivorship. But this is not a hard and fast rule; there have been significant changes in the relative standing of some of the major world regions. The rapid improvement of mortality in East Asia is

FIGURE 3. World Demographic Transition: 1950–85

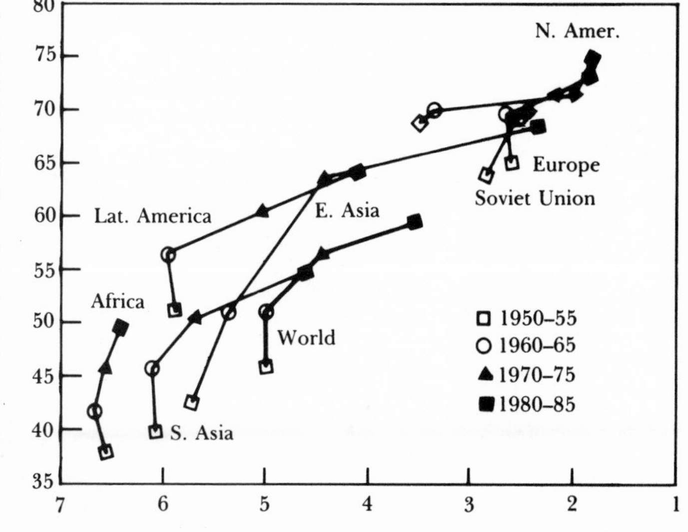

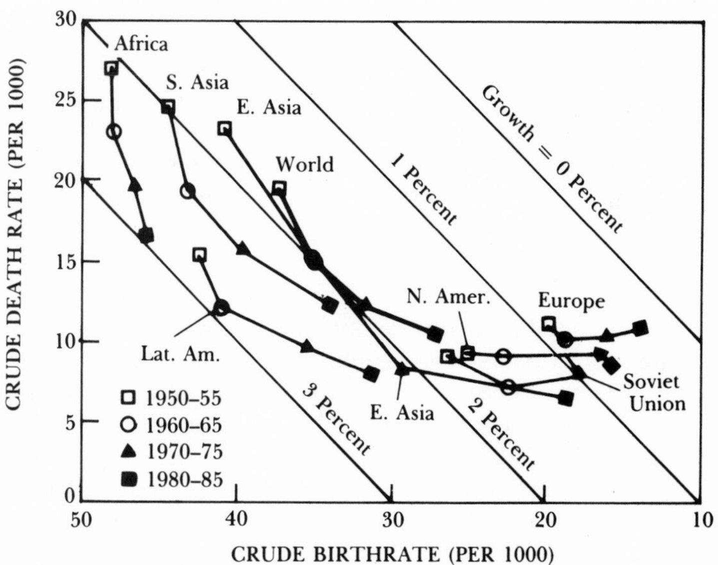

FIGURE 4. World Mortality Trends: 1950–2100 expectation of life at birth (both sexes) 1950–85: estimates; 1985–2100: projections

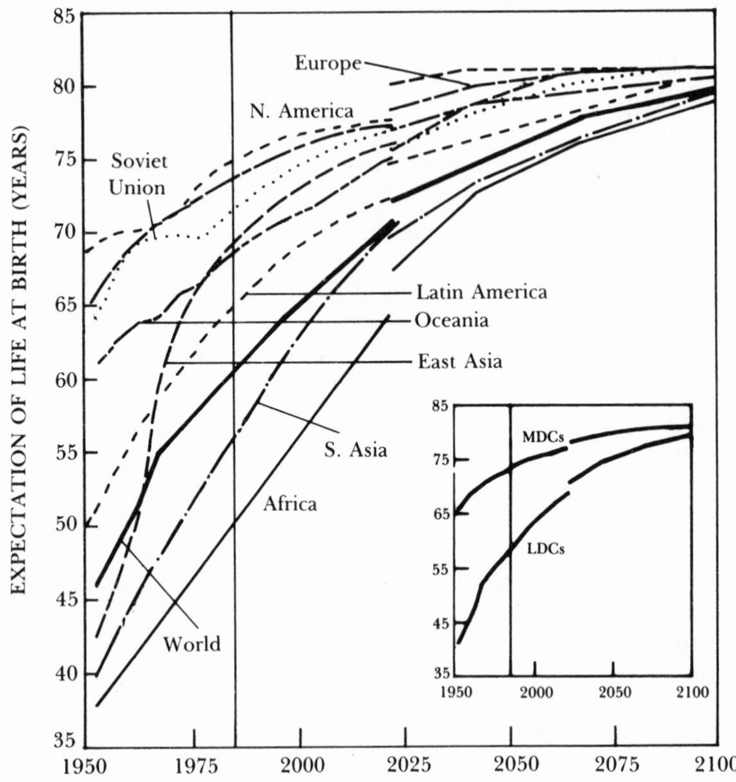

especially notable in this respect. For example, expectation of life in East Asia at the beginning of the period was lower than in Latin America by more than eight years. By the end of the period, despite major gains in Latin America, East Asia was ahead of Latin America by more than four years. Also, among LDCs the slowest gain was registered in Africa, even though mortality in that region was the highest to begin with, thus, in principle, offering the opportunity for especially rapid improvement. It should be noted, moreover, that the mortality levels indicated for Africa and, perforce, the amounts of mortality improvement shown are the statistically least well substantiated estimates presented in the table.

Weaknesses of the underlying statistics make it difficult to elaborate a refined picture of mortality change for higher mortality areas in general. It has been argued, for example, that since the 1970s the pace of improvement has slowed down compared to what could be expected from the record of the early postwar decades at any given level of mortality. But the evidence supporting this contention is far from conclusive.

Disputes about the factors responsible for the measured improvements in mortality also remain unresolved. As a result of early postwar successes of applying low-cost public health measures—for example, in reducing mortality from malaria—there has been a tendency to claim that, contrary to the historical experience of the now low-mortality countries, mortality change in contemporary LDCs depends primarily on the ability and willingness of each country to carry out appropriate health programs rather than on overall developmental advance. Econometric work seems to suggest that such claims are exaggerated: the two sets of factors may have had about equal influence on LDC mortality improvement in the post–World War II decades. The success of China in rapidly reducing mortality seems to demonstrate the possibility of considerable income-independent improvements in survival, but even there broader based socioeconomic factors were at work as well as narrow health interventions. It is believed that infant and early childhood mortality can be especially effectively reduced through relatively low-cost health interventions such as programs of prenatal care and immunization, and through making simple curative techniques such as oral rehydration known and accessible to mothers with small children. Indeed, maternal education has been found to have a greater influence on the level of infant mortality than do income and similar indicators of material progress.

Aspects of the mortality picture not touched on in this brief account include differential mortality within countries by socioeconomic status and by sex, the changing composition of mortality according to causes of death, and the relationship between measured mortality levels and the health status of the population at large. Important as these issues are, their significance pales compared to the issue of the overall level of mortality in any given population and the evolution of that level over time. A strong record on these scores virtually guarantees that examination of other aspects of mortality would also show good performance.

Fertility

The considerations that suggest that death rates are a poor measure of mortality apply, in principle, with even greater force to birthrates as a measure of fertility. Death, even if its probability varies greatly, occurs at all ages. Reproduction, in contrast, is limited to certain age groups. When based on birthrates, fertility comparisons, across countries and over time, will be distorted by variations in the proportionate size of the population of women of reproductive age and by variations in the age composition of women within the reproductive age span.

To more accurately gauge the level of fertility and changes in fertility over time, demographers use a measure called the total fertility rate (TFR): the average number of children women would have at the end of their childbearing years if between ages fifteen and fifty they were to bear children at the rate observed at each age in a given year. TFRs are sometimes simply referred to as the total number of children per woman, but the simplicity of the label is deceptive: the meaning and interpretation of this measure are not free of ambiguity. As a moment's reflection suggests, information about completed fertility as a straightforward observation can be obtained from women at age fifty or above. But then such an observation would be a historical datum: that is, women at age fifty in 1985 had their children largely in the 1950s, '60s, and '70s. As defined above, TFR gives *current* fertility, but current fertility does not necessarily predict how many children women now in the childbearing age range will actually end up with, on the average, once their childbearing is completed. Particularly when fertility is low and the timing of having children is a matter of voluntary choice, year-to-year variations in TFRs are apt to be larger than variation in completed fertility. Thus the observation that West Germany's TFR in 1983 was 1.32 and Keyna's 8.0 does not necessarily imply that German women who were of age fifteen to forty-nine in that year will on the average have 1.32 children and that Kenyan women will have 8; it merely means that they would have that number if fertility continued unchanged at its 1983 level in the years to come.

Table 3 presents numerical estimates of total fertility rates for world regions from 1950 to 1955 and from 1980 to 1985 along with the implied changes in fertility. The upper panel of Figure 3 depicts more detailed estimates of TFRs during this time period, in conjunction with changes in the level of mortality. TFRs are measured on the horizontal axis of Figure 3.

TABLE 3: Total Fertility Rate (number of children per woman), World Regions, 1950–55 and 1980–85

	Total fertility rate		Change from 1950–55 to 1980–85	
	1950–55	1980–85	Number of children	Percent
Northern America	3.48	1.83	−1.65	−47.4
Europe	2.60	1.87	−0.73	−28.1
Soviet Union	2.84	2.37	−0.47	−16.5
Oceania	3.83	2.66	−1.17	−30.5
Latin America	5.89	4.12	−1.77	−30.1
East Asia	5.71	2.35	−3.36	−58.8
South Asia	6.08	4.61	−1.47	−24.2
Africa	6.57	6.43	−0.14	−2.1
MDCs	2.84	1.98	−0.86	−30.3
LDCs	6.16	4.08	−2.08	−33.8
World	4.99	3.54	−1.45	−29.1

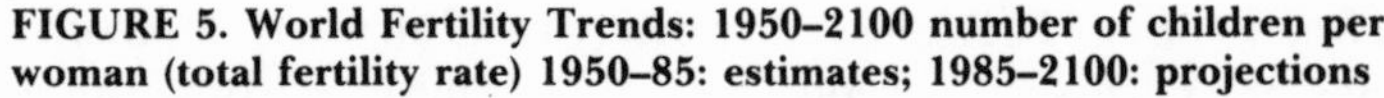

FIGURE 5. World Fertility Trends: 1950–2100 number of children per woman (total fertility rate) 1950–85: estimates; 1985–2100: projections

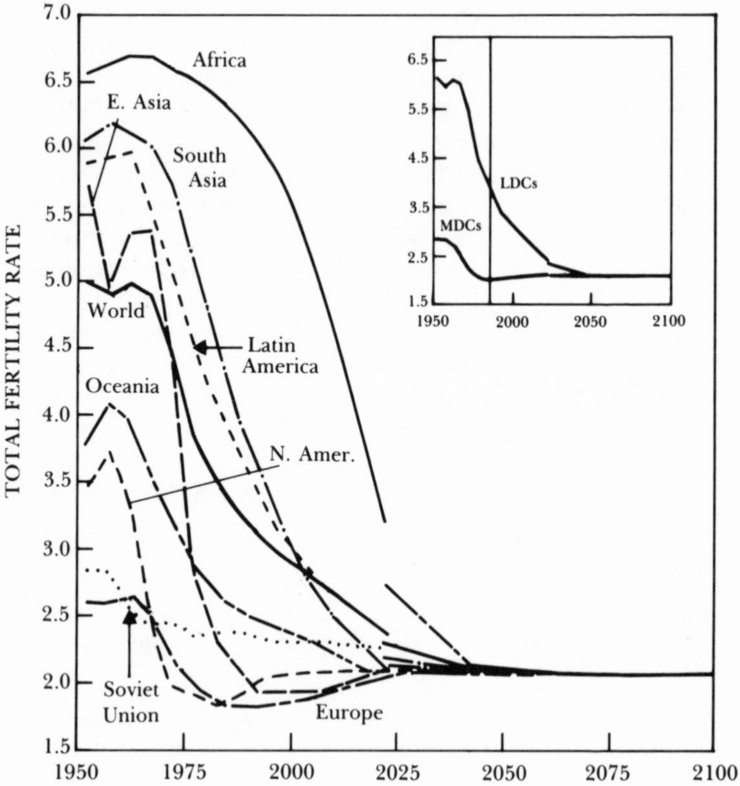

Since the dominant direction of fertility change, especially since 1960, has been downward, the scale is plotted in reverse order: from high to low fertility. Thus successive dates are read off the diagram in the "natural" fashion, as a progression from left to right. The full course of quinquennial estimates between 1950–55 and 1980–85 is shown on the left segment of Figure 5.

The picture that emerges from Table 3 and Figures 3 and 5 indicates major and pervasive declines in fertility during the period covered. In 1980–85, TFRs were estimated at more than 30 percent below their level three decades earlier in both LDCs and MDCs taken separately. (For the world as a whole the decline was slightly below 30 percent. This apparent contradiction between movement of the world average and its constituent parts is explained by the structural shift during the period: in the early 1980s the relative weight within the world of LDCs, where the level of fertility is more than twice as high as the level prevailing in MDCs, was greater than it was in the early 1950s.) Among regions the greatest declines were registered in East Asia (a near–60 percent drop in TFRs) and in Northern America (a near–50 percent drop). Other regions also show major declines in fertility: a 30 percent decline in Latin America and a 24 percent decline in South Asia are particularly notable. The single continent-size exception is Africa; there, estimated fertility in the early 1980s was virtually identical to fertility in the early 1950s.

A more detailed examination of the record of fertility change would show, however, that behind the rapid decreases there is considerable variation. Even outside Africa a number of areas experienced no fertility change or only modest changes. They include such large countries as Bangladesh and Pakistan, most of the Arab countries, and some smaller countries in Latin America. All told, if states of India are considered separately, the size of LDC populations that show no or only modest fertility change since the 1950s exceeded 1 billion in 1985.

Inspection of Figures 3 and 5 reveals that in LDCs where fertility did decline, much of this decline began in the 1960s and gathered momentum in the 1970s. The decline in East Asia—the most significant both because of its rapidity and because it affected a very large population—was largely concentrated in the 1960s and 1970s: in China a fifteen-year time span witnessed a halving of TFRs. A peacetime drop of this size during such a short time in a large population is without precedent in demographic history. The pattern of change in LDCs is less clear in the early 1980s. Data are more scarce for this period; hence estimates often involve extrapolations of earlier downward trends. Often these may be warranted and will be eventually borne out by empirical observations, but in a number of instances available country-level information suggests that extension of past trends is on tenuous ground. Around 1980, the momentum of fertility decline seems to have slowed down or even stalled at still relatively high levels of fertility in such countries at Sri Lanka, Malaysia, the Philippines, and Costa Rica.

What represents a "high level" is of course a relative matter. One advantage of the TFR as a measure of fertility is that it readily suggests a natural yardstick for fertility's influence on long-term population growth. If until the end of the childbearing years there were to be no mortality, a sustained TFR of 2 —an average of two children per woman by the end of the childbearing years—would just suffice to assure the long-run maintenance of the population at a constant size. However, since some newborn children do not survive to adulthood, a two-child average is not enough for zero long-run growth. Simple calculations suggest that the required number, the so-called replacement level fertility, is 2.1 children when mortality is very low—as is the case in the most advanced countries —and is in the neighborhood of 2.5 children when expectation of life is equivalent to the world average in the early 1980s, that is, about sixty years. By this yardstick it transpires that fertility sank below replacement level in the early 1970s in Northern America and in the late 1970s in Europe. Country-level information reveals that by the late 1970s a significant number of populations had TFRs appreciably below 2.1. The following data refer to TFRs in the years 1975–80:

West Germany	1.44	Hungary	1.81
Switzerland	1.52	Japan	1.81
Sweden	1.65	France	1.87
United Kingdom	1.73	Italy	1.92
Canada	1.77	United States	1.94

On the other end of the scale are the high-fertility countries. While estimates for these are less reliable, each of the following countries is believed to have had TFRs of 7.2 or higher in the period 1975–80: Kenya, Rwanda, Tanzania, Nigeria, Algeria, Libya, Jordan, and Syria. TFR estimates for 1975 to 1980 for some of the larger countries between these extremes are as follows:

Bangladesh	6.7	India	4.9
Pakistan	6.1	Indonesia	4.8
Vietnam	5.6	Brazil	4.2
Mexico	5.4	China	3.0
Egypt	5.3	Soviet Union	2.3

The long-term implications for the rate of population growth of a given level of TFR and the prevailing level of mortality can be readily calculated. Thus for West Germany current rates imply a decline of the total population by approximately one-third every generation, or roughly in every twenty-seven years. In contrast, under current rates the highest fertility countries can anticipate a threefold increase of their populations in each generation. But the assumption that current levels of fertility and mortality remain constant is unrealistic. Before turning to considerations of future demographic prospects, we shall examine more closely population growth actually observed in the recent past as a result of the joint effect of fertility and mortality and their interaction with age composition.

Natural Increase

The difference between birth and death rates is the "rate of natural increase"—that is, the rate of population growth calculated without taking into account the effect of net migration. For broad regional units, migration's effects on growth are usually so minor that the rate of population growth and the rate of natural increase tend to be nearly identical. The information presented in Table 4 on "vital rates" for 1950–55 and 1980–85 reveals the relative roles of the factors that represent the proximate determinants of population increase. For example, in LDCs as a whole these two five-year periods show the same rate of increase: the net addition of 20.2 persons per 1000 population per annum. But behind constancy of growth are major changes in both the birthrate and the death rate. Both of these measures dropped by 13.4 points per 1000 population during the period considered. A decline in the birthrate alone would have decreased the growth rate; a decline in the death rate alone would have increased it. The two effects cancelled out, but the underlying demographic situation has changed dramatically. The estimates for 1980–85 reflect a much more advanced stage in the process of the demographic transition than do the estimates for 1950–55.

TABLE 4: Vital Rates by World Regions, 1950–55 and 1980–85 (per 1000 population)

	Birthrate		Death rate		Rate of natural increase	
	1950–55	1980–85	1950–55	1980–85	1950–55	1980–85
Northern America	25.1	15.9	9.4	8.9	15.7	7.0
Europe	19.8	13.9	10.9	10.9	8.9	3.0
Soviet Union	26.3	19.0	9.2	9.1	17.1	9.9
Oceania	27.6	20.7	12.4	8.3	15.2	12.4
Latin America	42.5	31.6	15.4	8.2	27.1	23.4
East Asia	40.8	18.8	23.3	6.6	17.5	12.2
South Asia	44.6	34.1	24.6	12.4	20.0	21.7
Africa	48.3	45.9	27.1	16.6	21.2	29.3
MDCs	22.7	15.5	10.1	9.6	12.6	5.9
LDCs	44.4	31.0	24.2	10.8	20.2	20.2
World	37.3	27.1	19.6	10.5	17.7	16.6

Figure 3 gives a more detailed account of the transition process and its regional variations. The pure measures of fertility and mortality that appear in the upper panel are translated in the lower panel into birth and death rates, whose dynamics over time also reflect the influence of the age distribution. In LDCs during the earlier part of the period covered, the effect of declining mortality on the death rate was more important than the effect of declining fertility on the birthrate; hence rates of growth increased. The latter part of the period is dominated by declining birthrates; hence growth is becoming slower. Africa, still exhibiting accelerating population growth, is once again the exception to this generalization. In Northern America, Europe, and the Soviet Union, although mortality improved appreciably, aging population composition caused death rates to change little or not at all. Thus among MDCs, falling fertility and falling birthrates translated directly to falling rates of increase. The left segment of Figure 6 depicts in detail the course of these rates between 1950 and 1985. The picture shows the persistent striking differentials in the rates of growth, their initial acceleration in LDCs, and their overall dominant downward trend—except in Africa—since around 1970. The demographic transition, with the exception of Europe, is far from nearing completion, but in all major world areas outside Africa it is well advanced. The unsettled big question concerns the factors that will shape the transition process in the years to come and, in particular, the length of time that completion of the transition will require. After a brief look at the phenomenon of urbanization, we shall consider that question in the concluding section of this chapter.

Urbanization

In addition to fertility, mortality, and population growth, urbanization is a demographic process of particular interest. The shift in the distribution of a population from a predominantly rural to a predominantly urban residence tends to reflect increasing income levels and the consequent transformation of the industrial composition of the national product and of the labor force. But urbanization is also affected by the rate of population growth, and the size of urban agglomerations has a close relationship to the size of the population at large. The number of urban residents grows because of natural increase of the existing urban population, because of migration from rural to urban areas, and because of the statistical crossover of settlements formerly classified as rural to areas classified as urban. The latter can be the result of increasing population size within a given settlement or the absorption by growing urban centers of surrounding formerly rural areas.

Due to the combined effect of these factors, the urban population grew rapidly worldwide between 1950 and 1985. Basic data characterizing the urbanization process in world regions during that period are given in Table 5. LDCs have quadrupled the size of their urban population in thirty-five years, adding some 860 million urban residents to the initial stock of some 290 million in 1950. This translates to an average annual rate of growth of 4 percent. Since urban and rural rates of natural increase in LDCs did not differ significantly, a simple

TABLE 5: Urbanization by World Regions, 1950 and 1985

	Urban Population				Increase of the urban population 1950–85	
	(Millions)		(Percent)			Average annual increase
	1950	1985	1950	1985	(Millions)	(Percent)
Northern America	106	195	63.9	74.1	89	1.74
Europe	220	352	56.3	71.6	132	1.33
Soviet Union	71	183	39.3	65.6	112	2.71
Oceania	8	17	61.3	71.0	9	2.33
Latin America	67	279	41.0	68.9	212	4.06
East Asia	112	357	16.8	28.6	245	3.30
South Asia	113	433	16.1	27.7	320	3.84
Africa	35	165	15.7	29.7	130	4.40
MDCs	447	839	53.8	71.5	392	1.80
LDCs	287	1144	17.0	31.2	857	3.95
World	734	1983	29.2	41.0	1249	2.84

FIGURE 6. Average Annual Rates of Population Growth: 1950–2100 (1950–85: estimates; 1985–2100: projections)

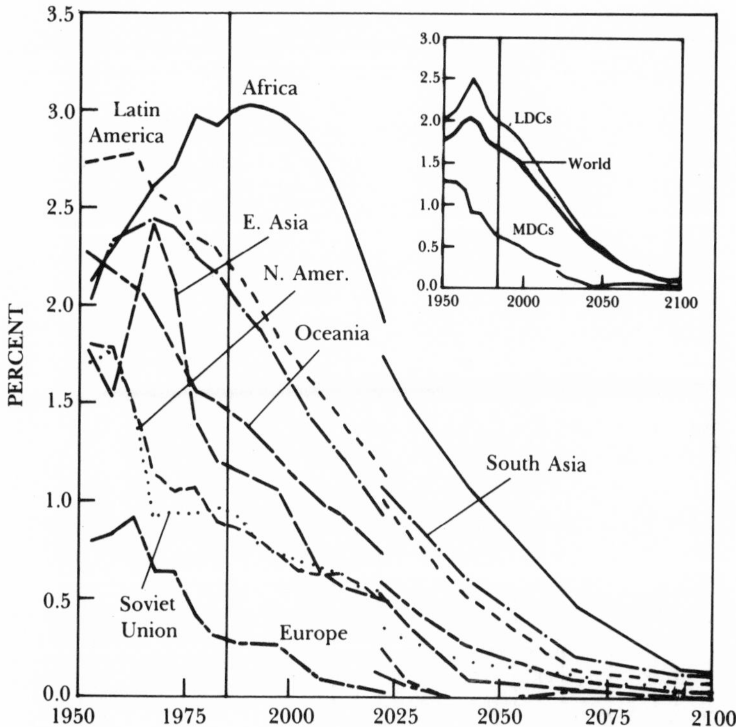

comparison of Tables 1 and 5 suggests that more than half of urban growth was directly attributable to the excess of births over deaths in the urban areas themselves; in other words, natural increase was a significantly more important factor in urban growth than migration from rural areas.

Indeed, urbanization proper, measured by the proportion of the urban population within the total population, was not especially rapid compared to the historical experience of the now developed countries. The urban share in LDCs grew from 17 percent in 1950 to 31 percent in 1985. Thus LDCs as a whole remained predominantly rural; internal migration failed to stem the continuing rapid increase of the rural population, which averaged 1.7 percent per year between 1950 and 1985, amounting to an absolute increase of more than 1.1 billion. The rural population increased in absolute terms during this period even in Latin America, the less developed region where urbanization is most advanced. The least urbanized region, South Asia, experienced a rural growth of some 540 million compared to the 320 million increase in urban areas. These comparisons suggest that, contrary to popular assumptions, the very rapid overall rate of population growth experienced by LDCs has retarded rather than accelerated the process of urbanization. The share of LDC urban population within the world total nevertheless increased from less than 40 percent in 1950 to about 58 percent in 1985.

This shift occurred despite continuing rapid urbanization in MDCs during the period. The urban share within MDCs grew from 54 percent in 1950 to over 71 percent in 1985—a greater percentage increase than that shown by LDCs. The MDC rural population declined at the average annual rate of 0.4 percent during the period, resulting in a total absolute decline of some 50 million.

A notable aspect of the rapid growth of urban populations, especially in LDCs, was the growth of large metropolitan centers. In 1950 the world's fifteen largest urban agglomerations ranged in size from 3.6 million (Milan) to 12.4 million (New York metropolitan area). In 1980 the fifteen largest centers ranged from 8.5 million (Seoul) to 17 million (Tokyo/Yokohama). In 1950, of the top fifteen urban centers ten were located in MDCs; three decades later nine of the top fifteen urban centers were in LDCs. Significantly, four of these nine were in China and India, countries with very low overall levels of urbanization.

Prospects of Demographic Change

What are the implications for the future of the demographic state of the world as outlined in the preceding pages? Although predictions of distant social phenomena can never claim a high degree of accuracy ex ante, demographic processes are characterized both by significant biological regularities and by a degree of behavioral inertia that make longer-range projections of past trends safer than projecting social changes in general. Barring catastrophic developments, some medium-term projections can be made with considerable expected accuracy, far more so, for example, than economic projections for similar time spans.

As an illustration, consider the problem of predicting changes in the size of the young adult population, young adults being defined as those between ages twenty and forty. Once we have the estimated age distribution and size of the population in 1985, the answer for the next twenty years is not difficult to obtain. For example, those aged twenty to forty in 2005 will be the survivors of those under the age of twenty in 1985. Thus, for some time to come, such a projection does not rely on estimating fertility—typically the most hazardous element in population projections—but only on predicting mortality. Mortality is relatively low in the age groups being considered; hence even a less than perfect mortality prediction will affect the accuracy of the projection only modestly. Yet the yield of such a twenty-year forecast—which in economic matters would be characterized as a long-range projection—is hardly trivial: changes in the size of the young adult population have a major bearing on such processes as the growth of the labor force and employment and the related accumulation of productive skills, changes in capital-labor ratios, labor mobility, comparative advantage in international trade, migration behavior, household formation, and, not the least, reproduction and population growth.

Comparisons between the size of the population aged twenty to forty in 1985 and as projected for 2005 are better appreciated if the corresponding population at an equidistant past date, 1965, is also taken into account. The figures for the young adult population in millions are shown in the table on page 60.

The contrasts between the demographic future of LDCs and MDCs with respect to this critical age group are striking. Between 1965 and 1985 both groups of countries experienced

	1965	1985	2005
MDCs	285	366	352
LDCs	636	1105	1674
World	921	1471	2026

rapid expansion even though at sharply differing rates. In absolute terms, in MDCs the number of young adults was 81 million greater in 1985 than in 1965; the corresponding figure for LDCs was 469 million. In the twenty-year period between 1985 and 2005 MDCs will experience an actual shrinkage of the number of twenty- to forty-year olds, at the average annual rate of 0.2 percent. LDCs will grow, in contrast, at 2.1 percent per annum. In absolute terms, in 2005 the young adult population in MDCs will be 14 million less than it was in 1985. In LDCs the size of this age group will grow by 569 million. Clearly, this is a forecast with potentially far-reaching economic, social, political, and demographic consequences.

It should be noted here that the forecast does not adequately take into consideration possible flows of international migration across the LDC–MDC divide. (In general, international migration is given short shrift in the present account: that important demographic process is the subject of another chapter in this volume.) It is clear from the above figures, however, that the demographic effects of such migration are bound to be highly asymmetrical. For example, a net migratory flow of 20 million young adults from LDCs would make a difference between decline of that age group and at least creeping growth in MDCs, and would represent a significant demographic addition there to the domestic stock of potential labor supply. Twenty million, in contrast, would be barely more than 1 percent of the projected number of young adults in LDCs in 2005 and would amount to about 3.5 percent of the expected net addition to the young adult population in those countries between 1985 and 2005. Outmigration from LDCs in the assumed volume, if evenly spread among sending countries, would therefore make nary a ripple in LDC demographic dynamics.

Demographic projections involving the total population are, however, on less firm footing than the special example given above, and their expected reliability decreases rapidly as the time horizon is extended forward. They should be considered as numerical exercises spelling out the implications of specified assumptions concerning the future course of mortality and fertility. If those assumptions are accepted as valid, the picture depicted by the projection in question is accurate by definition. As was noted in connection with Figure 2, the United Nations has prepared three sets of projections up to the year 2025—"high," "medium," and "low"—and some World Bank projections are extended to 2100. Against the background of observed and estimated fertility and mortality trends between 1950 and 1985, Figures 4 and 5 illustrate the assumptions underlying the "medium" U.N. projections and those made by the World Bank for the period 2025 to 2100. Although the World Bank's projections are close in spirit to those of the U.N. medium projections (and incorporate the same "cohort component" methodology), there is a discontinuity in the graphs at the year 2025. This discontinuity is a reminder (but not an adequate gauge) of the growing arbitrary element in specifying the most plausible course of mortality and fertility as far ahead as a distance of forty years.

With respect to mortality, the governing assumptions are straightforward: trends in expectation of life will continue apace along the pattern of past improvements. The now laggard regions will more or less retrace the average past record of progress, while the more advanced regions will be experiencing continued gradual slowdown as they approach the presumed upper limit, set at a life expectancy of about eighty years. These assumptions imply a continuing pattern of regional mortality differentials over time. Absolute differences do narrow down, but the time lag between leaders and followers in attaining particular levels of life expectancy remains fairly stable.

The underlying fertility assumptions can be characterized in an even more lapidary fashion. The projections specify a jolt-free headlong rush to replacement-level fertility from current levels. In all regions, with the exception of Africa, this convergence to a TFR of near 2.1 will be essentially completed by about 2020. By that time Africa, too, will have experienced a 50 percent decline in its fertility from 1980–85 levels, but replacement-level fertility will be reached only around 2040. In all areas, once replacement-level fertility is attained it is firmly and permanently hewed to.

The implications of these assumptions are spelled out in Figures 6, 7, and 8 in terms of three indexes of demographic change: rates of population growth, annual additions to population size, and total population size. As to the rate of population growth (Figure 6), the already well established declining trend is shown to continue at a rapid pace, although in Africa the downturn occurs only after the turn of the century. But the calculated time path of the growth rate shows a much more moderate pace than is suggested by the posited precipitous drops in fertility. To some extent this is because of the assured mortality improvements. Although the hypothesized future increases in life expectancy will be a less potent factor in adding to and in sustaining growth than were gains in life expectancy in the past, they do contribute significantly to population increase, particularly in areas of still relatively high mortality. A more important engine that works toward prolonging the attainment of zero growth, however, is the momentum inherent in the young age distributions caused by past high fertility in LDCs. Even if replacement-level reproduction could be achieved instantaneously, populations with the age composition of typical LDCs would add 50 percent or more to their present population size before a no-growth state is eventually reached.

Absolute annual increases are shown in Figure 7. Given the underlying fertility and mortality assumptions, despite declining growth rates, absolute increases would continue to swell beyond the 1980s in all major LDC regions, except in East Asia. Peak absolute growth would occur around 2000 in South Asia and in Latin America, and in the second decade of the twenty-first century in Africa. Thus the projections imply that in terms of this important index, in major LDC areas the brunt of the population explosion is yet to come.

FIGURE 7. Average Annual Population Increase (Millions): 1950–2100 (1950–85: estimates; 1985–2100: projections)

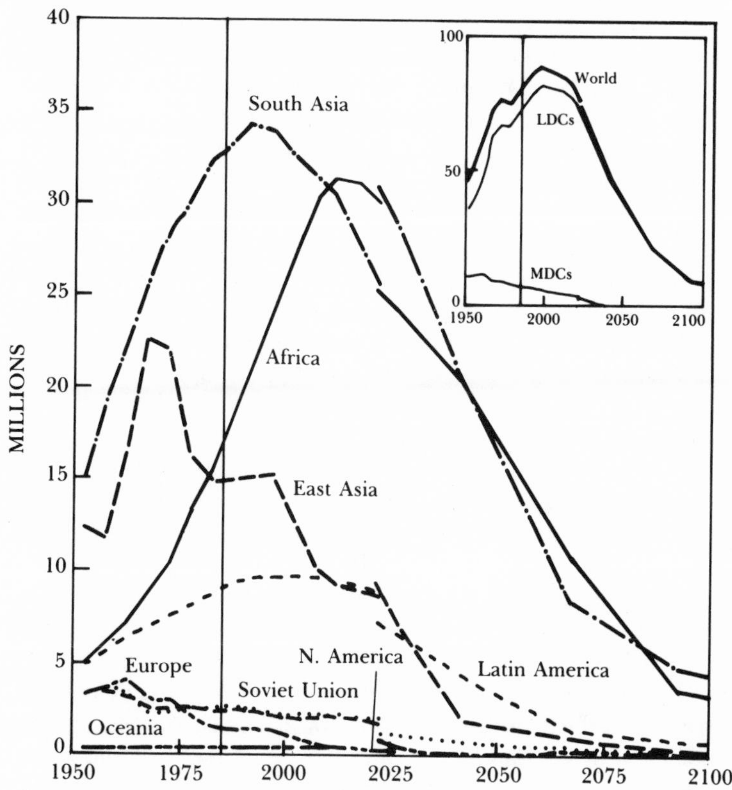

Finally, the implications of the projections in terms of population size are depicted in Figure 8 (in which populations are plotted against a logarithmic scale). According to this figure, in the year 2000 global population would be 6.1 billion and would rise to 8.2 billion by 2025, to 9.4 billion by 2050, and to 10.4 billion by 2100. This overall growth would be accompanied by major shifts in the regional composition of the global population. For example, by the end of the twenty-first century, Europe's share would be 5.2 percent, half of its 1985 level; Northern America's share (still comparable to that of the

Soviet Union) would be down to 3.1 percent (from the 1985 level of 5.5 percent); Africa's share would be 24 percent, up from the 1985 level of 11 percent. In 2100, the present area of the LDCs would contain 87 percent of the world's total population. By that time, however, all regional components of the world population would be in the stationary state, implying only minimal further demographic shifts either with respect to size or composition.

Anyone dissatisfied with or skeptical of such forecasts must go back to the underlying assumptions shown in Figures 4 and 5 and reject them. Substituting more defensible hypotheses then can spawn a new, preferred set of projections. To obtain specific numerical outcomes requires simple, albeit laborious, calculations, but the direction of change compared to the reference projections in most instances can be readily perceived even without such calculations.

For instance, is global population stabilization feasible well below the 10 billion mark implied by the projections presented in Figure 8? What modifications of the underlying mortality and fertility assumptions would be needed to bring about a smaller ultimate world population size?

Modifying the specified courses of mortality may not seem very promising for the purpose. As is, the assumptions seem rather pessimistic; for most of the LDC region they exclude the possibility of the kind of rapid improvement already achieved by China and discount the possibility of rapid transfer and successful application of new death-control technologies in LDCs. In MDCs, the assumption of eighty years as the near–upper limit of the average length of human life even by the end of the next century is also rather timid. More optimistic assumptions would, of course, lead to more rapid growth and higher population size.

On the other hand, mortality setbacks such as the major famine-induced excess mortality in China during the Great Leap, or the more recent deterioration of life expectancy in the Soviet Union (affecting especially the male population) are excluded in Figure 4. But such setbacks, even if they occur, are likely to be temporary, with limited longer-term demographic

FIGURE 8. World Population Growth: 1950–2100 (1950–85: estimates; 1985–2100: projections)

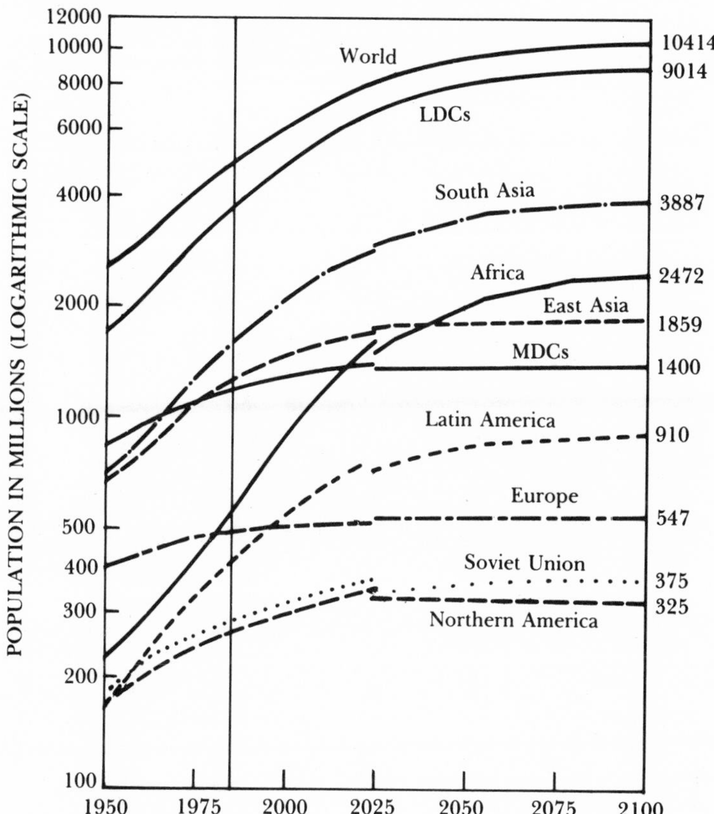

impact. More significant is the exclusion of a more drastic "Malthusian" adjustment: a balancing of birth and death rates by return of the death rates to levels resembling the state that preceded the onset of demographic transition. Arguably, that is not only an undesirable but also an impossible eventuality. Sustaining a world population of 5 billion–plus requires a high-level technical civilization and a highly interconnected world economy. Their effective functioning is hardly compatible with death rates rising to medieval levels: rising mortality would be likely to lead not to equilibrium but to demographic collapse.

Almost certainly, the crucial variable shaping humankind's demographic future will be the course of fertility. Can the picture shown in Figure 5 be "improved" upon to yield a faster approach to zero growth than is presented in Figures 6 and 7? If so, what mechanisms are envisaged to bring about a more rapid decline of fertility? For instance, will Africa, early in the next century, somehow imitate the much maligned policies that China introduced in the 1970s? Or can a faster decline than envisaged in Figure 5 come about through the influence of other forces? Will these be rising expectations and the market-generated appeals of the high-consumption society, or pressures of crushing poverty and the specter of sinking below already attained standards of living? In countries that are successfully developing, is it realistic to assume that fertility will naturally drop to replacement level without pause, or will couples prefer to turn some of their income gains into larger than two-child families? Once replacement fertility is attained, might future baby booms occur after all, echoing earlier Western experience? Will some populations with already below replacement-level fertility remain there permanently, thus heading to extinction? Answers to these and other similar questions are likely to suggest that possible demographic futures could deviate greatly from those pictured above, especially in directions that might generate an overall global population trajectory well above that shown in Figure 8, yet permit changes in the opposite direction in some of the regional populations. Conducting the contemporary debate on international population policies in the thrall of a presumed most likely course of the world's demographic future without confronting these questions would be a serious mistake.

2

Are the Economic Consequences of Population Growth a Sound Basis for Population Policy?

SAMUEL H. PRESTON

The political debate that has produced robust U.S. support for efforts to reduce rates of population growth and for family planning as the means to this end has been predicated on the presumed negative effects of continuing rapid growth on economic development and on individual welfare. This chapter will review some of the evidence currently available on the economic consequences of high versus low fertility. But the primary focus of this discussion will be on whether the economic consequences of population growth, as we now understand them, are a sound basis for population policies of

---

SAMUEL H. PRESTON is author or editor of several books and many articles on population, particularly mortality and population trends. Most recently, he was involved in the preparation of a National Academy of Sciences report, *Population Growth and Economic Development: Policy Questions,* which contains citations to many of the references appearing here. Dr. Preston is active in research, in professional conferences here and abroad, and in the leadership of professional associations. He chairs the Department of Sociology at the University of Pennsylvania. Dr. Preston gratefully acknowledges comments on this chapter by Marc Nerlove, Jere Behrman, Landis McKellar, Jane Menken, Susan Watkins, Jerry Jacobs, and Michael Teitelbaum.

various types. The analysis will apply the apparatus of welfare economics to this question. It will consider the question of whose welfare we are considering, the state or the individual, and, among individuals, it will distinguish among effects on various interested parties to a childbearing decision.

The recent policy of the United States has been one of support for voluntary family planning programs. A few countries, China being the most notable, have decided that their population problem was severe enough to justify policies that went beyond family planning in an effort to stem population growth. Much of the welfare economics analysis is pertinent to the discussion of such policies. Therefore, although these policies are not now under direct consideration for U.S. support, this chapter will also consider the question of whether and when the effects of individual fertility decisions justify policies that go beyond enabling a couple to reach their childbearing goals. To set the stage, we will first consider the relative magnitudes of various influences on economic growth and the measures that have conventionally been used to study them.

Per Capita Income and Population Growth

We are all taught that in matters of human well-being it is per capita measures that really matter. Goods and bads are to be divided by the size of the population that enjoys or suffers them in order to assess how well we are doing, on average.

Accepting per capita measures as the definitive indicators of human welfare immediately creates an apparent link between population size and social progress. In fact, per capita measures of well-being appear to give population size coequal importance with whatever appears in the numerator. Given the size of the numerator, growth in population spreads the "goods" more thinly and results in a loss of well-being. The logic of the connection is unassailable. Since many of the goods involve products of nature—land, minerals, energy, species—and since the abundance of nature is seen as more or less fixed, it becomes reasonable to think that population growth diminishes the per capita availability of most goods. It seems fair to say that this is the predominant way that the issue of the economic effects of population growth has traditionally been considered. It is an approach that traces back at least to Malthus.

At the same time, a host of the "bads" are seen as man-made. Crime, war, pollution, social disarray, even poverty increase at least proportionally with population size. To many, it appears reasonable to believe that social problems increase even faster than population because larger numbers of people are forced to contend over more limited resources, producing many forms of social disorganization. According to a recent statement by the chairman of the board of the Environmental Fund, Thomas Brokaw:

> [Americans] are treated to the spectacle of millions of well-meaning people working diligently to overcome the effects of over-population. Here I refer to law enforcement agents, educators, environmentalists, transportation authorities, health and social workers, and many others, but most of all politicians. All of them are busily ignoring the basis of the problems that they are working to correct.

At the extreme, such views are a self-parody. In only slightly less extreme form, they can pass for conventional wisdom. These modes of thought seem to come particularly easily to biologists and ecologists, who as a group are almost surely endowed with an above-average reverence for nature and are inclined to view man's intrusions as violations of a sanctified order. More importantly, they often reason about human affairs by analogy to species that do not systematically and purposively *construct* the environment from which they derive sustenance. For such species, it is plausible to view the fixity of nature as presenting immutable constraints. But does this constraint apply equally to humans?

Natural and Other Resources

Man constructs his own environment, and therein lies the basic fallacy of much reasoning in matters of population growth. The availability of natural resources has simply played a minor role in modern economic growth. European countries in the eighteenth century had far more resources per capita than they do today, but they also had per capita income levels that were shockingly poor by modern standards. Economic growth occurred through the accretion of physical and human capital, the development of supportive institutions, and above all through the accumulation of knowledge about techniques of production.

Japan provides a more vivid and contemporary example. After World War II, Japan's per capita income lay below prewar standards. Resource poor, it appeared to many contemporary observers to be "overpopulated." According to Irene Taeuber in her classic 1958 book, *The Population of Japan,* the Japanese government's Population Planning Commission concluded in 1946 that "unparalleled surplus population is now an undeniable fact"; and the Population Problems Council argued in 1949 that "the solution of our problems demands suppression of population expansion through birth control but also through emigration overseas." However, the population of already dense Japan was to grow by 40 percent between 1950 and 1980, while per capita income grew by a factor of 7.4. Hong Kong, South Korea, Singapore, and Taiwan have, of course, made great economic strides despite being resource poor. More recently, China has expanded its food production by a dramatic 55 percent over a six-year period largely through an institutional change that has replaced a command system with markets. The fact that these examples are all Asian enhances rather than diminishes their demonstration value, because it suggests the dependence of economic growth on institutional, cultural, and human resource factors.

On the other hand, Zaire is extraordinarily rich in resources, including agricultural land. According to a recent study by the Food and Agricultural Organization, it could feed the entire projected population of Africa in the year 2000 several times over if the best of currently available production techniques were employed. Yet Zaire is exceptionally poor, with the seventh lowest gross national product (GNP) per capita in 1982 among the 126 countries for which the World Bank provides such estimates.

The success stories cited above are well known, but their lesson is easily neglected. Most of the things that we appear to value as a species are not fixed in abundance. They are produced by people using man-made tools and relying on techniques that are derived from an ever-growing storehouse of knowledge. The techniques accumulate rather than erode because of the cultural inventions of speech and language, books and education. As Julian Simon has stressed, in view of the importance of the human factor in production, it makes no sense to assume that the number of "goods" in the numerator of a per capita index is unrelated to the size of the denominator.

Demographers and economists have long recognized the vital role of physical and human capital in producing goods and services. Nevertheless, their habits of thought drove them in the same direction as the layperson: to represent economic processes through relatively simple formulas in which the size of the population or labor force was one element and the relationship between population size and the dependent economic indicator remained the same over time. The effect of population growth could then be studied by performing mental (or computer) experiments which varied the size of population. The results from these early models have been questioned on several grounds: that the relationships may not be fixed over time or at all population levels; that the economic indicators (e.g., capital/labor ratios) may not be as relevant as once thought; and that the models omitted prices, which direct the behavior of individuals and firms in adaptive ways.

Demographic-Economic Models and the Sources of Economic Growth

An early economic-demographic model by Ansley Coale and Edgar Hoover focused on the effects of population growth on capital supply and, through capital/labor ratios, on per capita income. They concluded that high fertility was likely to reduce the supply of capital, capital/labor ratios, and per capita income because it was associated with a higher "burden of dependency": the larger population of youths would tend to divert income so that, instead of being saved, it would go into immediate consumption in the form of larger expenditures on food, health, schooling, and other social programs. Many qualifications have been raised about the Coale-Hoover model. It has been argued, for example, that population growth itself might be expected to increase the demand for capital, that a rise in the rate of return to capital induced by capital shortages could be expected to increase investment, and that educational expenditures might be treated as a form of investment rather than of consumption. Despite these qualifications, a recent review of evidence in the matter by the National Academy of Sciences concludes that capital/labor ratios would be expected to be modestly higher in a slower-growing population compared to a similar but rapidly growing population.

But capital/labor ratios, like natural resources, have left the center stage of the debate. Their importance was undercut by the empirical demonstration that the growth of capital stock has played a far smaller role in economic growth than had previously been believed. In a highly influential series of studies, Denison, Abramovitz, and others show that the principal factor in economic growth in the United States, Europe, Japan, and certain developing countries had not been growth in the volume of capital or labor or in the two combined but a change in production techniques, gains in the amount and value of output that could be extracted from given physical quantities of inputs.

In retrospect, it does not appear reasonable to attempt to represent the millions of daily decisions in a modern economy, and the extraordinarily variegated structure within which that economy operates, by a few indexes, mechanically combined. But framing the issue in terms of simplified formulas was useful precisely for demonstrating that results typically were inaccurate in the direction of underpredicting economic growth. Using fixed formulas to relate inputs to outputs usually produces pessimistic biases in economic predictions, because it neglects the unidirectional changes in accumulated technical knowledge (at least since the Dark Ages). The bias is present whether we deal with fixed factors of production alone (e.g., land) or whether we add produced factors of production (e.g., factories).

Focusing exclusively on the economic success stories can also produce biased accounts. While resource scarcity has not prevented many countries at different times in world history from enjoying rapid economic growth while undergoing rapid population increase, resource availability remains an important element in economic well-being in many poor countries today precisely because the essential elements for economic growth have been missing. Telling Bangladesh that what it needs is to be more like Hong Kong is like telling an unemployed man in the South Bronx that what he needs is to go to Harvard. What is needed is advice on how to get the next steps up the development ladder, in full awareness of the conditions at hand.

The situation in Bangladesh is wretched, and population growth has probably helped bring it about. A.R. Khan presents evidence that real agricultural wages in Bangladesh in the 1970s were below their level in the 1830s. Much of the decline occurred in the period of most rapid population growth, after 1950. The decline in real wages was accompanied by an apparent large increase in landlessness between 1951 and 1977 and by a reduction in average calorie consumption and a rise in the proportion of the population living in poverty. Several economists—Boserup, Hayami and Ruttan, and others—have demonstrated convincingly that greater density of population can promote technological change in agriculture that takes advantage of more abundant labor. But others, including Ghatak and Ingersent, note that once Bangladesh's density is reached there may be no technological tricks left in the bag.

There is other evidence that Malthus's dismal scenario is not always averted: time-series evidence on real wages and population in England, France, and a composite of European countries between about 1300 and 1750 leave little doubt that exogenous changes in population, induced by epidemics, plagues, weather changes, and wars, affected average wages.

Periods of unusually small population numbers had unusually high wages. Ronald Lee's estimates for preindustrial England suggest that a 10 percent increase in population depressed real wages by 22 percent and raised rents by 19 percent. Robert Evenson reaches similar conclusions from cross-sectional data in contemporary northern India: a 10 percent increase in population density is associated with a 3.3 percent decline in per capita output and a decline of 6.4 percent in wages of the landless, even after all of the adaptive changes in technique are factored in.

So it is reasonable to believe that the economic consequences of high fertility and rapid growth vary with many features of the national setting. One would expect the effects to be most serious in poor, dense, agrarian countries where ratios of natural resources to population are most consequential for economic processes.

What policy implications follow from a demonstration that population growth has negative effects on per capita income? What kinds of population policies can be justified in an effort to increase well-being? A clear answer to these questions requires that we give some thought to whose well-being we are concerned with.

The State, the Individual, and Externalities

An exclusive focus on characteristics of the aggregate, such as per capita income, income distribution, life expectancy, or mean years of schooling, greatly simplifies the analysis of development. The conventional approach to studying the impact of population growth focuses on these aggregate indicators. However, it is obvious that many of these indicators can be made to improve by implementing population policies that actually reduce individual welfare. For example, per capita income will almost certainly rise in the short run (through reduced dependency burdens) if all couples are forcibly sterilized; per capita measures of income distribution will improve if low-income people are selectively prevented from reproducing; mean levels of schooling will rise if the illiterate are forced out of the country. Even though the aggregate measures improve, no one is necessarily made better off by these policies, and many may be worse off. In the sensitive area of population policy, it makes little sense to talk about improvements in well-being as though they could be disembodied from the policies that bring them about.

In other words, governmental musing over population growth is not equivalent to parents musing over the size of their own families. If it were, we could simply collectively examine the costs and benefits of additional children for some national indicator such as per capita income, and decide how many babies we wanted. Many debates over population growth seem to assume that this is the way nations do, or at least should, proceed.

On the contrary, the gains and losses from economic growth, as well as from children, count only to the extent that they are registered in *individuals'* well-being; governing structures do not "enjoy" income—they are insensible—nor do they bear children. It is parents who bear the brunt of the costs and enjoy the bulk of the benefits, many of them noneconomic, from children. If parents are willing to pay the price of their behavior, why should nations interfere, even if per capita income in the family and nation is reduced by an additional birth? As Paul Demeny notes, the situation is analogous to individual work/leisure decisions. Per capita income would surely rise if the government decreed that everyone must work on Sunday. But who is made better off by the decree?

Welfare Economics

A more appealing framework for population policy discussions than looking simply at per capita measures is provided by the apparatus of welfare economics. Here a good policy is one that increases the welfare of someone or some group without making anyone worse off. More broadly, a reasonable policy is one in which individual gains exceed individual losses such that the losers could be fully compensated and still leave the gainers better off. Whether or not the compensation actually occurs is a separable issue having to do with choices about the distribution of well-being (or income), and we will for the most part leave this issue aside, simply noting some distributional consequences if compensation does not occur.

Forcible sterilization, to take an extreme example, would be rejected by the criterion of welfare economics unless it could be shown that the benefits to the nonsterilized exceed the welfare losses among the sterilized. Obviously there are moral and human rights features of such policies that must be considered; here we are dealing only with what are in principle quantifiable economic gains and losses.

There is, however, one type of population policy that clearly benefits those whose fertility is affected and for which a demonstration of benefits to others is, therefore, not required. Family planning programs that provide couples with the means to achieve their desired family size have positive payoffs for the couples who use the services. Because they empower couples to achieve their personal goals, they increase the private welfare of users, at the expense of a (usually small) tax on nonusers. (This assumes, of course, that the means employed by the users are acceptable to the nonusers; otherwise an additional cost to nonusers is entailed.) The voluntary nature of family planning programs accounts for much of their appeal as a policy instrument. To some extent, the rationale for government involvement in family planning programs is much like that for government involvement in health information or agricultural extension activities: there is a high informational content to such programs, and private firms may have no incentive to spread the proper information, e.g., about the rhythm method or the health consequences of sterilization. Furthermore, the required size and organizational complexity of family planning programs may be so great that no private companies would be willing to undertake the risk of supplying the services.

While this justification seems entirely valid, there are many other areas in which people could profit from information and services supplied by governments but where corresponding programs are essentially absent in poor countries: job placement services, home-building advice, assessments of household water quality, and so on. Such programs use scarce resources, as do family planning programs, and most governments have chosen not to bear the costs. It is safe to say that much of the special interest in family planning programs historically reflects a belief that the benefits derived therefrom extend *beyond* the couple that is making the childbearing decision to other members of society. These benefits reflect presumed social gains from the effects of slowing rates of population growth. Thus, while one rationale for family planning programs does not require us to examine the benefits and costs to anyone other than the childbearing couple, the policy context directs our attention to these external effects. And if the effects are indeed present, then a properly constituted policy *should* be aware of them and set program intensities accordingly.

"Externalities"

Welfare economics has a well-developed framework for examining the effects of one person's behavior on aggregate welfare, recently elaborated with regard to population issues by Marc Nerlove, Robert Willis, and others. Central to this framework is the notion of an "externality." An externality exists when resources could be reshuffled in such a way as to make someone better off without making anyone else worse off. More generally, it exists if on balance the benefits produced by this reshuffling exceed the losses incurred. Economists have shown that if fully competitive markets existed to accurately reflect the costs to producers and benefits to consumers for all commodities, externalities could not exist; they reflect the failure of markets to fully represent these costs and benefits in setting prices. When an externality is present, prices no longer provide the correct information about the social value of resources used in production and consumption. In the presence of such failure, governments could intervene in markets to improve the average level of well-being.

A classic example of an externality is untaxed air pollution by a factory. Such pollution imposes a cost on those outside the factory, but this cost is not reflected in the price—zero—that the factory owner is charged for creating such pollution. A suitable tax could be found such that the factory owner's decisions reflected the full social cost of air pollution, and such a tax would be expected to reduce air pollution. The expected gain to sufferers from air pollution can be shown to exceed the loss to the factory owner and consumers of the product of the factory.

The fact that one person's behavior has an *effect* on others does not constitute a prima facie case that an *externality* exists. For example, when one wheat producer expands his output, it may drive down the price of wheat for all other producers, but it also increases the amount of wheat that consumers can buy for a certain amount of dollars, and no net welfare loss is entailed. A welfare loss would result, however, if the government prevented him from marketing his wheat, or if it paid him above market prices for producing the wheat and then let it rot, or even sold it at market prices (in which case too many resources would be devoted to wheat production and too few to the production of other goods). It is easy to see why these interferences with market mechanisms produce a net loss of welfare.

An analogous situation exists with respect to fertility. When one family has an extra child, it can be expected (marginally) to drive down the wages paid to members of other families decades hence. But at the same time, it increases rates of return to owners of other factors of production (capital or land). Lee's work on preindustrial England and Evenson's on north India reveal precisely these effects: rapid population growth depressed wages and increased rents. If markets adjust in this fashion to a larger population, there is no necessary or likely average loss of welfare for other families. Economists, using simple supply and demand curves and assuming a downward sloping demand curve for labor, have shown that the loss in wages is approximately equal to the gain in returns to other productive factors. If all of the capital is owned by the family having the child, everyone else would be made worse off, on average; if it is all owned by others, they will be made somewhat better off. In this situation, fertility does not create an externality and, therefore, would not satisfy the strictest welfare economics criterion for governmental action.

These are not notions known only to the professional economist. Much of the controversy over immigration policy in the United States today reflects the conflicting position of unions representing wage earners, who correctly perceive that faster immigration could be expected to depress wages, and owners of land and factories, whose profits could be expected to be higher when wages are lower. The connection was also known to slave owners who encouraged the reproduction of their slaves in order to increase the returns from their land.

The relative effects of population growth on wages and on payments to other factors of production require elaboration. The reduction in rates of return to labor from faster population growth, and the increase in rates of return to other factors of production, would be expected to exacerbate income inequality. Owners of capital and land typically have above average incomes, and those who earn the bulk of their income through wages usually have below average income. So faster population growth could be expected to increase income inequality and raise the fraction living in poverty. In theory, these effects could be essentially offset by increased taxes on rents and redistributions to laborers. However, it would not be sensible to suppose that such redistributions are likely to occur. To the extent that we care about income inequality, the example provides a basis for social intervention in childbearing. It is important to recognize that it is a *distributional* ground, reflecting relativistic judgments about how much various groups should have, and not an *externality* ground.

Thus far, we have considered only wages. But if the labor markets are, in economists' jargon, "sticky," in that they fail to adjust to population growth in such a way as to equate supply and demand at an equilibrium wage, then one family's childbearing might also be expected to reduce employment levels for other families. In this situation, high fertility would lead to an externality; a market failure is present that is exacerbated by population growth. A review in the recent National Academy of Sciences report of the limited evidence available fails to find an empirical connection between population growth and unemployment. Rates of labor force growth across countries and over time are not found to be statistically related to unemployment levels. The low-wage informal sector in developing countries evidently has substantial capacity to "absorb" labor. It takes very few saved or borrowed resources to set up shop as a petty trader on the streets of cities in developing countries, for example. The incentives to find some form of work are very great when one is very poor; as the aphorism says, the poor can't afford to be unemployed. In this situation, wages rather than unemployment statistics are where we would expect the consequences of population growth to appear.

In summary, evidence is lacking that effects of population growth on employment, wages, and returns to land and capital typically lead to externalities. Where markets are operating effectively, the influence of population growth on rates of return to labor and other factors of production do not represent true externalities. But there are other instances where market imperfections are known to create externalities from childbearing. The most important of these are probably the following.

Externalities from Childbearing

Subsidized Schooling and Other Social Programs for Children

Parents do not pay the full cost of schooling in developing countries. For a variety of reasons, the state usually subsidizes schools, at least up to a certain grade level. These subsidies impose a cost of one family's childbearing on other families. The social cost could, of course, be eliminated by making parents pay the full cost of schooling. Short of that, it could be reduced by imposing other kinds of penalties on parents for childbearing, thereby reducing the total burden of externalities.

There is another side to this coin, however. Educated children grow up and pay taxes that subsidize the education of other people's children. No one has, to my knowledge, computed the net balance of lifetime charges against and contributions to the educational system of an additional birth. The costs are incurred before the benefits are received. Economists typically "discount" the value of benefits received at a later date to take into account the time lag during which there is no return on the investment in education. It is likely that this calculation would result in each child's representing a net cost rather than a net benefit, although in a high-fertility population each child whose education is subsidized may in turn subsidize the schooling of several children in the next generation.

Societies could react to higher fertility by spreading the same amount of resources among more school-age children, thereby sacrificing some of the social benefits expected from subsidized schooling, or by spending the same amount per child and hence raising the total costs of education, or by some intermediate strategy. T. Paul Schultz recently used cross national data to examine how societies actually do react. He finds no association between the rate of growth of the school-age population and the rate of per capita enrollment growth. Faster growth does not appear to compromise schooling attainment. He does, however, find a strong inverse association between population growth and school expenditures per child. This finding indicates that the quality of education may suffer in faster-growing populations, although a strong relation between school expenditures per child and output measures (e.g., test scores) has been difficult to demonstrate either in developed or developing countries. An externality produced by subsidized schooling is likely to remain whatever the social reaction to high fertility, and the burden of this externality would be mitigated by reduced fertility.

It is interesting to consider the externalities created by social programs in socialist countries, where more resources are allocated by the state than in market economies. The size of this type of externality from childbearing, accordingly, becomes larger, to the point where it almost makes sense to think that governments are the relevant actor in childbearing decisions: paternalistic governments literally taking on the role of parent. This logic may explain why population policies have typically been more vigorous in socialist countries. In the Soviet Union, for example, the main rationale for prohibiting emigration has been the resources that the state has invested in the potential emigre. But while resources invested in individuals by the state are greater, so are resources donated by individuals to the state. The net balance, over the life cycle, of contributions to and withdrawals from the public trough is unclear, especially as programs for the elderly are added to programs for children. Socialist governments do not appear on balance to be any more pronatalist or antinatalist than other governments, simply more active in adopting and implementing population policies, befitting their greater assumption of parental responsibilities.

Common Property Resources

From the standpoint of welfare economics, the most clear-cut externalities from childbearing result from the existence of common property resources. These are resources that, for one reason or another, are not "owned" and, hence, to which access is not effectively limited. The absence of ownership usually results either from the fact that the resource is not very valuable or from the difficulty of policing access. Note that ownership that effectively limits access need not be private but could be collective, as in the case of national forests in the United States or oil reserves in some kingdoms. Public schooling can be thought of as a special case of a common property resource because access is not purposefully limited but rather made available upon presentation of a claim.

Natural Resources. Let us deal first with natural resources. When a natural resource is owned and effectively managed, its price will reflect supply and demand conditions. Added demand that may result from population growth will be expected to increase the price of the resource, a disadvantage to the prospective purchasers but an advantage to resource owners. Many examples can be cited of how natural resource prices respond to changes in supply and demand conditions and direct the search for additional deposits and for substitute materials. However, if there is no ownership of the resources, additional claimants resulting from population growth will simply add congestion and represent a net loss to other users, who will have to share the resource more widely. There is no owner whose accounts register the greater scarcity value of the resource, and no market to restrict uses to the most highly valued. The problem is that the actual price of the resource—zero—is different from the price that a market would determine to be appropriate for balancing supply and demand. The resulting inefficiency, which produces over-use of the resource, is typically exacerbated by population growth.

The class of common property problems is quite broad. It pertains to land in much of Africa and parts of Asia and Latin America, to air and water resources nearly everywhere, to many forests and species of plants and animals, and, in selected cases, to mineral resources. To some, the earth and all upon it are common property resources; those who take this point of view are typically the most distressed by the prospect of rapid population growth. It is, however, an incorrect view that works only as an attention-getting metaphor. Were access to all resources of the earth truly unlimited, it would by now be a barren wasteland. Resource ownership promotes conservation. When a resource is unowned, users have no incentive to save it for future use or to avoid its degradation, because they realize only a tiny fraction of the gain from taking such steps. There is simply no way to guarantee themselves access to the resource that is saved or enhanced.

Allowing a resource to remain freely available to any potential user, regardless of the value that he or she places on it, is clearly not an efficient social management strategy. But such instances do indeed arise. Sometimes they arise because of the sheer technical difficulty of preventing access. The clearest such instance is probably the siltation of water resources resulting from soil erosion. Policing this process is extremely difficult because it results from thousands or millions of individual actions over a widely dispersed area. According to Pierre Crosson, the cost of such siltation exceeds the cost of erosion on the farmland itself. Policing access to forests is also quite difficult, and it is very likely that population growth is exacerbating externalities in much of the developing world through over-rapid deforestation. In the United States, on the other hand, forest management (chiefly by private companies) has produced a rising trend in wood growth per acre since 1952, and in Puerto Rico deforestation has been effectively reversed through sensible management.

Many resources remain common property simply because their value is low: it is not worth the effort, socially, to establish and enforce rules for access. When the resources become scarcer, it is reasonable to expect that institutions will adapt to promote more efficient use. The possibilities for "institutional adaptation" occupy a lively new branch of study in economics, and population growth has played a major role in much of this work. In particular, the growth of population has been shown to be an important factor—perhaps the dominant one—in establishing property rights to land in preindustrial Europe, in tropical Africa today, and in several Asian countries during the past century. Population growth is not the only factor capable of promoting ownership rights; some analysts stress the importance of the penetration of international markets in explaining the evolution of property rights to land in certain Asian countries, for example, although they also reserve a role for population growth. And institutional adaptations are surely not automatic. The Economic Commission for Africa recently noted that government efforts to establish more secure user rights over agricultural land have met with considerable resistance by tribal groups and individuals in Burundi, the Comoros, and Zaire.

Nevertheless, the possibility that population growth may stimulate the development of property rights, and in the long run promote conservation, is clearly an important qualification to the "tragedy of the commons," reasoning that views population growth as an unmitigated environmental disaster. The link between property rights and soil conservation is clearly recognized by Chinese authorities, who in recent years have promoted long-term contracts for cropland to arrest land degradation. An important by-product of establishing property rights is an improvement in capital markets by virtue of the collateral that is created. While this change is expected to be reflected in lower agricultural wages, as noted above, economic historians have also suggested that it had the favorable effect in preindustrial Europe and twentieth century Asia of helping to liberate labor from the restrictive institutions of corvée, indentured servitude, and serfdom.

In sum, population growth is likely to exacerbate inefficiencies resulting from common property natural resources. Where holding resources in common essentially reflects technological difficulties in restricting access, as in the case of water siltation and, to a lesser extent, deforestation, the disadvantages of population growth are likely to occur over the long term as well as the short term. In instances where institutions are capable of adapting to the greater resource scarcity resulting from population growth, effects may be limited to the short run if adequate institutional change takes place. Once property rights are established, the losses to one group resulting from greater resource scarcity and higher prices are matched by the gains among resource owners. This process typically would lead to a worsening of income inequality, an important policy concern in many developing countries. But it does not reflect externalities.

How important are these common property problems? Relative to many other problems besetting poor countries—lack of skills, poor techniques of production, and shortage of capital—they appear quite minor. Indeed, when technical or institutional means exist to correct the problem, the fact that they are not implemented suggests that the problems are a minor concern. With relatively little expenditure, Chinese industries could treat their waste products before dumping them into rivers, but most wastes are discharged untreated. If the lumber or fuel obtained from forests and bushlands being used for slash-and-burn agriculture in parts of Africa were valued sufficiently highly, it would be sold rather than burned. Such arguments are not appropriate for water siltation, where means for correcting the problem would be very expensive to implement; and in other cases, conflict between groups or a lack of popular participation in government may impede the implementation of appropriate measures. The problems exist, but in most times and places they do not seem to pose major obstacles to economic advance. If the social loss of common property resources resulting from population growth were fully represented (e.g., by taxation) in childbearing decisions, it seems unlikely that it would raise the private costs of childbearing by more than a few percent. In parts of West Africa where depletion of common forest resources has raised the price of fuel wood to the point where it represents a quarter of a household's budget, the problem is obviously much more serious.

Other Common Property Resources. We have spoken so far only of common property natural resources. But there are other resources that are created by man and that turn into common property resources to which access is unlimited. A classic example is national defense. It is virtually impossible to exclude a resident from a nation's defense umbrella. More pertinent to economic processes are roads, ports, and other transportation lanes. While such lanes present opportunities for restricting access, they provide no incentives for restriction until congestion occurs, since otherwise the marginal cost of use is nearly zero. In a larger population, the costs of "public goods" like defense, roads, and government sponsored agricultural research can be spread among more potential users, creating positive externalities to population growth. Research by Julian Simon suggests that some populations have, in fact, responded to the cheaper costs of transportation systems in denser areas by increasing the provision of transport more than proportionally to population size. The greater incentive to create transportation systems in a larger population is probably the most unambiguously positive externality from population growth, although an extra individual's contribution to creating such systems must be weighted against whatever extra congestion costs he or she poses for existing systems. The National Academy of Sciences report cites research by Simon, Boserup, Evenson, and others in support of the claim that infrastructural investments in rural areas are typically (though not invariably) stimulated by population growth.

This discussion would not be complete unless we noted that many valuable social and intellectual achievements also become common property resources: Shakespeare, Mozart, Confucius, the theory of relativity, participatory democracies, yoga, the French language, miracle wheat strains, and moon voyages are more or less freely available to all of us in one form or another. The fact that these boons to happiness are created by people does not mean that there will be more such creations the more people we have. Though entirely plausible where conditions are supportive, such a connection remains undemonstrated. But it is important to recognize that the number of such intellectual and social achievements is not fixed and, unlike the case of poorly managed natural assets, one person's enjoyment of them need not come at the expense of others.

Intergenerational Relations

We already have considered the impact of a family's childbearing on the economic well-being of other families. But fertility levels also have important effects within a particular family, especially upon the children born into it. It is clear that nature does not assign these children much if any market power that they could use to influence the childbearing decision of their parents. So while the "market" may work perfectly well in reflecting the wishes of current participants (the parental generation), one could argue that it fails to give "proper" weight to the wishes of future generations. It is perhaps more straightforward to think of the issue as one of the distribution of income between generations, rather than in the context of the market failure framework that we have been employing.

A substantial literature demonstrates that children drawn from small families tend to enjoy better schooling and better health. While some of the observed effects may reflect greater "tastes" for child quality among those wanting and having fewer births, some of the effects apparently also reflect the greater pressure on resources in homes where unwanted births occur. Gerry Rodgers reviews scattered evidence showing that child mortality tends to be higher in families where unwanted childbearing occurs, and Mark Rosenzweig shows that school achievement in India is lower among children in families where twins are born, a special kind of unanticipated childbearing. Whatever the mechanism that produces the relationship, it is reasonable to believe that a reduction in family size would present advantages for the children who are born.

Most studies of the relations between child mortality and family size reveal U-shaped effects, with death rates typically beginning to increase beyond a family size of three or four. James Trussell and Anne Pebley, for instance, calculate on the basis of World Fertility Survey data that eliminating all births beyond three in the typical developing country would reduce infant mortality rates immediately by 8 percent. While not everyone will consider these effects large, they are persistent across societies. Family planning programs that enable parents to space their births over longer intervals are also likely to be beneficial whatever the completed family size; analyses of World Fertility Survey data by John Hobcraft and others show extremely large mortality benefits from longer birth spacing, effects that swamp those pertaining to completed family size.

In addition to health and education effects, one could expect greater per child endowments of other family resources such as land and housing in a lower-fertility population. As noted above, these resources are probably especially important in poor, dense, agrarian countries, where natural resources are most likely to be scarce and, hence, to be owned and passed on from generation to generation in a family.

Let us summarize this discussion. First, family planning programs can be expected to enhance the welfare of users, who are better able to achieve their childbearing objectives. Second, the programs are also likely to improve the health and educational levels among children of users and to result in higher endowments per child of other family assets such as land.

The impact of successful family planning programs on the well-being of other families, including nonusers, is more ambiguous. The most direct effect is that the nonusers of family planning services are typically paying some form of minor tax to subsidize services for the users. On the benefit side of the ledger, the programs would ease short-term pressures on common property natural resources such as land and forests. However, in the longer run, they reduce the incentives to establish the access rules for such resources that help guarantee their long-term availability. They also raise the per capita cost to nonuser families of man-made common property goods such as transportation systems and agricultural research. In regard to social programs, when the major program is subsidized education, the net effect on other families of reduced fertility is most likely to be beneficial.

Beyond Family Planning

The United States has not supported policies that would attempt to alter fertility levels other than through voluntary family planning, but many urge support for such policies. Much of the discussion above is also pertinent in assessing programs that go "beyond family planning." Conceptually, the simplest such policies are incentive schemes that would explicitly or implicitly raise the costs of children to parents, and quantity restrictions that would simply place a limit on the number of children parents could have. Singapore and Bangladesh have experimented with the former type of policy and China with the latter.

The most obvious disadvantage of such programs relative to family planning is that those whose fertility is reduced by the program are not necessarily made better off by it. Couples whose fertility is reduced below desired levels by quantity restrictions are obviously made worse off. As Gerry Rodgers points out, the loss of welfare is likely to be greater for poorer couples, so that inequality in outcomes is likely to be exacerbated. Couples who are induced to reduce fertility through incentive schemes are presumably better off under the new conditions than if they maintained their previous behavior, but it is not possible to say, in general, whether they are better off than if previous conditions had remained in effect. What can be said is that if a nation chooses one of these policies, an incentive scheme results in a smaller loss of parental welfare than does rationing. If parents are induced to avert a birth by a rise in the cost of a child, then it is a reasonable inference that the child was worth less to them than the extra cost imposed or reward given. It is the births least valued by parents that are expected to be averted by an incentive scheme. On the other hand, quantity restrictions avert births without regard to their potential value to parents, and a larger welfare loss can be expected.

Despite these negative or ambiguous effects on parental welfare, such schemes could still be justified if the externalities from childbearing were sufficiently high. Family planning programs, after all, simply allow parents to choose the number of children that is in their own self-interest. They do not, except for the minor tax or subsidy involved in mounting the program, reflect the costs and benefits to others of their own childbearing.

Our review of these externalities suggests that the advantage of fertility reductions for those who are not a party to the childbearing decision is far more clear-cut for children in the same family than it is for members of other families. There are both positive and negative externalities for other families that work through social programs and through common property resources. The net balance of these is not clear, and it does not seem likely to be quantitatively large in most circumstances. On the other hand, the advantages for children in the same family of having fewer siblings seem reasonably well documented.

Do these advantages justify a program that would go beyond

family planning? Here, the apparatus of welfare economics offers little guidance. The basic issue is whether the interests of future generations in the same family are "adequately" protected by parental childbearing decisions. Most parents are obviously concerned with the well-being of their own children. Yet nothing prevents them from choosing family sizes that result in the gradual impoverishment of successive generations or in less rapid advance than would otherwise have occurred. Maybe their altruistic behavior is not, from a social point of view, strong enough.

The issue basically boils down to one of intergenerational comparisons of welfare. If we wanted to, we could take many social steps to ensure a brighter future for our descendants, e.g., refusing to use any fossil fuels for the rest of the twentieth century, or arbitrarily reducing consumption to increase investment. Many economists, such as Paul Samuelson, have argued that such steps will worsen intergenerational income inequality, since our descendants are already very likely to be richer than we are. Complicating this discussion in the case of population policy is the fact that we are simultaneously choosing the number of and conditions among the next generation. How many would prefer that their parents had lived in a society where an incentive scheme succeeded in eliminating half of the births that actually occurred?

In the absence of any compelling logic or evidence to the contrary, governments and societies have in the main assumed that parents act in the best interests of the family aggregate, including children already born and those who may or may not yet come. Reproductive rights are ceded to the family in nearly all societies, and family sovereignty in reproduction has been repeatedly affirmed in United Nations declarations. There are clear instances—child labor laws, compulsory schooling, or vaccination—where the state has intervened in child-rearing practices. Except for China and a brief episode in India, however, the state has not imposed legal or quasi-legal restrictions on childbearing. That is not to say that it would not do so if the case became compelling; reproductive rights, like other rights, exist at the sufferance of the collectivity that guarantees them. But the main justification for interfering in such rights at present relates to childbearing effects on descendants in the same family, rather than effects on members of other families. This justification appears to be an unsteady basis for going beyond family planning.

Discussion

Underpinning this account is the notion that couples make decisions about childbearing. Some would argue that this view is naive, that most couples in poor countries exist in a cultural and institutional context in which childbearing is under social rather than individual control: couples simply carry out the behaviors expected of them from centuries of accumulated cultural norms. If this were true, then the coercion of government would be little different than the coercion of culture, and the door would be opened to many forms of government intervention, including quantity rationing of children.

One must distinguish situations in which culture and institutions play a major role in influencing individual choices from a situation in which childbearing is not, in any meaningful sense, under individual control. Nothing in our account requires that the prime motivation for childbearing be economic; it is obvious that cultural expectations and institutional constraints play a major role in many countries in determining the value of children. Analytically, these values are readily incorporated into the functions that express individuals' tastes and preferences over alternative outcomes. The analytic apparatus is intact as long as individuals want to exert some purposeful control over the childbearing process, control that reflects the value that they attach to an additional birth.

Do couples make purposeful decisions about childbearing? I would contend that this is a reasonable assumption in nearly all countries. Cross-sectional variations in fertility levels are usually consistent with our notions of what would be in a couple's self-interest. Fertility is generally lower where the costs of children are higher, e.g., in urban areas or where children contribute less to a family's economic enterprise. Improving means to control fertility has apparently resulted in fertility declines in Mexico, Indonesia, Thailand, and elsewhere, a result that is difficult to interpret if childbearing simply reflects deeply embedded cultural norms. As Rudolpho Bulatao has shown, parents in many developing societies are able to provide extensive information about their perceived values and costs of children. Ethnographic studies in Bangladesh and sub-Saharan Africa present convincing portraits of how childbearing responds to the incentives provided by the social structure. Surely we do not understand all of the motives for childbearing in all societies, and there appear to be interpersonal forces at work in fertility decline, both in developing and developed countries, that do not admit to ready interpretation. But abandoning the assumption that childbearing reflects self-interested decisions appears unjustified.

Recognition that fertility behavior is conditioned by culture and institutions does open many possibilities for governmental intervention that we have not discussed. Regarding institutional changes (e.g., land redistribution, improvement in markets, minimum wage laws, compulsory education), the most that can be said is that many of these changes can be expected to influence fertility, and that fertility effects should be borne in mind in framing policies. Welfare economics has nothing to say about the wisdom of governments altering cultural patterns, since it takes as given the tastes and preferences that reflect that culture. It is not possible to compare the relative merits of two outcomes based on different sets of preferences. The prospect of government's altering cultural values will make many people uneasy, since it is difficult to evaluate government actions except from the point of view of the values embedded in a particular culture. There are no standards by which to evaluate government as standard maker, and any action could be justified as a cultural corrective. However, most countries do not have a single, readily identified value system, and the competition among value constructions admits and sometimes even encourages government intervention regarding traditional practices (e.g., with respect to female circumcision).

"Couples making decisions" is obviously a shorthand expression for what is likely to be a complicated process in most countries and most families. There can be substantial conflict between spouses, and the outcome of the conflict is likely to reflect their relative power. Programs that intervene in the fertility process can alter this power balance by giving one spouse, usually the woman, more direct influence in an important area of family life. So population programs can have some effect on redistributing power between the sexes, and social policy that concerns itself with this distribution should obviously take account of these effects. Finally, when there is concern with the distribution of power and resources between human beings and other species of animals and plants, it is obvious that programs to affect rates of population growth can be used to alter this balance as well.

Summary

Many intuitions about the economic effects of population growth overestimate the importance of natural resources in economic processes. The key to advance in rapidly growing economies has been the development of skills, techniques, and institutions. Nevertheless, there remains poor, dense, agrarian countries such as Bangladesh, Rwanda, Burundi, and Haiti where per capita resource endowments are an important element in economic well-being precisely because the development of these other features has been inadequate. Such countries are also expected to have the most acute family-level trade-offs between numbers and quality of children, as well as the least institutional adaptability to added population growth. Especially in such countries, fertility reductions appear likely to speed the growth of per capita income.

This aggregate-level relation does not provide any direct policy guidance. Governments do not bear children, people do. Formulating sensible policies requires that we examine the expected costs and benefits to various groups. In this paper, we distinguish among effects on the couple whose fertility is reduced, effects on their children, and effects on members of other families.

The economic effects on members of other families do not appear to be a strong basis for antinatal policy. It is difficult to make the case that other families suffer a net loss or gain from one family's childbearing, although such effects are surely possible in certain circumstances. Nevertheless, it is generally to be expected that higher fertility will result in higher levels of income inequality because it will depress wages and raise rates of return to other factors of production.

Most policies to reduce rates of childbearing would probably result in gains in health, education, and family asset endowments for children in the family whose fertility is reduced. It is, however, possible that certain kinds of incentive schemes could wind up withdrawing assets from children by virtue of the penalties attached to large families.

Of the policies considered here, only family planning programs can be reasonably assumed to increase the well-being of the couples themselves whose fertility is reduced. The case for going beyond family planning would have to rest mainly on the claim that parents are not acting in the best interest of their own children. Governments have been reluctant to press this claim, perhaps in part because it undermines the entire structure of informal norms and practices under which families carry out their array of critical social functions.

Therefore the present emphasis of population policy on family planning programs appears well justified. The programs benefit the users and their children, and they are also likely to reduce income inequalities and poverty levels by raising wages relative to rates of return to other factors of production. They cannot make a poor country rich, but they can help make it less poor.

3

Population Trends and Economic Development

ANSLEY J. COALE

In 1956, Edgar Hoover and I were in the middle of a research project in which we spent about two years studying the relationship between choosing continued high fertility or choosing substantially reduced fertility and the ensuing welfare of the population making the choice. We concluded that in both India and Mexico the choice of a 50 percent decline in the rate of childbearing in the ensuing twenty-five years would lead to better social and economic conditions in the 1980s than would the choice of continued high fertility of the sort that had prevailed in both populations up to the mid-1950s.

It is perhaps unfortunate that the short title of our book *Population Growth and Economic Development in Low Income Countries* suggests that our analysis dealt mostly with alternative rates of increase of the population. In fact, our analysis con-

---

ANSLEY J. COALE is William Church Osborn Professor of Public Affairs, professor of economics, and associate director of the Office of Population Research at Princeton University. Dr. Coale's teaching, consulting, and work in professional associations have reflected his long-term interest in population issues. A recent focus of his research has been population issues in China.

centrated on a thirty-year time perspective in which the principal effect of the choice of lower fertility would be to reduce the number of children in the population, with inconsequential effects until after thirty years on the size and rate of increase of the labor force.

Recent arguments minimizing the adverse implications of continued high fertility have emphasized that the empirical relation between the rate of increase in per capita income and the rate of increase in populations among different countries is negligible. Surprisingly enough, this lack of association between the rate of increase of population and rate of increase of per capita income is perfectly consistent with the research that we reported in our book. Hoover and I analyzed the prospects in India at considerable length and then more briefly analyzed the prospects in Mexico as exemplifying the potential effects of lower fertility under contrasting circumstances. It happens that in India both the rate of increase in population *and* the rate of increase in per capita income were lower than in Mexico. This fact was irrelevant to our conclusion that reduced fertility would improve social and economic prospects in *both* countries.

I have assembled figures on the rate of increase in per capita income from 1960 to 1982 in different major regions in the less developed world and compared this rate of increase with the rate of increase in population, with the expectation of life at birth in 1982, with the total fertility rate in 1982, with the reductions in fertility from 1952 to 1982, and with the proportion of the population under age fifteen in 1982. India, China, and Turkey are considered as separate entities. (The regions contain as many as eleven countries. The values compared are the population-weighted average values for the countries within each region.) Data on growth in gross national product per capita, growth in population, life expectancy, and total fertility rates are taken from the World Bank's *World Development Report* of 1984. The proportion under fifteen and the change in total fertility rate (TFR) are taken from *World Population Prospects as Assessed in 1982* by the Population Division of the United Nations.

Percent Increase in Per Capita Income (versus percent increase in population)

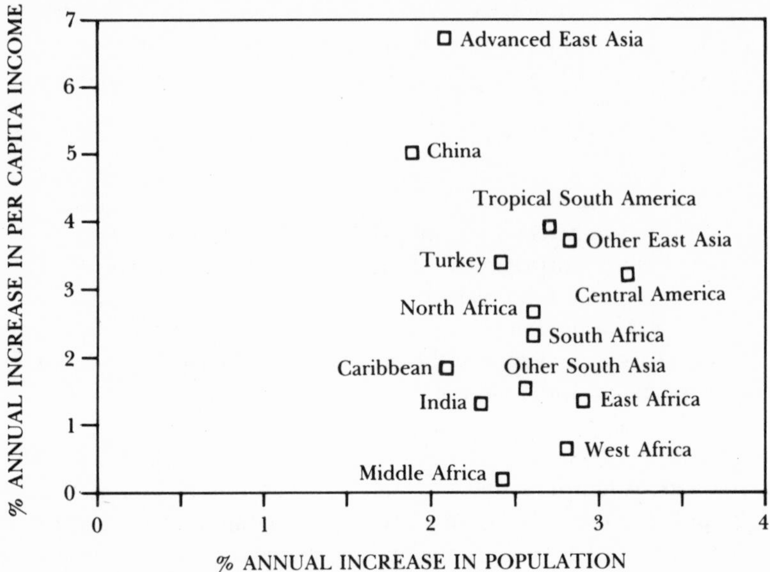

The scatter diagrams confirm what has been widely noted—the absence of any substantial relation, positive or negative, between the rate of increase in population and the rate of increase in per capita income. There is a clear positive relation, however, between the rate of increase in per capita income and the expectation of life at birth; there is a substantial negative relation between rate of increase in per capita income and the total fertility rate. Populations that have experienced a rapid rate of increase in per capita income generally have lower mortality and lower fertility than those where per capita income has grown more slowly. Because both fertility and mortality are lower in such countries, the rate of increase (the difference between the birthrate and death rate) can be either greater or less.

Particularly interesting relations are the negative associations between the rate of growth of per capita income and the

Percent Increase in Per Capita Income (versus total fertility rate)

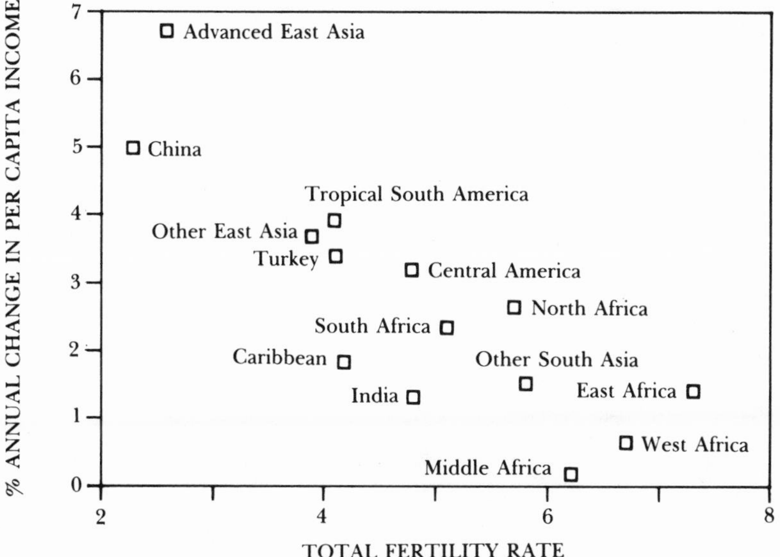

proportion of the population under age fifteen, between growth in per capita income and the decrease in fertility in a thirty-year period. Hoover and I concluded that social and economic advantages would accrue from reduced as opposed to sustained fertility primarily as a result of the smaller number of children that reduced fertility would yield. The empirical negative relation between growth in per capita income and the proportion of the population under age fifteen (and the thirty-year change in fertility) that is apparent in the figures presented here is not proof that our analysis was correct, but is certainly consistent with it.

In looking back I would qualify one point that Hoover and I made. The lower level of investment that we saw as associated with continued high fertility is far from a certain effect, as we only partially recognized at the time. Household savings are not necessarily the major source of net investment

Percent Increase in Per Capita Income (versus life expectancy at birth)

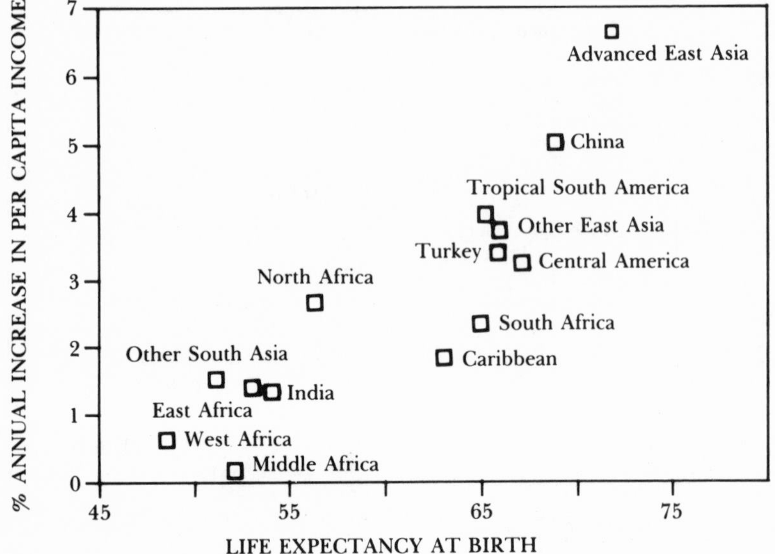

in less developed countries; therefore, a smaller number of dependent children may not have a consequential effect on the level of investment achieved. The major source of higher income per person caused by reduced fertility is simply the division of the national product among fewer persons.

In reconsidering the current situation (thirty years later) in India and Mexico, however, it does seem obvious that the welfare and the prospects of the children who have been born during these thirty years would be better if fertility had declined beginning thirty years ago rather than remaining constant until very recently. A smaller number of children would have grown up in households that were less crowded, with better diets, better health conditions, more parental care, and greater access to education. As I noted in a lecture in 1978, the population attending school in Mexico was multiplied by 3.6 between 1950 and 1970; the proportion of children six to

Percent Change in Per Capita Income (versus change in total fertility rate)

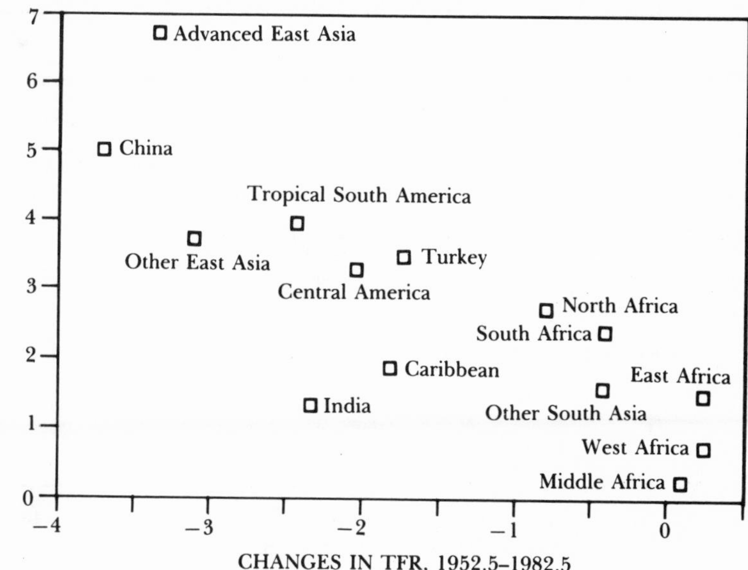

fourteen attending school rose from about 38 percent to about 64 percent. Nevertheless, the number of children *not* attending school was greater in 1970 than 1950. Had fertility dropped so that after twenty-five years it reached half its earlier level, school enrollment could have approached 100 percent.

The greatest advantage that reduced fertility would have brought to those born during this period in both countries is much better future prospects. Qualified observers agree that there are an insufficient number of adequately productive jobs in most less developed countries, including India and Mexico. The lack of minimally rewarding jobs does not necessarily show up in the form of high levels of unemployment, since unemployment is conventionally defined as an active search for work by persons who are out of work. In many less developed countries a redundancy of labor takes the form (espe-

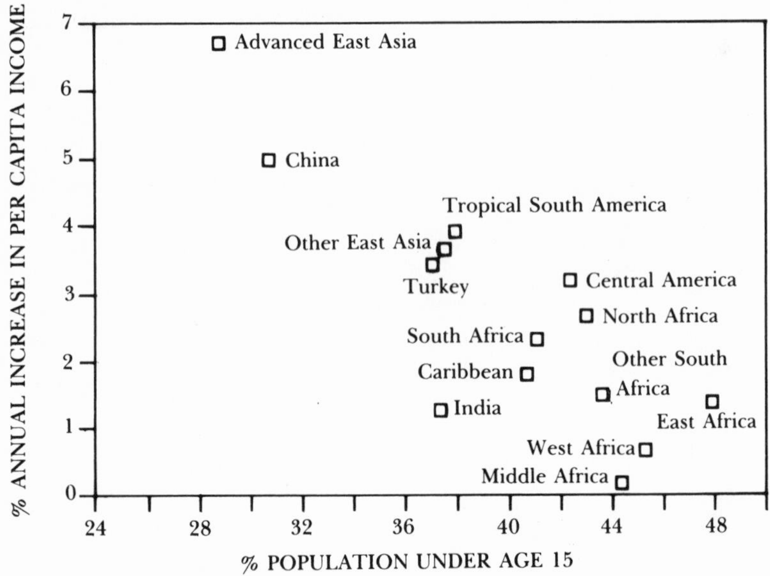

cially in agriculture) of spreading traditional jobs among a large number of persons. Few seek alternative employment because there are few visible opportunities. In urban areas the number of small shops with pitiful inventories, the number of barbers offering a shave or a haircut on the sidewalk, and the number of porters at the railroad stations and airports are greater than would be needed to provide full service for the maximum number of potential customers. In other words, retail services, barbering, and portering could be adequately provided by a much smaller number than those who now eke out a living in these pursuits. Changing technology has contributed more to rapid growth in national product than it has to expansion in productive employment. In Mexico the number of persons aged fifteen to sixty-five expected twenty years from now is more than double the current number. The future of young people today would certainly be brighter if the prospective number were only 60 percent greater than today, as would be the case had fertility declined by 50 percent in the last generation.

Productive employment prospects are further worsened in many less developed countries by the concentration of the labor force in the agricultural sector. In Bangladesh, where 74 percent of the labor force is in agriculture, few experts would contend that an increase in the number of persons in agriculture in the next twenty-five years would be advantageous to the modernization of the sector. The projected population in Bangladesh at ages fifteen to sixty-four in twenty-five years is more than twice the current number. If the persons of labor force age and dependent on agriculture remained at the current 38 million, the number dependent on the nonagricultural sector would have to increase by a factor of five.

If there were solid progress in agriculture in Bangladesh, the number dependent on agriculture for a livelihood would be reduced. A fivefold increase in employment opportunities in the nonagricultural sector is clearly impossible. Therefore, a substantial fraction (perhaps an unchanging fraction) of people of labor force age will still depend on agricultural activities. Underemployment in agriculture and in other sectors will be as acute or more acute than today. Prospects for the young people who will be added to the labor force in the next twenty-five years would surely be better if fertility had been reduced in the last twenty-five years so that the increase in numbers would be less.

It is, of course, too late to achieve the more favorable outcome for the persons born in the last twenty-five years or thirty years by a reduction of fertility that might have begun in the mid-1950s. The prospects of young people a generation from now will be better if high-fertility populations initiate a reduction in fertility beginning today. The maintenance of high fertility in many populations has been interpreted as a logical reflection of the self-interest of the couples who continue to have large families. Perhaps. I think it probable that high fertility often reflects the continued force of traditional values rather than rational calculation about practicing or not practicing contraception. However, even when the parents' choice is a calculated one, it need not reflect an accurate perception of, or even a strong concern for, the lifetime prospects of the children being born. In considering the welfare argument that people do what's best for them, bear in mind that the children are not consulted about their welfare. If the decision to have another child were subjected to the vote of their prospective siblings rather than decided by the parents, fertility choices might be very different.

4

The Transition in Reproductive Behavior in the Third World

JOHN BONGAARTS

Fundamental changes in reproductive behavior occur during the development process that transforms a traditional agricultural society into a modern industrial one. Before this transition, fertility is high—typically six to seven births per woman— and the use of contraception is virtually absent. In contrast, the large majority of couples in developed societies limit their family size to an average of around two children by practicing contraception, and, to a lesser extent, induced abortion. A large increase in the practice of contraception is therefore the most important change in reproductive behavior over the course of the fertility transition.

There are, however, other factors that have crucial effects on fertility levels and trends. In pretransitional societies traditional practices such as breastfeeding and abstinence for a

---

JOHN BONGAARTS is senior associate at the Center for Policy Studies at the Population Council and an adjunct professor in the Department of Population and Family Health at Columbia University, where his teaching concentrates on his central professional interest, the sociobiological determinants of fertility. He is coeditor of *Family Demography: Methods and Their Applications,* his most recent of many publications.

period following childbirth operate to reduce fertility. During the early phases of the fertility transition these traditional controls are largely abandoned, thus putting upward pressure on fertility that has to be compensated by the uptake of modern contraception before fertility can fall. This shift from traditional to modern control of reproduction occurs in all societies that eventually experience a sustained decline in fertility. The timing of this decline is determined by the interaction between the changing patterns of traditional and modern birth limitation practices. A more detailed understanding of this process is therefore of particular interest to policy makers concerned with excessive population growth in countries that are still in the early phases of the fertility transition.

The first three parts of this chapter deal with reproductive behavior and fertility patterns in, respectively, pretransitional, early transitional, and midtransitional societies. The fourth part considers likely future trends in fertility and their implications for contraceptive practice.

Traditional Patterns of Reproduction

Behavioral and Biological Determinants of Natural Fertility

The term "natural fertility" is used to describe fertility in populations in which the practice of contraception and induced abortion is absent or negligible. Virtually all countries of the Third World had natural fertility up to the middle of the twentieth century. A large number of these countries have experienced declines in fertility since 1950, but in most of sub-Saharan Africa and in several countries in Latin America and South Asia fertility has remained close to natural.

On average, about six or seven children are born per couple in societies with natural fertility. This rate of childbearing is sometimes considered "excessive" because it results in a birthrate that considerably exceeds the death rate in contemporary developing societies. While this natural level of fertility is indeed high compared with the average family size achieved in developed countries, natural fertility is only a fraction of its biological potential, since most women are capable of bearing more than about seven children over the reproductive life span, which extends from age fifteen to age forty-five or fifty. A full-term pregnancy takes only nine months, so that child-bearing at a rate of one per year is biologically possible, yielding a theoretical upper limit of about thirty births per woman during a thirty-year reproductive age span. There are, in fact, examples of a few women who have approached this limit, but on average, natural fertility is only a fraction of its biological maximum. Why are observed "high" natural fertility levels so low? The explanation for this finding lies in the fertility reducing effects of a number of biological and behavioral factors (the so-called proximate determinants of fertility).

Biological Factors.

(1) *Difficulty in achieving fertilization.* Among couples who do not use contraception and who have intercourse at a typical average frequency of once every few days, only about half will achieve a fertilization in any given month. This is primarily due to the relatively short viable life spans of ova and sperm (about six and thirty-six hours, respectively).

(2) *Spontaneous abortion and embryo mortality.* Fewer than half of all fertilized ova end up as live births. Mortality risks are highest during the first weeks of pregnancy when most fertilized ova and embryos with genetic or chromosomal abnormalities are expelled spontaneously.

(3) *Sterility.* A significant proportion of couples are incapable of reproducing. This proportion increases from a few percent among women in their early twenties who are permanently sterile, to virtually 100 percent when the woman reaches age fifty. As a consequence, the age at last birth among couples who do not use contraception is on average only about forty years, even though a very small proportion of women continue to bear children until they are age fifty.

Together these biological factors reduce maximum biological fertility to about fifteen children per woman, half of the theoretical limit of thirty births. Natural fertility levels are, of course, well below fifteen births per woman. The reasons for this further reduction are the following behavioral factors.

Behavioral Factors.

(1) *Breastfeeding.* In traditional societies virtually all infants are given breast milk for at least the first several months of their lives, and for many infants breastfeeding is continued until the mother becomes pregnant again. Breast milk is more than a convenient, nutritionally balanced food: it saves the lives of many infants. In traditional societies breast milk substitutes are often nutritionally inferior and easily contaminated, so that infants who rely on these alternative foods experience higher mortality and morbidity than their breastfed counterparts. Although its main function is the provision of nutrition to infants, breastfeeding has also an important effect on fertility because it delays the return of ovulation after each birth. The duration of this interval of anovulation depends on the intensity and duration of breastfeeding. Periods of anovulation of one and one-half to two years are not unusual among women who practice prolonged breastfeeding. The effect on lifetime fertility can be very substantial. For example, if a woman bears a total of seven children and each birth is followed by an anovulation interval of 20 months, then 140 months, or nearly half of her actual reproductive life span, is spent in the anovulatory state. Clearly, prolonged breastfeeding can be a crucial determinant of fertility.

(2) *Abstinence from sexual relations among breastfeeding women.* The resumption of sexual relations is delayed by at least a few weeks after a birth in most populations. In some societies, however, abstinence is much longer. In parts of tropical Africa couples believe that "semen poisons the milk," and abstinence can last until the child is weaned at age two or three. In such cases abstinence increases the birth interval and reduces fertility if the abstinence interval exceeds the duration of anovulation.

(3) *Delayed marriage.* To be exposed to the risk of childbearing throughout the potential reproductive period, a woman would have to marry (or enter into a socially sanctioned union)

at menarche. There is a substantial delay between menarche and marriage in most traditional societies. This lost reproductive time can have a significant effect on fertility. For example, if menarche occurs at age fourteen or fifteen and marriage at eighteen, then perhaps one birth has been lost over the woman's lifetime, due to this delay.

(4) *Marital disruption.* The termination of marriage by either divorce or widowhood occurs in all populations. The demographic significance of these events is highly variable, in part because the divorce risk is very culture-specific and in part because the probability of remarriage differs widely among societies. The only generalization that can be made with confidence is that the risk of widowhood is closely related to the overall level of mortality in the population.

The joint effects of these behavioral and biological factors on the reproductive pattern are summarized in Figure 1. The first bar in this figure outlines the average timing of childbearing in a not atypical traditional society. Between marriage in the late teens and the onset of sterility at about age forty a woman has an average of seven births at intervals of three years. This average birth interval is much longer than the nine months needed for a full-term pregnancy because an anovulation interval of twenty months as well as a seven-month waiting time to conception ending in a live birth are added. Also presented in Figure 1 is the average childbearing pattern of the Hutterites, the current world record holders in fertility. The Hutterites are members of an Anabaptist sect descended from Swiss settlers in the northern United States and Canada. They live in small communities in which strict social and religious control exists over most aspects of daily life, including reproductive behavior. Their extremely high average fertility of nine births per woman is made possible by spacing births about two years apart during their reproductive years beginning with marriage in the early twenties. The average birth interval of the Hutterites is substantially shorter than in most traditional developing countries because breastfeeding is less prolonged so that the anovulation period following each birth is only about six months.

FIGURE 1. Average Timing of Reproductive Events in Selected Types of Societies

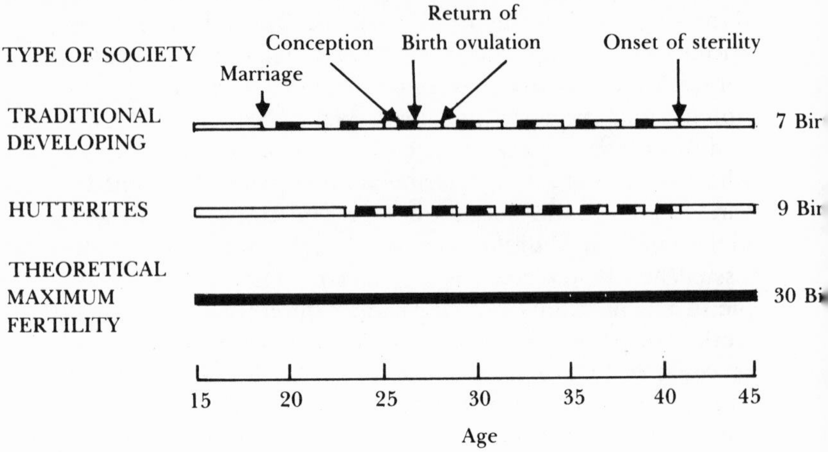

TYPE OF SOCIETY
Marriage
Conception
Birth
Return of ovulation
Onset of sterility
TRADITIONAL DEVELOPING — 7 Bir
HUTTERITES — 9 Bir
THEORETICAL MAXIMUM FERTILITY — 30 Bi
15 20 25 30 35 40 45
Age

Achieving Desired Family Size

Virtually all couples in traditional societies want large families. Average ideal family size as measured in surveys in developing countries with natural fertility ranges from four to over eight children. Although children provide a variety of social and psychological benefits to their parents, the primary motivation for wanting a large family is economic. Surviving children, and in particular sons, are valuable sources of labor in these largely agricultural societies. In addition, and equally important, children are often the only source of support in old age in countries where savings, pensions, and social security are either unknown or available only to a small elite. Under these circumstances it is not surprising that women are expected to bear and raise many children and that the use of contraception is negligible.

A substantial proportion of couples in traditional societies do not achieve their desired family size. There are two reasons for this: subfertility and high child mortality.

Subfertility. The overall description of natural fertility patterns presented earlier emphasized the reproductive experience of the average couple. Individual fertility can and does vary considerably from this average. For example, in a population in which the average woman bears seven children by the end of the reproductive years, there are always some women who have no births and some who have more than ten. This variability in fertility is caused by individual differences in the biological and behavioral determinants of natural fertility. Assuming no deliberate attempts to avoid pregnancy, a couple that fails to have a birth at all could have a permanently sterile partner or the woman could be biologically incapable of completing a pregnancy to term. At the other extreme, women who have more than ten or even fifteen births would have to marry in their teens, remain fecund until their late forties, and space children at intervals of about two years. The following table provides data on the proportion of women with relatively few or many births over their reproductive lifetimes.

TABLE 1: Proportion of Women with Relatively Few or Many Births

		Percent of women with	
	Average number of children	fewer than 4 births	more than 10 births
Mexico	7.0	18.7	18.1
Pakistan	7.0	13.5	9.5
Bangladesh	7.1	13.4	10.8

Note: Data as reported by women age 40–44 in surveys carried out by the World Fertility Surveys Organization in the mid-1970s; these women started childbearing in the 1950s when fertility was close to natural.

A fairly large proportion of women deviate substantially from the average childbearing experience. The large majority of women with fewer than four births had fewer births than they desired.

Child Mortality. The survival of children until age fifteen or twenty is essential to parents since the economic benefits they expect from their offspring are not realized until children reach maturity. Raising children is, therefore, as important as bearing them. The chances of survival from birth to adulthood depend on the level of health and nutrition prevailing in a population. In the early part of the twentieth century, close to half of all children born failed to reach adulthood in most parts of Africa, Asia, and Latin America. Since World War II, mortality has declined substantially in the Third World, but in the 1970s there were still countries, particularly in the rural areas of sub-Saharan Africa, where a third of all children died before age twenty.

Given the substantial levels of subfertility and child mortality and their unpredictable occurrence, it is not surprising that these societies select reproductive strategies to maximize the chances of producing surviving offspring. This implies resistance to the use of contraception and induced abortion; in addition, women will maintain prolonged breastfeeding. Even though breastfeeding reduces fertility, it is essential for child survival and hence a necessary practice to maximize family size.

Do Malnutrition and Poor Health Reduce the Capacity to Reproduce?

The possibility that malnutrition and poor health impair fecundity was viewed with alarm by policy makers concerned with the welfare of populations in the Third World. If this link turned out to be a strong one, it could have implications for food aid and public health programs because these programs would then have the undesirable side effect of raising birthrates in addition to their desired impact on morbidity and mortality. Fortunately, intensive research efforts in the 1970s to study the hypothetical link between fecundity and nutrition and health have been reassuring. The results of this work can be summarized as follows.

Effects of Chronic Moderate Malnutrition. In theory, malnutrition could affect reproductive performance through a variety of mechanisms. It could raise age at menarche and lower age at onset of sterility; it could increase the probability of anovulatory cycles and the risk of spontaneous abortion; and it could prolong the duration of anovulation associated with breastfeeding. Detailed reviews of the available scientific evidence have identified only three mechanisms with a measurable impact. Chronic malnutrition apparently increases the age at menarche by two to three years above levels prevailing in developed countries. However, the impact of delayed menarche on actual fertility is minimal, because marriage typically takes place a few years after menarche, and the link between the timing of these two events is often weak. The other small effects of malnutrition are a slight lengthening of the anovulation interval after each birth by one or two months and a few percent increase in the risk of spontaneous abortion. In practice, none of these fecundity-reducing effects can be considered of demographic importance. It should be emphasized, however, that this conclusion only applies to the chronic moderate malnutrition prevailing in the poorest classes of the many developing countries. In contrast, acute but necessarily temporary starvation during famines does have a substantial impact on fertility. The causes of this effect are not well understood. A temporary reduction in the biological ability to reproduce, anovulation induced by stress and anxiety, infrequent intercourse, voluntary efforts at contraception, and spousal separation in the search for food, all have been suggested as possible contributing factors.

Effects of Poor Health. After reviewing the available evidence, Ron Gray in *The Determinants of Fertility in Developing Countries* concluded that general poor health is unlikely to have a substantial impact on fecundity because morbidity severe enough to inhibit reproduction afflicts only a minority of disadvantaged women. An important exception to this generalization is the relatively high prevalence of disease-induced sterility in a few populations, primarily in parts of tropical Africa. Venereal disease is apparently the principal cause of this sterility.

The conclusion that neither chronic malnutrition nor general poor health provides significant constraints on fertility is, of course, consistent with observed fertility differentials between contemporary populations. The highest birthrates are found in the least developed and most disadvantaged societies with low levels of nutrition and health.

The Onset of the Transition in Reproductive Behavior

Third World populations that enter into a sustained fertility decline have, with very few exceptions, the following general characteristics: first, these societies have experienced at least some socioeconomic development and institutional change; second, couples have access to contraceptive supplies; and, third, mortality levels have declined substantially. These three factors can in practice be considered preconditions for a reproductive transition to occur. Later chapters discuss in detail the fertility effects of socioeconomic development and an increase in the availability of birth control methods. The present discussion is, therefore, limited to the reproductive consequences of a mortality decline.

Relationship between Mortality and Fertility Declines

Supporting evidence for the contention that lowered mortality is required before fertility can be reduced is provided in Figure 2. It plots levels of fertility (average number of children per woman, on the vertical axis) and mortality (life expectancy in years, on the horizontal axis) in the late 1970s for each of ninety-six contemporary developing countries. The figure shows a clear pattern linking fertility and mortality. In countries with life expectancies below fifty years, fertility is high, and in virtually all of these societies fertility has been close to natural for centuries. At the other extreme, populations with life expectancies over sixty years have, with few exceptions, experienced substantial fertility declines with the average number of children per woman ranging from about five to near the replacement level of two. These data support the conclusion that life expectancy has to rise to between fifty and sixty years before a substantial fertility decline can be expected to occur. Since life expectancy was near or below thirty years in most of the Third World before the twentieth century, the implication of this finding is that life expectancy typically has to double from traditional levels before a population enters into the fertility transition. (The few outliers in Figure 2 are also of interest. Among the countries with lower than expected fertility are India and Indonesia with massive and fairly effective family planning programs, Gabon with an unusually high prevalence of pathological sterility, and South Africa where spousal separation may play a role in reducing fertility. Countries with higher than expected fertility include Kenya and several Mideast countries, such as Jordan and Syria, where desired family size is among the highest ever measured.)

Mortality Factors Significant in Fertility. Why is a substantial decline in mortality apparently required before a reduction in fertility can be expected? Although an answer to this question is necessarily in part speculative, the following factors are probably crucial.

(1) *Increase in the "supply" of children.* In most traditional societies high fertility is not seen as an end in itself but rather as a necessary part of a process that produces a substantial number of surviving children. Typically couples want at least four or five children who reach adulthood. Considering reproduction from this broader perspective implies that achieving success in attaining desired family size depends on the level of mortality as well as on fertility. For example, an increase in life expectancy from thirty to sixty years would raise the number of children surviving to age twenty from an average of 3.5 to 6 per family if 7 is the natural total fertility rate. An average family size of 3.5 would be smaller than desired for most couples and would therefore not provide an incentive for reducing fertility. On the other hand, 6 surviving children per couple would be more than most couples want, thus providing an incentive to use birth control.

(2) *Reductions in the uncertainty of achieving family size goals.* As

FIGURE 2. Total Fertility Rates and Life Expectancies at Birth for 96 Developing Countries (average for 1975–80 period)

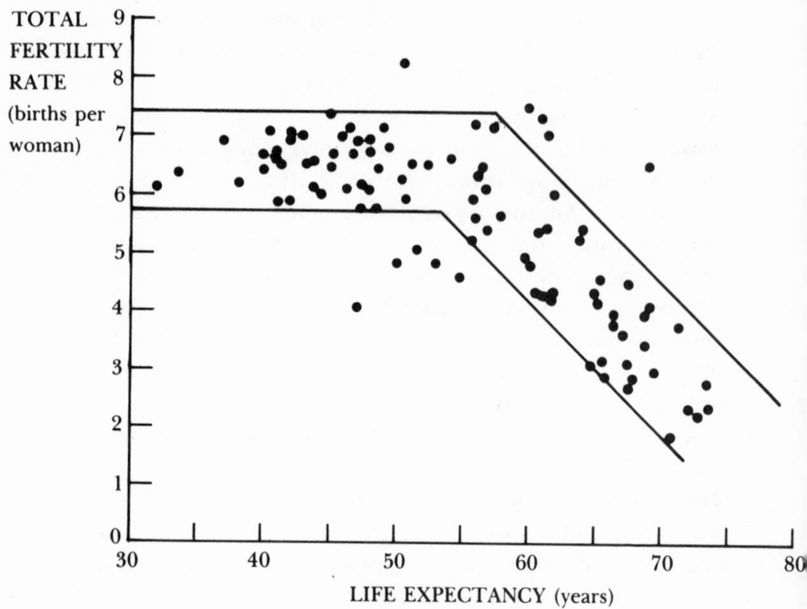

noted earlier, a substantial proportion of couples do not reach their desired family size either because they are subfertile or because they experience a number of infant deaths. The chance element introduced by high mortality is easily documented. For example, in a population with a life expectancy of thirty years, virtually all couples will experience the death of one of their children before the age of twenty, and in the large majority of families, more than one such child death will occur. An important consequence of this fact is that even among couples who have had four or five births in succession and whose children are still young, there is a strong incentive to continue childbearing to offset the likelihood of future child mortality. This high risk of future loss of offspring is probably a key reason for maintaining high fertility in societies with high mortality. A sharp reduction in mortality is needed to remove this element of uncertainty from the family-building process.

(3) *Reduction in the risk of widowhood.* In pretransitional populations with high mortality (e.g., with a life expectancy of thirty years or less) about half of all newly married women become widows before they reach the end of the childbearing years. Since the life of a widow with only small children is often a miserable one, it is to be expected that women want to bear children rapidly in the early years of their marriages. The presence of mature sons or daughters at the time of the death of the head of the family is essential to the economic survival of the family unit. A decline in mortality and in the risk of widowhood would reduce the need to produce offspring as insurance against the often disastrous effects of the loss of a husband.

Together these three factors provide a powerful incentive to maintain a high rate of childbearing in populations with high mortality. It is, therefore, not unexpected that sharp reductions in mortality have always preceded sustained declines in fertility in contemporary developing countries.

The Initial Phase of Fertility Decline

Rise in Contraceptive Prevalence. Once the necessary preconditions (such as socioeconomic development, availability of contraception, and reduced mortality) are met, increasing proportions of couples desire lower fertility, and they begin to practice contraception to achieve this objective. A rise in contraceptive prevalence is therefore a key sign that a society has begun to abandon traditional reproductive patterns. As noted earlier, in the long run, large reductions in fertility are achieved primarily by the widespread adoption of contraception. However, in the early phases of the reproductive transition, an increase in contraceptive use does not necessarily imply a decline in fertility. Fertility may remain stable or even rise temporarily, because the social, economic, and demographic conditions that bring about the increase in contraceptive use also lead to changes in the other behavioral determinants of fertility.

Changes in Other Determinants of Fertility.

(1) Traditionally, breastfeeding intervals are long and supplements are often given at a late age. As a society modernizes, both the duration and frequency of breastfeeding decline, thus reducing the fertility-inhibiting effect of breastfeeding. Factors that tend to encourage this change in feeding patterns include the availability of hygienic and nutritionally adequate food supplements; an improvement in health conditions, which makes breastfeeding less of a requirement for child survival; and changes in women's labor force participation that may make it difficult to continue time-consuming breastfeeding.

(2) Since the duration of prolonged postpartum abstinence is generally tied to the breastfeeding interval, a shortening of the latter would also reduce the abstinence interval. Furthermore, with modernization, traditional beliefs supporting abstinence erode.

(3) In the least developed countries of the Third World, the mean age at first marriage is typically between ages fifteen and twenty. With increases in literacy and school enrollment, changing roles of women, and other social and economic developments, age at marriage rises. As a consequence, the mean age at marriage in a substantial number of developing countries now slightly exceeds twenty years.

(4) Declining levels of mortality inevitably reduce the risk of widowhood. The effect of this trend on the proportion of women that is married and, hence, on fertility depends on the proportion of widows that remarries. However, even when the majority of widows remarry and do so relatively soon after their spouses have died, a reduction in mortality will still tend to increase fertility by reducing the number of years widowed.

Changes in these factors, together with an increase in contraceptive use, are the principal features of the transition from traditional to modern reproductive behavior. The fertility impact of these changes in the various fertility determinants are summarized in Table 2.

TABLE 2: Fertility Impact of Changes in Fertility Determinants

Expected change in determinants of fertility	Fertility effect
Decline in breastfeeding and postpartum abstinence	+
Increase in age at marriage	–
Reduction in widowhood risk	+
Rise in contraceptive prevalence (and induced abortion)	–

The combined impact of these variables on levels and trends in fertility depends both on the amount of change in each determinant and—equally important—on the timing of these changes. Since several determinants of fertility are involved, and since the extent and the timing of change in each of them varies considerably among societies, a wide variety of trends in fertility can result at the onset of the transition. To simplify the presentation, only three general types will be discussed here (see Figure 3).

Three Types of Transition. If the changes in the factors with a positive fertility effect (e.g., decline in breastfeeding) are substantial and occur before contraceptive prevalence and age at marriage rise, then fertility will increase temporarily above its pretransitional level (type I transition). An example of a society with this type of transition is Kenya, where fertility has risen over the past two or three decades to a record breaking eight births per woman, largely as a result of reductions in breastfeeding and abstinence. Several other countries, especially in Latin America, apparently also experienced an upward trend in fertility in the middle of this century, but in most of these societies fertility has declined rapidly since the 1960s.

If the timing of the onset of the change in the different determinants of fertility is more or less simultaneous, the positive and negative effects tend to offset one another, and as long as their magnitudes do not differ greatly, fertility will remain

FIGURE 3. Alternative Fertility Trends for Different Types of Fertility Transition (see text for further details)

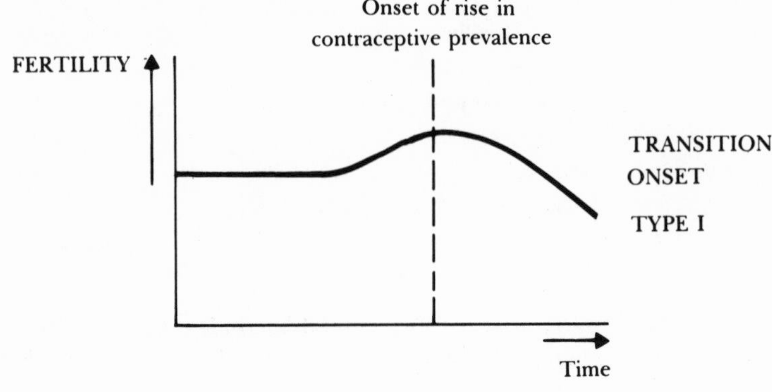

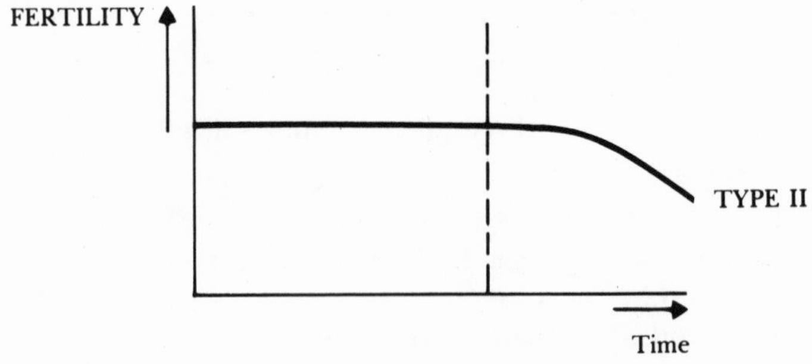

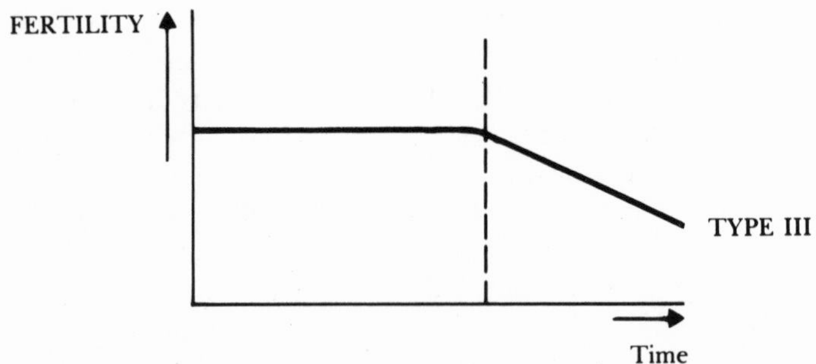

relatively stable (type II transition). This implies that a significant rise in contraceptive use is accompanied by very little change in fertility. Zimbabwe is a country where reproduction may have changed in this way. According to a 1984 survey, 39 percent of couples were practicing contraception, yet the fertility level was 6.4 births per woman, which is probably not very different from past levels. Of course, if contraceptive prevalence continues to rise, fertility will drop eventually.

If the changes in the factors that reduce fertility are large and occur before the other factors change, then fertility will decline relatively early in the reproductive transition (type III transition). In this type of transition the onset of fertility decline usually coincides with the rise in contraceptive use, because contraception is the main fertility-inhibiting factor. Countries such as Indonesia and India approach this transition pattern. In both countries strong family planning programs have contributed to substantial rises in contraceptive use, but breastfeeding behavior is not being modified rapidly.

These illustrations indicate that the onset of the fertility decline involves the interaction of a number of fertility determinants whose combined effect can yield a range of different patterns in fertility. The main finding of interest to policy makers is that the onset of fertility decline occurs earliest in societies where traditional fertility-inhibiting behaviors such as breastfeeding and abstinence are maintained longest.

Societies in Transition

As described earlier in this volume, most countries in the developing world entered the fertility transition between 1960 and 1980. From pretransitional levels of between 6 and 7 births per woman, fertility had declined in 1980 to 2.6 in East Asia, to 4.9 in South Asia, and to 4.3 births per woman in Latin America. Only in Africa have reductions in fertility on average been negligible. For the developing world as a whole, the total fertility rate was 4.3 in 1980. These rapid and unprecedented recent declines raise several questions about their proximate causes.

Contraception

Once a fertility decline is well under way, trends in fertility are largely determined by trends in contraceptive behavior. The crucial role played by contraception in explaining levels and trends in fertility is evident from Figure 4, which plots current contraceptive prevalence and total fertility rates for eighty-three countries around 1980. According to the regression line fitted to these data points, contraceptive prevalence explains 85 percent of the fertility variation between countries. Fertility is highest in countries with near zero contraceptive prevalence and declines at an average rate of 0.6 births for each 10 percent rise in prevalence. Most contemporary developed countries with fertility near two births per woman have contraceptive prevalence levels between 65 and 80 percent. Both fertility and contraceptive prevalence levels vary widely among the major continents of the world.

Table 3 presents by region contraceptive prevalence levels and the mix of contraceptive methods used. Prevalence ranges from a low of 11 percent in Africa to 69 percent in East Asia (which is dominated by China). The developing regions combined had an estimated prevalence of 38 percent, which is slightly more than half of the 68 percent prevalence found in the developed world. In each continent, prevalence rose, often dramatically, between 1960 and 1980: from 5 to 11 percent in Africa, from 14 to 43 percent in Latin America, from 13 to 69 percent in East Asia, and from 7 to 24 percent in South Asia. These changes in contraceptive behavior closely correlate with declines in fertility over the same period. With respect to the mix of contraceptive methods selected by couples, the pill was the preferred method in Africa and Latin America, while most women chose the IUD in East Asia and sterilization in South Asia. For all developing regions combined, sterilization was the most popular method because it was selected by 40 percent of all couples who used contraception. Remarkably, sterilization is one of the least popular methods in the developed world, where more than half the couples selected "other"

FIGURE 4. Total Fertility Rates and Contraceptive Prevalence Levels for 83 Countries, Circa 1980

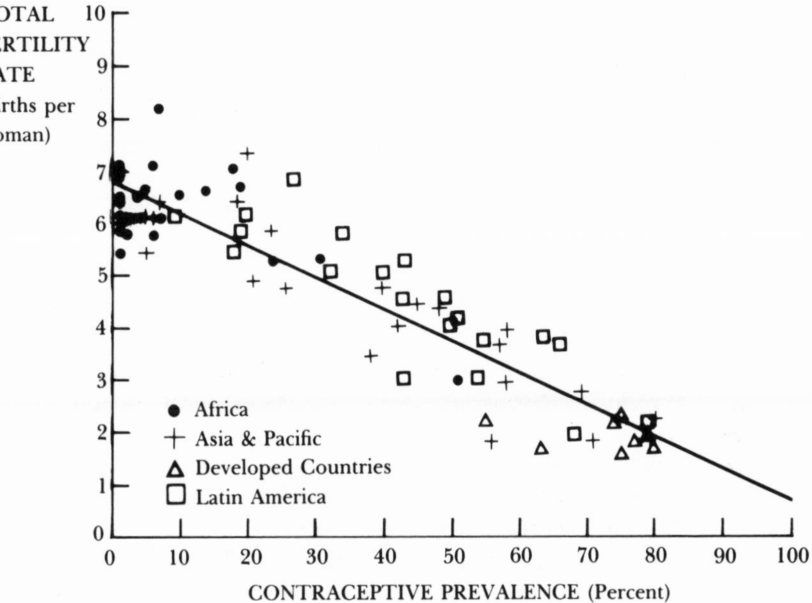

methods (e.g., condoms, diaphragms, spermicidal agents, withdrawal, rhythm).

Although contraceptive prevalence is the most important determinant of trends in fertility once a society is in transition, other proximate determinants can still play a significant role. This is clear from Figure 4 where some countries deviate substantially from the regression line. The correspondence between given levels of fertility and prevalence is far from exact. For example, in countries with prevalence under 10 percent, fertility ranges from five to eight births per woman. Similarly, in countries with prevalence near 60 percent, total fertility rates range from two to four. The primary causes of this variation in fertility (which is not attributable to differences in contraceptive prevalence) are differences in other proximate

TABLE 3: Contraceptive Prevalence Levels and Mixture of Contraceptive Methods by Region, 1980–81

Region	Contra-ceptive prevalence (percent)	Contraceptive method used (percent)				
		Total	Sterilization	IUD	Pill and injectibles	Other
Africa	11	100	8	14	55	22
Latin America	43	100	24	14	34	28
East Asia*	69	100	36	49	8	6
South Asia	24	100	54	7	19	19
All developing regions	38	100	40	33	14	13
All developed regions	68	100	14	7	23	56

*Excluding Japan
Source: United Nations Population Division (1984).

determinants of fertility. For a given level of prevalence, a short duration of breastfeeding and postpartum abstinence, a low age at marriage, a low incidence of marital disruption, induced abortion, and pathological sterility, and a high remarriage rate all imply higher than expected fertility and vice versa. Given this multiplicity of factors that can influence levels and trends in fertility, it is difficult to generalize about their impact. However, the effects of these other proximate determinants on fertility trends are typically both positive and negative, so that they tend to offset one another (e.g., declining breastfeeding combined with rising age at marriage). As a consequence, contraceptive prevalence is the key determinant of fertility trends in the majority of countries in transition. On the other hand, as explained earlier, other proximate determinants can play a key role in the earliest phase of the transition. As shown in Figure 3, there is only a loose connection between the onset of fertility decline and the initial increase in contraceptive prevalence.

Induced Abortion

Although induced abortion is practiced by some women in virtually all societies, it has played only a minor role during the first phase of the fertility transition of the Third World in the 1960s and 1970s. In all but a handful of developing countries laws are in effect that either prohibit or severely restrict the use of induced abortion. The only nations in which relatively liberal laws (permitting abortion on demand or for socio-medical reasons) have been adopted are China, Cuba, Hong Kong, India, Korea, Singapore, Tunisia, Vietnam, and Zambia. However, even with liberal laws women do not make much use of this method of birth control. In the developing countries for which estimates of legal abortion rates are available for 1980, these rates were at an average level that would result in 0.6 abortions per woman by the end of the reproductive years. The demographic significance of this abortion rate is further diminished by the fact that, on average, an abortion averts less than one birth. (This is in part because some pregnancies terminated by induced abortion would have been aborted spontaneously, and in part because after an induced abortion a woman returns to the fecundable state sooner than would have been the case if the pregnancy had ended in a birth followed by a postpartum anovulation interval.) Reliable estimates for parts of the Third World in which induced abortion is illegal are not available, but it is plausible to assume that these rates are, on average, substantially below those prevailing in countries with liberal laws. As a consequence, the reduction in the total fertility rate due to the practice of induced abortion in the Third World in 1980 was probably well below one-half of a birth per woman.

Future Trends in Fertility

A key question of interest to policy makers in many countries of the Third World is whether the very rapid increases in contraceptive prevalence and the corresponding declines in fertility in the 1960s and 1970s will continue into the future. Standard projections of future demographic trends typically assume that countries that have experienced fertility reductions will continue on a downward trajectory until they reach the replacement level of near two births per woman. No doubt in the long run fertility will indeed fall to levels approaching those now observed in the developed world, but it is by no means clear that the decline will be a smooth or uninterrupted one.

There is now growing evidence from a number of developing countries that fertility and contraceptive prevalence are leveling off at values well short of those found in the developed world. Some countries, such as China, Taiwan, and Hong Kong, have indeed made the full transition to total fertility rates near two and to prevalence rates of 70 to 80 percent. The list of countries that apparently are stalling in midtransition, however, is steadily lengthening. Previously rapid changes in fertility and prevalence have slowed down considerably or have stopped altogether between the mid- or late 1970s and the early 1980s in countries as diverse as Sri Lanka, Thailand, Philippines, Malaysia, Costa Rica, and Mauritius, and probably also in Colombia, Brazil, and Mexico. In fact, in the Philippines prevalence appears to have declined from 39 to 32 percent between 1978 and 1983, and in Costa Rica the total fertility rate rose from 3.8 to 3.9 between 1975 and 1979. In most countries in which stalling occurs, levels of fertility are between three and four births per woman and prevalence is between 45 and 65 percent.

Reasons for the Reduced Pace of Fertility Decline

What is the cause of this stalling? Since the phenomenon is a very recent one, it has not yet been studied in detail by demographers, and, in any case, there is not likely to be a single cause that explains all trends in all countries. A plausible explanation that has probably played a role in most cases, however, is a substantial reduction in the gap between actual and desired fertility. In other words, during the initial phase of rapid fertility decline, the number of unwanted children was reduced by the increasing use of contraception, but once actual fertility approached desired fertility the motivation for further reductions in fertility was much smaller. Support for this hypothesis can be found in data on desired family size gathered through the World Fertility Surveys (WFS) conducted in thirty-nine developing countries in the mid- and late 1970s. Average family size desired by married women at the beginning of the reproductive years varied by region, as shown in Table 4.

TABLE 4: Average Desired Family Size by Region

Region	Number of countries	Average desired family size (women aged 15–19)
Africa	9	6.7
Asia and Pacific	10	3.2
Latin America and Caribbean	13	3.3
Middle East and North Africa	7	4.2

Variation among individual countries was even greater than among regions, but in no case did desired family size average fewer than 2.6 children. If these estimates of desired family size are reasonably representative of the ideal rate of childbearing in the years following the survey, then they are roughly consistent with fertility plateaus between three and four births per woman in Asia and Latin America. In any case, they can be considered inconsistent with a rapid fertility decline to total fertility rates near two because family size preferences tend to change only slowly over time.

An additional factor that justifies skepticism about continued rapid fertility declines is the lack of perfect birth control. Except in societies where sterilization is the only form of contraception, substantial proportions of couples experience contraceptive failures. This in turn implies significant levels of unwanted births unless all such undesired pregnancies are aborted. A simple numerical example helps to illustrate the magnitude of the problem. Assume that in a hypothetical developing country all women marry at age 20 and desire exactly 3 children. Assume further that these women space their births at intervals of 2.5 years and remain married until the end of their reproductive years. In that case, the 3 desired births occur at ages 22.5, 25, and 27.5 respectively, and the couple then has approximately 12.5 years of reproductive life left during which they have to avoid pregnancy. (The end of the actual reproductive years is taken to be age 40 years for the woman, which is the average age at last birth in societies with natural fertility.) The number of unwanted pregnancies that occurs during these 12.5 years depends directly on the effectiveness of contraception being practiced (Table 5).

TABLE 5: Effectiveness of Contraception and Number of Unwanted Pregnancies

Effectiveness of contraception (percent)	Approximate average number of unwanted pregnancies in 12.5 years
100	0.0
95	0.7
90	1.3
85	2.3

In the absence of induced abortion these unwanted pregnancies would, with few exceptions, turn into unwanted births. For example, with 90 percent effective contraception and no induced abortion, about 1.2 unwanted births would be added to the 3 wanted ones, yielding a total fertility rate of 4.2 (for simplicity, no replacement of children who die is assumed). The corresponding total fertility rate with 95 percent effective contraception would be about 3.6. Although this exercise makes a number of simplifying assumptions, it demonstrates the key issues involved and gives the approximate magnitude of risk of unplanned pregnancies. That these results are not implausible is indicated by reported rates of contraceptive failure. For example, in Costa Rica fully 35 percent of births were accidentally conceived, according to respondents in the 1976 WFS survey. This proportion would, of course, have been lower if induced abortions were more widely used. It would also have been lower with more effective contraception. In Costa Rica in 1976, 19 percent of couples using contraception were sterilized, 37 percent used the pill, 9 percent used the IUD, and 35 percent used other methods. Average effectiveness was probably less than 90 percent, because standard levels of effectiveness assumed to prevail in the developing world are 95 percent for the IUD, 90 percent for the pill, and 70 percent for other methods. (Few reliable studies of effectiveness have been made in developing countries, and these estimates are therefore only approximate.) These method-specific estimates imply that even if most women were to switch to modern methods, such as the IUD or pill, it would be difficult to reach average effectiveness levels of above 95 percent, unless much larger proportions of couples were to resort to sterilization. It is consequently difficult to avoid significant numbers of contraceptive failures.

The main conclusion from this brief discussion of levels of desired family size and the risks of contraceptive failure is that a leveling off of fertility and contraceptive prevalence as observed in a number of developing countries is not a surprising phenomenon. Countries that have seen very rapid declines in fertility and growth in prevalence are likely to see considerably slower rates of change in future years, and in a number of cases, the fertility transition will stall temporarily.

Implications of Future Fertility Trends for Contraceptive Practice

Barring unforeseen circumstances, average fertility in the developing world is likely to continue to decline in the future, although the rate of decline will almost certainly be lower. Long-range forecasts of the size and other demographic variables of the population of the world, as well as of regions and countries, are now routinely made by international agencies such as the United Nations and the World Bank. In the United Nations projections published in 1985, the total fertility rate of the developing regions as a whole is projected to decline from 4.0 in 1984 to 3.1 in 2000 and then to the near replacement level of 2.3 in 2025. Projected trends for each of the major regions of the Third World are given in Table 6.

TABLE 6: Total Fertility Rate Interpolated from U.N. Medium Projections, by Region, for Selected Years from 1984 to 2025 (1982 assessment)

	Total fertility rates				
Region	1984	1990	2000	2010	2025
Africa	6.4	6.2	5.6	4.6	3.2
Latin America	4.0	3.6	3.0	2.7	2.4
East Asia*	2.3	2.0	1.9	1.9	1.9
South Asia	4.5	3.9	3.0	2.5	2.1
All developing countries	4.0	3.5	3.1	2.8	2.3

*Excluding Japan.

Due to China's one-child policy, East Asia is expected to have below replacement fertility in the first quarter of the next century. Latin America and South Asia are projected to reach near replacement fertility in 2025, and only in Africa is fertility expected to remain high, although even there fertility could decline to a total fertility rate of 3.2 in 2025. This is not the place to comment on the plausibility of these trends, but it is worth noting that past United Nations projections have been fairly accurate, and the estimates in Table 6 are not likely to be far off the mark. (Note that they assume a reduction in the rate of fertility decline after 1984.)

What are the implications of these fertility trends for future contraceptive use in the developing world? A recently developed methodology provides tentative answers to this question. Estimates of the number of women using contraception in selected future years obtained by this methodology are given in Table 7.

TABLE 7: Estimated Number of Married Women Practicing Contraception, by Region, for Selected Years from 1984 to 2025

Region	Women practicing contraception (millions)				
	1984	1990	2000	2010	2025
Africa	11	16	35	74	168
Latin America	32	41	58	73	90
East Asia*	132	160	180	184	171
South Asia	81	120	190	250	307
All developing countries	256	337	462	581	736

*Excluding Japan.

In 1984 approximately 256 million women were practicing contraception; of that number more than half lived in East Asia (i.e., China). By the year 2025 this number is projected to grow almost threefold to 736 million. The largest increases in numbers of users between 1984 and 2025 are expected in South Asia (from 81 to 307 million) and in Africa (from 11 to 168 million). These projections make clear that a rapid expansion of family planning services provided by both the public and private sectors will be required for at least the next several decades. This need for additional services is greatest in South Asia and Africa.

Conclusion

The 1970s will go down in history as the decade when most of the developing world entered the fertility transition. The principal proximate factor responsible for this decline is a substantial increase in the use of contraception. By 1984 approximately a quarter of a billion women in the Third World were practicing contraception, which is at least ten times more than in the 1950s. This generally encouraging picture is clouded by two issues. First, a substantial number of poor countries, especially in Africa, have yet to experience significant declines in fertility. In fact, it is quite possible that in some of these societies fertility will rise temporarily as traditional fertility controls, such as breastfeeding and abstinence, are relaxed before the use of contraception becomes widespread. Second, there is increasing evidence that fertility declines are slowing down or even stopping altogether in countries where recent fertility change has been most rapid. Optimism about continued rapid declines to the low fertility prevailing in the developed countries is not justified, unless desired family size drops well below current levels. If this stalling phenomenon becomes more widespread and prolonged, then population growth rates in the Third World could well exceed expectations in the near future.

5

Intersections: Immigration and Demographic Change and Their Impact on the United States

MICHAEL S. TEITELBAUM

A nation's population change is determined by the confluence of three quite separable elements—fertility, mortality, and international migration. The first two are well known: in the modern epoch, mortality decline has been the engine of rapid population growth, and fertility decline has been the focus of government policies to restrain the growth thereby generated. These two elements taken together explain the sharp differences between rates of population change in developing and developed countries.

Meanwhile, international migration, neither fish nor fowl,

MICHAEL S. TEITELBAUM is program officer at the Alfred P. Sloan Foundation. He has developed his professional concentration on population issues through university teaching and research at Oxford and Princeton Universities; government service, including directorship of the House Select Committee on Population; work with foundations; and leadership in professional associations. He is the author or editor of six books and numerous articles. Dr. Teitelbaum gratefully acknowledges constructive comments on a first draft provided by Carl Hampe, Charles Keely, Albert Rees, Jack Rosenthal, and Robert Warren, none of whom is responsible for any errors of fact or interpretation.

floats rather awkwardly in a different dimension. Migrations across national borders are large and apparently growing, though they have only recently attracted the attention of most students of world population dynamics. International migration now represents an important and growing point of intersection between the rapid demographic growth of many developing countries and the much slower growth of the industrialized countries of Western Europe, North America, and Australia/New Zealand.

International Migration as a Changing Concept

Human migrations have been fundamental to the history and evolution of the species, but the form of such migrations has changed in basic ways from epoch to epoch. Early human migrations were by hunter-gatherers in search of food. Later migrations were in search of new lands, employment, trade, or conquest.

In one sense, modern international migrations can be seen simply as movements of individuals across space, differing from other migrations only in the distances traveled (and sometimes not even in this respect, when internal migrations within large countries can span thousands of miles). But in another sense, modern international migrations differ qualitatively and fundamentally from other types of migration. This is so because the basic organizational structure of the modern world is that of the sovereign nation-state, and the control of entry by noncitizens is one of the few fundamental and universally agreed attributes of such sovereigns.

While the human species has always been migratory in some sense, it is important to recognize that the very nature of international migrations has literally been transformed over the past two centuries for at least three reasons: the modern universality of the nation-state system, the dramatic demographic expansion of the period, and the significant technological advances in transportation and communication.

Modern Universality of the Nation-state System

The modern international system, with all its weaknesses and lethal conflicts, became predominant in the last century and well-nigh universal with the postwar rise of independent nation-states from the European colonial empires in Africa and Asia. Suffice it to say that national claims to sovereignty have been applied now to essentially the whole of the world's land mass (and much of its water surface as well); the only significant exception is the frigid continent of Antarctica, in which territorial claims have stopped short of formal sovereignty.

This political order has changed the meaning of human migration in many regions. A migration from Spain to Mexico, from Mexico to California, or from East Bengal to West Bengal today brings the migrant in contact with quite fundamental aspects of state sovereignty that simply did not exist in these same areas only two centuries ago. The change is even more dramatic in Africa, where national boundaries cutting across tribal groups were established by the ebb and flow of European colonial competition but are now embraced and fiercely defended by indigenous African leaders.

Demographic Expansion

There is a second fundamental factor that has transformed both the reality and the potential for human migrations, and this is the factor that forms the basis of this volume. Put simply, the unprecedented demographic expansion of Europe in the nineteenth century and the even more rapid expansion of the developing countries since World War II have sharply increased the density of human populations worldwide. Not only does this mean that in some unfavored areas there have been ever-larger numbers of residents seeking to move elsewhere in search of survival or advancement, but also that would-be immigrants are no longer able to find many unpopulated or sparsely populated regions with favorable life chances that are seeking or welcoming large numbers of additional people. (There are exceptions to this, but not many.)

In fact, the following generalization can be made with but a few caveats: only 100 years ago there were large areas of the world (the United States, Canada, Australia, New Zealand) whose leadership welcomed immigrants to people their frontiers and staff their farms and factories. Today, most of these same countries no longer seek mass immigration for such purposes, although immigration, both lawful and unlawful, continues due to limited needs for additional workers, the pressures of domestic politics, humanitarian concerns, and family reunification.

Technological Advance

There is a third factor that has been significant in changing the nature of international migration: the development and spread of modern technologies of transportation and communication. Only two centuries ago, much of international migration represented a slow, expensive, and quite dangerous adventure. Within the past century, the advent of the ocean-going steamship made large-scale intercontinental movements possible for the first time. With the post–World War II arrival of the jet plane and modern road transportation, the option of long distance migration was even more widely disseminated. Moreover, the relative wealth and attractiveness of Western life styles can now be communicated to quite remote rural areas of deep poverty in a way that could not have been imagined before the advent of television, radio, cinema, and telephone.

Immigration Trends and Directions

Discussions of international migration are often bogged down or misdirected by a tendency toward national and definitional parochialism. In particular, discussion of international migration is often restricted to a single-nation perspective rather than a global one, and frequently a spurious accuracy is offered by referring only to those immigrants who are legally admitted and recorded by government agencies. To avoid such pitfalls, let us start from the mountaintop, by first asking how many international migrants, and what varieties of these migrants, can be accounted for over the past decade or so.

The absolute totals are quite large. Perhaps 40 to 50 million persons currently reside outside their homelands as a result of movements over the past ten years or so. Of these, the largest fractions are not the traditional two categories of legal permanent immigrants and refugees, but instead a mixed category who are thought to be migrants of a more irregular and/or temporary character. Perhaps 10 to 15 million have been legally admitted to their countries of residence for temporary stays. These are the "guest workers" of Western Europe and the "temporary workers" of the Persian Gulf states. Another 10 to 15 million have migrated unlawfully, especially to such countries as the United States, Venezuela, India, and parts of Western Europe.

Meanwhile, the more traditional categories of immigration (those of "immigrant" and "refugee") seem to be of somewhat smaller magnitude. Over the past decade, on the order of 10 million persons have migrated internationally and lawfully for permanent residence. Of these, perhaps one-half have moved to a single country, the United States.

The number of refugees in the world today is hard to estimate, but, if the term is limited to the internationally agreed definition, it too is probably on the order of 10 million or so, over half accounted for by Afghans, Ethiopians, and Palestinians.

There is another overarching and important fact that makes current migration patterns radically different from those of the not very distant past: international migration today is principally from the developing countries of the Third World to industrialized countries or to more favored Third World countries. The volume of migration between industrialized countries or from industrialized countries to Third World countries comprises only a small fraction of international migration. This represents a major shift from the international migration patterns of only fifty years ago, when the principal source countries were in Europe.

Some insight into the future potential for international migration from developing countries can be garnered from Paul Demeny's discussion in chapter 1 of this volume of the recent and prospective growth in the young adult population, the age group that provides the overwhelming bulk of international migrants. The rapid expansion of this age group in Third World countries since 1965 surely has contributed to the increasing migration pressures experienced over that period. Demeny notes that robust projections for this same age group up to 2005 show even greater increases—some 569 million—than those of the recent past. Related to such trends are labor force projections for the Third World indicating twenty-year increases of 600 to 700 million; for perspective, such an increase over twenty years exceeds the total combined labor forces of all industrialized countries today.

U.S. Immigration: A Mixed History

Immigration policy in the United States has a complex and sometimes unsavory history. Moreover, the popular images of U.S. immigration history are full of exaggeration, misunderstanding, and mythology, all of which have clouded past and recent debates on the subject.

It is not much of an oversimplification to say that there have been essentially four broad phases of American immigration experience.

Phase I, 1790 to 1875. No numerical limits of any kind. Active legal importation of African slaves until 1807, with illegal slave smuggling of unknown magnitude thereafter. Periods of active unofficial labor recruitment.

The United States of the late eighteenth and the nineteenth century was the classical resource rich and labor short developing country of that period. In the colonial period and during the early years of the Republic, agricultural labor in the South was supplied by the forced immigration of African slaves. The numbers of slaves held in bondage grew quite large, stimulated especially by the development of the cotton plantation toward the end of the eighteenth century. Legislation in 1807 made the importation of slaves unlawful, but the international slave traffic from Africa to the New World continued for another half-century, with unknown levels of illegal trafficking to the United States.

The nineteenth century was one of rapid geographical expansion for the United States, by purchase, treaty, and conquest. The Louisiana Purchase of 1803, the annexation of the state of Texas in 1845, settlement of a dispute with the British over the Oregon Territory in 1846, and the Treaty of Guadalupe Hidalgo of 1848, in which Mexico ceded California and the New Mexico territories, made the United States into a fully continental state embracing an enormous landmass. However, much of this territory was sparsely populated frontier, vulnerable to potential encroachment by neighboring countries or European colonial powers. At the same time, the United States had developed in its Northeast and Midwest regions a rapidly expanding industrial base for which a growing labor force was required.

Thus the United States in the last half of the nineteenth century faced two imperatives (in addition to resolving the national unity and slavery issues that led to the 1860–65 Civil War), one political and the other economic. The first imperative was to settle and establish effective control over its frontier regions, while the second was to staff its factories and farms. During this same period, European countries experienced a series of economic and political upheavals (e.g., the failure of the potato crops in Ireland and Germany), which, in the context of their rapidly growing populations, made them ready reservoirs for exportable labor.

Together these forces led to substantial growth in immigration flows to the United States from the 1840s to World War I, as can be seen in Table 1. In formal legal terms, U.S. immigration policy was neutral, but migration numbers were wholly unrestricted, and there were considerable unofficial efforts at labor recruitment as well. Labor recruiters found fertile terri-

TABLE 1: Legal Immigration to the United States, 1820–1985

Year	Number of persons	Year	Number of persons	Year	Number of persons	Year	Number of persons
1820–1883	51,406,446						
1820	8,385						
1821–1830	143,439	1851–1860	2,598,214	1881–1890	5,246,613	1911–1920	5,735,811
1821	9,127	1851	379,466	1881	669,431	1911	878,587
1822	6,911	1852	371,603	1882	788,922	1912	838,172
1823	6,354	1853	368,645	1883	603,322	1913	1,197,892
1824	7,912	1854	427,833	1884	518,592	1914	1,218,480
1825	10,199	1855	200,877	1885	395,436	1915	326,700
1826	10,837	1856	200,436	1886	334,203	1916	298,826
1827	18,875	1857	251,306	1887	490,109	1917	295,403
1828	28,382	1858	123,126	1888	546,889	1918	110,618
1829	22,520	1859	121,282	1889	444,427	1919	141,132
1830	23,322	1860	153,640	1890	455,302	1920	430,001
1831–1840	599,125	1861–1870	2,314,824	1891–1900	3,687,564	1921–1930	4,107,209
1831	22,633	1861	91,918	1891	560,319	1921	805,228
1832	60,482	1862	91,985	1892	579,663	1922	309,556
1833	58,640	1863	176,282	1893	439,730	1923	522,919
1834	65,365	1864	193,418	1894	285,631	1924	706,896
1835	45,374	1865	248,120	1895	258,536	1925	294,314
1836	76,242	1866	318,568	1896	343,267	1926	304,498
1837	79,340	1867	315,722	1897	230,832	1927	335,175
1838	38,914	1868	138,840	1898	229,299	1928	307,255
1839	68,069	1869	352,768	1899	311,715	1929	279,678
1840	84,066	1870	387,203	1900	448,572	1930	241,700
1841–1850	1,713,251	1871–1880	2,812,191	1901–1910	8,795,386	1931–1940	528,431
1841	80,289	1871	321,350	1901	487,918	1931	97,139
1842	104,565	1872	404,806	1902	648,743	1932	35,576
1843	52,496	1873	459,803	1903	857,046	1933	23,068
1844	78,615	1874	313,339	1904	812,870	1934	29,470
1845	114,371	1875	227,498	1905	1,026,499	1935	34,956
1846	154,416	1876	169,986	1906	1,100,735	1936	36,329
1847	234,968	1877	141,857	1907	1,285,349	1937	50,244
1848	226,527	1878	138,469	1908	782,870	1938	67,895
1849	297,024	1879	177,826	1909	751,786	1939	82,998
1850	369,980	1880	457,257	1910	1,041,570	1940	70,756

Year	Number of persons	Year	Number of persons	Year	Number of persons	Year	Number of persons
1941–1950	1,035,039	1961–1970	3,321,677	1976–1980	2,557,033		
1941	51,776	1961	271,344	1976	398,613		
1942	28,781	1962	283,763	1976 TQ*	103,676		
1943	23,725	1963	306,260	1977	462,315		
1944	28,551	1964	292,248	1978	601,442		
1945	38,119	1965	296,697	1979	460,348		
1946	108,721	1966	323,040	1980	530,639		
1947	147,292	1967	361,972				
1948	170,570	1968	454,448				
1949	188,317	1969	358,579				
1950	249,187	1970	373,326				
1951–1960	2,515,479	1971–1980	4,493,314	1981–1985	2,894,397		
1951	205,717	1971–1975	1,936,281	1981	596,600		
1952	265,520	1971	370,478	1982	594,131		
1953	170,434	1972	384,685	1983	559,763		
1954	208,177	1973	400,063	1984	543,903		
1955	237,790	1974	394,861	1985 (est)	600,000		
1956	321,625	1975	386,194				
1957	326,867						
1958	253,265						
1959	260,686						
1960	265,398						

*Denotes "transitional quarter," reflecting shift in federal government fiscal year.

tory in Ireland, Germany, China, Mexico, and in eastern and southern Europe.

Phase II, 1875 to 1921. Still no numerical limitations of any kind. Gradual accretion of qualitative restrictions. Continued active unofficial labor recruitment. Exclusion of Chinese, then Japanese, then all Asian immigrants.

As early as the 1850s, an organized opposition to unfettered immigration arose in the Know-Nothing movement, and in California, state legislation was adopted to restrict the recruitment of Chinese "coolies." Anti-immigrant sentiments subsided during the tumult of the Civil War, but re-emerged thereafter. The first federal legislation restricting immigration was passed in 1875, aimed at excluding criminals and prostitutes. This and subsequent legislation for nearly half a century imposed no numerical limitations on immigration, but instead sought to exclude certain categories of immigrants such as convicted felons, anarchists, the mentally ill and retarded, alcoholics, polygamists, and beggars. In 1882 political pressure from California led to congressional passage of the Chinese Exclusion Act, which excluded a whole nation from eligibility as immigrants. This was extended to Japanese in 1907 by the "Gentlemen's Agreement," and, in 1917, to all Asians. Also excluded in the 1880s, under pressure from organized labor, were contract laborers who were being used as strikebreakers.

These qualitative restrictions of the 1870s and 1880s had no quantitative effect, however. Sustained economic growth led to rising demand for labor in America, while in Europe there were fundamental shifts in the source countries of would-be immigrants. Migration from eastern and southern Europe grew rapidly in the 1880s, exceeding that from western and northern Europe by 1876. A sharp recession in the late 1890s temporarily reduced immigration numbers, but the trend into the new century was clearly upward.

By the first decade of the twentieth century, there was a vigorous political effort to limit both the countries of origin and the numbers of immigrants. This campaign was permeated with the biological beliefs of the period, influenced as it was by social Darwinism and eugenics. For it was widely held that the "races" of the world (with "race" having a more general definition than today's, as in "the British race," "the French race," etc.) possessed notably differing biological characteristics and capabilities, including varying capacities to adapt to democratic society. From 1907 to 1911, a Joint Commission on Immigration, established by the U.S. Congress and known as the Dillingham commission, embraced many of these arguments as to the inferiority of immigrant "races" and recommended legislative restrictions that took such considerations into account.

Phase III, ca. 1921 to 1968. First numerical limitations on legal immigration, with effective bias toward northern and western Europeans. Substantial temporary worker program from Mexico from 1942–1964, with accompanying illegal immigration.

World War I concentrated national attention upon other, more pressing, concerns. Although the literacy test mentioned above was adopted in 1917, the first acts limiting the volume of immigration were not passed until 1921 and 1924. The full effects of these legislative changes were not felt until 1929, but it seems likely nonetheless that they restrained immigration flows during the late 1920s, which earlier experience suggests would otherwise have increased greatly during this economic boom period.

The centerpiece "national origins quotas" of the 1921 and 1924 acts were deliberately skewed to limit immigration from eastern and southern Europe. Yet no numerical limits were placed upon immigration from Mexico and Latin America. Economic interests in the Southwest no doubt had something to do with this, but the relative population sparsity in the region at that time meant there was little prospect of substantial immigrant flows. For example, in 1900 the total population of Latin America and the Caribbean was less than 75 million, with that of Mexico less than 14 million; today the same region's population exceeds 400 million, with Mexico alone approaching 80 million.

Immigration from 1930 to 1945 was sharply constrained by the convergence of three developments: the full implementation of the 1924 numerical restrictions in 1929, the unrelated financial crisis of that same year and the ensuing Great Depression, and the limits on European outmigration imposed by harsh realities of World War II. Indeed, the return migration of European immigrants during the years leading to World War II means that net immigration during this period may have been slightly negative in some years. The labor shortages caused by military mobilization did lead to the creation of a "temporary worker" program for agricultural workers from Mexico (known as *braceros,* "strong-armed ones"). Although its significance was not appreciated at the time, this *bracero* program laid the foundations for a pattern of illegal immigration that accompanied it and continued after its termination.

From the end of World War II to 1952, the immigration policies framed in the 1920s were continued, albeit with continuation of the *bracero* program at the insistence of growers who had become dependent upon this labor supply, and with the ad hoc admission of significant numbers of refugees displaced by the European war. In 1952 a major recodification and revision of immigration law was adopted, the Immigration and Refugee Act of 1952, also known as the McCarran-Walter Act. This legislation, passed during both the cold war and the Korean War, was very much a product of its times. It codified and continued in modified form the national origins provisions of previous law and embraced the existing exclusions of Communists embodied in the Internal Security Act of 1950. It also allowed for continuation of the "temporary worker" or *bracero* program, initiated a full decade earlier in wartime 1942.

Although the McCarran-Walter Act generally is seen as limiting immigration, it did little to restrain illegal immigration. A 1956 account of the evolution of this legislation by Eleanor Hadley in *Law and Contemporary Problems* reported that Senator Pat McCarran, who strongly supported limitations upon legal immigration, "defended the illegal traffic over our southern border on the grounds that legal entry of Mexicans for employment in American agriculture and industry involved too much red tape." There was also the general assumption that such migration would be only for short periods at times of planting and harvest, and hence would not constitute permanent immigration.

Indeed, the McCarran-Walter Act included a fateful provision, the now-notorious "Texas Proviso," that has served over the past three decades to facilitate the employment of illegal aliens. This provision, originally passed three months earlier and then recodified in the McCarran-Walter Act of 1952, makes interesting reading in the United States of 1986 (the proviso is the underlined portion of the following section prohibiting harboring of illegal aliens):

[Any person who] willfully or knowingly conceals, harbors, or shields from detection . . . in any place . . . any alien . . . not duly admitted . . . shall be guilty of a felony, and upon conviction thereof shall be punished by a fine not exceeding $2,000 or by imprisonment for a term not exceeding five years, or both, for each alien in respect to whom any violation of this subsection occurs: *Provided, however, that for the purposes of this section, employment (including the usual and normal practices incident to employment) shall not be deemed to constitute harboring.* (Immigration and Nationality Act, Section 274(a), emphasis added)

The illegal immigration encouraged by the *bracero* program and the Texas Proviso was of little concern in the 1952 congressional deliberations, but just over a year later Attorney General Herbert Brownell paid a visit to the California border. According to Hadley, Brownell described the border situation he saw as "shocking," and his earlier support for reductions in border patrol workers as "the most penny-wise and pound-foolish policy I've ever seen." He returned to Washington to push for increased border patrol workers, and later encouraged the development of Operation Wetback, a concentrated task force operation in the Southwest whose large-scale apprehensions served as a deterrent to additional illegal immigration for many years.

In subsequent years, opposition to the *bracero* program grew among labor and church groups, and eventually it was allowed to terminate in 1964, fully twenty-two years after it was initiated as a "temporary" measure during the war emergency.

Phase IV, 1968 to Present. Continued numerical limitations on legal immigration, with effective bias toward more recent immigrant groups (mostly from Asia, Latin America, and the Caribbean). Substantial continuing illegal immigration.

The next major reforms of immigration law took place in 1965. These amendments to the Immigration and Nationality Act abolished at last the national origins quota system originally established in the 1920s. It also eliminated immigration discrimination "on grounds of race, sex, nationality, place of birth or place of residence," thereby abolishing the earlier provisions that had sharply limited immigration from Asia.

Finally, the 1965 amendments shifted emphasis in the immigration preference system away from those with skills needed in the U.S. labor market and toward those with family ties with U.S. citizens and resident aliens. By so doing, it unintentionally replaced the bias of the McCarran-Walter Act favoring immigrants from northern and western Europe with a new bias favoring immigrants from countries providing recent immigrants. Under these terms, immigrant visas now are more readily available to would-be immigrants from Latin America and parts of Asia than to similar people from Europe or Africa.

But the 1965 reforms did not deal with illegal immigration, and in the early 1970s legislation sponsored by Congressman Peter Rodino was passed twice by the House of Representatives to penalize employers who knowingly employ illegal aliens. This legislation (known by the shorthand term "employer sanctions") was blocked in the Senate by then-chairman of the Judiciary Committee James O. Eastland, who strongly represented the interests of agricultural employers in insisting upon a new "temporary worker" program as a quid pro quo for employer sanctions.

By the mid-1970s, there was increasing awareness and concern expressed about growing abuses of immigration laws. An Interagency Task Force on Illegal Immigration was established by President Gerald Ford in January 1976. Its report served as raw material for a Cabinet committee on the subject established by newly elected President Jimmy Carter in 1977, which framed legislation proposed by the president to delegalize the knowing employment of illegal aliens while offering amnesty to large numbers who had entered the country before 1970. Once again, Congress failed to act on these proposals, instead choosing to defer the decision by establishing a Select Commission on Immigration and Refugee Policy at the urging of Senator Edward M. Kennedy, then-chairman of the Senate Judiciary Committee. This commission was asked to issue its report *after* the 1980 elections, and did so in 1981.

Meanwhile, Congress was able to manage reforms in U.S. refugee policy, driven by the experiences of the Vietnam "boat people" crisis of 1978–79. The definition of "refugee" incorporated in the 1952 McCarran-Walter Act, with its heavily cold war tone drawn from the McCarthy period, was transformed to that of the internationally-agreed refugee definition of the 1951 United Nations Convention on the Status of Refugees and its 1967 Protocol. Whereas in the 1952 law most persons qualifying as refugees were required to have fled

> persecution or fear of persecution on account of race, religion or political opinion . . . from any Communist or Communist-dominated country or area, or . . . from any country within the general area of the Middle East. . . .

the 1980 law extended eligibility of persons from all countries by redefining a refugee as:

> any person who is outside of any country of such person's nationality . . . and who is unable or unwilling to return to . . . that country because of persecution or a well-founded fear of persecution on account of race, religion, nationality, membership in a particular social group, or political opinion. . . .

Numerical Trends in U.S. Immigration, Both Absolute and Relative

Official data on legal immigration to the United States are available from 1820 onward. These data have numerous limitations which cannot be discussed in detail here. For example, they exclude all illegal immigrants, which makes them misleadingly low during periods of substantial illegal movements, such as the early 1950s and since the late 1960s. No data are collected on emigration by past immigrants or native-born, making it necessary to estimate net legal immigration. Furthermore, although the numbers of refugees admitted to the United States for permanent residence have been quite large in recent years, these are not entered into the official immigration numbers until refugees "adjust their status" to that of permanent resident alien, which involves variable but usually multiyear delays.

A comprehensible and balanced picture of the numerical significance of U.S. immigration can be obtained only by considering legal immigration data in both absolute and relative terms and by including a range of reasonable estimates of illegal immigration.

Legal Immigration—Absolute Numbers

In absolute terms, legal immigration was on a generally rising trend from the 1820s to the 1880s, with several peaks and troughs. Most of the immigrants of this period were from northern and western Europe, with the United Kingdom, Ireland, and Germany looming large. After a temporary trough, there was then a sharp increase in immigration numbers from the 1880s through the 1920s, peaking in the decade 1901–1910 when an annual average of 880,000 immigrants was recorded. The source countries of this large migration were no longer the traditional ones of northern and western Europe, but instead of eastern Europe (Austria-Hungary and Poland) and southern Europe (especially Italy).

During the sharply constrained immigration situation that prevailed from 1930 to 1945, only 699,383 legal immigrants were recorded, or less than 47,000 per year. Indeed the total number of immigrants over this fifteen-year period was less than the number admitted in *every single year* between 1903 and the onset of World War I in 1914.

This period from 1930 to 1945 proved to be an interlude, for after World War II legal immigration grew substantially. The average annual immigration in the period 1945 to 1950 was about 173,000, more than three times higher than the average from the abnormally depressed levels between 1930 and 1945. Each subsequent decade saw further substantial increases in immigrant numbers.

Legal Immigration—Two Relative Measures

A clear understanding of immigrant numbers requires that they be considered in relative terms, taking into account both the size of the population base of the United States *and* its rate of growth. The first expresses immigration in relation to the overall *size* of the receiving population; the second, as a percentage of the overall *increase* in the receiving population. Both comparisons are meaningful, in different ways; neither on its own presents a fair picture of the relative demographic significance of immigration.

During the period of numerically unlimited immigration from 1790 to 1930, the volume of immigration in relation to the U.S. population base generally increased, and reached an extraordinary peak in the decade of 1901–1910. In that single decade an immigration stream equivalent to fully 10 percent of the resident population entered the country. The magnitude of this immigration flow surely contributed to the strong political pressures that led in the 1920s to the first numerical restrictions on entry.

As was the declared intention of these restrictions, rates as high as those described above were not seen again. Legal immigration as a percent of population was near zero during the 1930s and World War II. Although it has been rising significantly throughout the 1950s, 1960s, 1970s, and 1980s, the large size of the U.S. population base means that it is still substantially less than 1 percent. (Legal immigration numbers equal to 1 percent of the current U.S. population of 238 million would exceed 2 million immigrants per year.)

Over the same period, dramatic shifts in the level of U.S. fertility and mortality have affected the other relative measure, that expressing legal immigration as a percentage of overall population increase. Because U.S. fertility was declining throughout the nineteenth century, this percentage increased more rapidly than did immigration as a percentage of the total population. Although immigration declined sharply during the 1930s, so did U.S. fertility, and the postwar increase in immigration was paralleled by the dramatic fertility increase known as the "baby boom." Thus the extent of change in legal immigration as a percentage of population growth was moderated in this century by parallel changes in fertility, until the 1960s at least.

This pattern changed significantly in the mid-1960s, when the trends in immigration and fertility diverged sharply and dramatically. Immigration numbers rose with the 1965 liberalization described below and the accompanying increase in illegal immigration (see discussion below). Meanwhile, fertility declined dramatically in what is now known as the "baby bust" or the "birth dearth." So substantial was this decline that the total fertility rates in the late 1970s were about 50 percent lower than those twenty years earlier. The combined effect of rising immigration numbers and declining fertility was to sharply increase the relative magnitude of the former, i.e., the percentage of population growth accounted for by immigration rose to the highest levels seen since the first numerical restrictions on immigration a half-century earlier.

Illegal Immigration—The Numbers Game

Measurement of illegal or undocumented immigration poses the most profound data problems, for the obvious reason that a clandestine and unlawfully present population cannot be expected to present itself for governmental enumeration. Illegal aliens fall into at least three major categories—those who cross the U.S. border without permission or inspection (EWI or "entry without inspection"), those who enter via ports of entry using fraudulent or counterfeit visas, and those who enter using valid temporary visas and then overstay or otherwise violate the terms of their admission. Efforts to estimate the gross numbers of such persons have provided fertile territory both for objective scholars with an interest in creative measurement techniques and for the numerous politically motivated advocates who seek apparently objective numbers to support their positions.

Making and criticizing estimates of this population has been a remarkably popular pastime in some circles. In part this is because the numbers are important to a range of policy issues, e.g., the question of whether "amnesty" or legalized status should be offered to those illegally in the United States. If the numbers are small, this proposal is more likely to be acceptable than if they are large. At the same time, those interested in stimulating public and political concern about illegal immigration are often drawn to larger estimates, while their opponents prefer smaller ones.

There are also nonpolitical reasons for disagreement. Executives and management consulting firms are accustomed to tapping the knowledge and insights of administrative and sales personnel to obtain estimates of important economic and social trends that are not accessible via standardized quantitative data. Meanwhile, quantitative social scientists tend to eschew such insights as "nonscientific" or "speculative," preferring instead to use official data or indirect estimates drawn from "objective" data even if they are of uncertain quality.

Origins of Disagreements. Even within either of these two approaches, there is enormous scope for disagreement. In a 1984 article, Eduard Bos points to four sources of such discrepancy.

(1) The exclusion of different categories of illegal aliens. For example, estimates based upon U.S. census data typically exclude large numbers of "visa-abusing tourists and foreign students, aliens engaging in fraudulent marriages, and aliens using bogus passports or permits for resident "aliens." Other studies exclude those using border "shopping permits" to commute unlawfully to work in the United States, on grounds that they are resident elsewhere.

(2) Use of data drawn from different time periods. Since some part of the illegal alien population is thought to be seasonally present, different dates of measurement could lead to substantially different estimates, even within the same year.

(3) Inaccuracy of U.S. data on legal immigration. Many indirect estimates of illegal alien numbers have been modeled upon techniques developed to adjust census data for undercounts on the basis of prior census and birth and death registration. However, illegal immigration estimates from such methods are heavily dependent upon the accuracy of data on net legal immigration. Since U.S. data on net legal immigration are of poor quality, various analysts have adopted different assumptions that result in different estimates of the illegal alien population.

(4) Lack of evidence as to age, sex, and other demographic characteristics of illegal aliens. Some indirect estimates (e.g., those based upon unexpectedly high mortality rates) require assumptions about the age and sex characteristics of the illegal alien population. In the absence of direct evidence on such matters, various estimators have adopted different assumptions that can have important effects upon their ultimate estimates.

Range of Estimates. Given such fundamental problems, it is hardly surprising that a wide range of estimates has been elaborated. In general, those based upon administrative judgment have been the highest, ranging up to 6 to 8 million in the mid-1970s. Earlier and more speculative estimates of 12 million and higher have been largely discredited. Those based upon indirect techniques are the lowest, ranging as low as 1 to 2 million. So profound is the analytical divide that one enthusiastic expert on indirect estimation techniques has gone so far as to characterize administrative estimates as "coming out of the blue."

In view of the numerical murkiness and strongly held opinions that afflict this debate, this discussion will not join the fray. Although there has been a profusion of estimates and a tendency toward analytic arrogance, in fact the range of responsible estimates is not as wide as might be thought. Almost everyone agrees that the likely number of illegal aliens in the United States is in the millions. A reasonable lower bound has been established, with some 2 million estimated to have been counted in the 1980 census. The upper bound is far less certain; one's view here depends upon what fundamentally must be a guess as to what fraction of this clandestine population was counted in the 1980 census. Some hold that at least half were counted (implying an upper bound of 4 million illegal aliens), while others believe the percentage counted was much smaller, and the upper bound therefore higher (for example, if the percentage of illegal aliens enumerated in the 1980 census was closer to 25 percent than to 50 percent, the estimated 2 million counted would imply a total of 8 million in the population). Thus, estimates of the upper bound are very sensitive to one's guesses about the percentage enumerated, and unfortunately there is no firm basis for judging the completeness of enumeration of a clandestine population.

Despite the rhetoric and exaggerated claims for one or another method, the fact is that *illegal immigration is essentially inaccessible to accurate measurement,* as are other clandestine processes such as organized crime, drug abuse and trafficking, the "underground economy," and incest. No one, and certainly not this author, can know with any great accuracy what are the true current size and growth rate of the illegal alien population, nor is firm evidence likely ever to become available. Although there are powerful indirect techniques for estimating demographic rates such as births and deaths when official data are absent or unreliable, such methods are far more subject to error in measurements of clandestine behaviors, which many of those involved seek consciously to shield from detection. Most advocates and some researchers will continue to have a taste for the numbers game, and no one will be able to provide convincing proof that almost any numerical claim within a plausible range (between, say, 4 and 8 million) is empirically wrong. The best anyone can expect is a reasonable range of estimates that is adequate for policy formulation. Even though our understanding of these phenomena has been improving, assessing the size and impacts of the illegal alien population remains akin to many other areas of public policy for which truly firm and reliable quantitative data are unavailable, such as the intentions of the Soviet Union or the true magnitude of child abuse.

Impacts of Recent Immigration

To a degree unusual among the nations of the world, Americans have a generally positive image of immigration. Although only a small percentage of current residents of the United States is foreign-born (smaller, incidentally, than in several other countries such as Canada, Australia, New Zealand, and Israel), most Americans are proud to live in a "nation of immigrants" and often consider themselves to come from immigrant stock, even if the immigrant was a distant forebear. For this reason, among others, ethnic diversity is celebrated in the United States, and most Americans appreciate the fascinating variety of cuisines, languages, and cultural traditions that contribute so much to the quality and energy of American life.

There is also, however, a national ambivalence about immigration, arising out of longstanding concerns about its cultural, economic, and political impacts. Such concerns tend to be suppressed as long as economic conditions are robust and immigration flows are moderate in size and culturally diverse, but appear with predictable regularity during periods of economic stress and when immigrant influxes are large, visible, and culturally concentrated. As a result of such large and concentrated immigrations, there have been significant anti-immigration backlashes in recent years in regions such as southern California and south Florida.

Unfortunately, the available empirical evidence on the impacts of immigration to the U.S. has been freely distorted and exaggerated by the many activists and scholar-advocates who have energized the public debate on immigration policy. This is hardly surprising; most of the opposition to the current policy regime usually derives from its perceived negative consequences, while support for the current situation usually comes from those who find the trends favorable or at least acceptable in economic, political, or cultural terms. The purpose of this section is to summarize available evidence as objectively as possible, excluding most of the special pleading that plagues the debate. When there is disagreement among reputable nonadvocates, both sides are described.

Impacts in three categories are discussed: economic impacts; implications for provision of education and social services; and political, social and cultural effects. As will be seen, much of the political debate has concentrated upon argued economic costs and benefits of legal and illegal immigration, which has tended to obscure the noneconomic aspects that may be of greater public concern to residents and immigrants alike.

Economic Impacts

Assessments of the economic impacts of international migration are freighted with ideological considerations. For example, the 1986 Annual Report of the Council of Economic Advisors, then a two-member council chaired by a prominent monetarist, Beryl Sprinkel, sought to prove that unrestricted immigration has economic virtues similar to those of free trade in goods, services, and financial claims. On the basis of such arguments, an earlier unpublished draft went so far as to publicly oppose measures supported by President Reagan to reduce illegal immigration, thereby generating considerable controversy and an ultimate disavowal from within the administration.

The economic effects of immigration are usually discussed in terms of their "macro" effects upon the larger economy; their "micro" effects upon specific regions, industries, firms, and population groups; and their effects upon productivity. In all cases, attention must be paid to the distinctions between legal and illegal immigration and between short-run and long-run impacts.

"Macro" Impacts. Standard economic theory would see the macroeconomic effects of immigration quite differently depending upon whether conditions of relative labor scarcity or surplus prevail, and also depending upon whether the focus is upon the short to medium term or the long term. For example, during medium-term periods of economic boom (such as that in West Germany in the 1960s) or wartime distortions (such as those during World War II), the large-scale importation of labor from low-wage countries could resolve important bottlenecks in the economy and thereby further growth and reduce inflation. Conversely, during a period of economic stagnation or slow growth, in which unemployment and underemployment rates are high, large-scale immigration of low-skill workers from low-income countries might lead to higher growth in aggregate but lower growth in per capita gross national product (GNP) and productivity. The returns to labor would be restrained, while profits and other returns to capital might benefit over the short to medium term. However, the economic incentives favoring investment in increased productivity would also be reduced, which might thereby exacerbate long-term problems of competitiveness in an increasingly difficult international economy.

"Micro" Impacts. At the micro level of the industry, firm, region, and individual, there would be clear winners and clear losers from such a policy. Industries, firms, and regions making heavy use of low-wage imported labor would be expected to gain over the short to medium term, while those unable or unwilling to employ such labor would be relatively disadvantaged. Thus there would tend to be a gradual shift of economic activity toward sectors with such a low-cost labor supply, to the detriment of those lacking same. Certain labor-intensive industries in which there is substantial international competition from low-income countries (such as the garment industry) would be expected to benefit or at least to retard the losses incurred from imports. Similar benefits could not be claimed by other industries (such as construction, services, etc.) in which international trade is limited.

At the level of individual workers, such labor importation would be expected to depress wages, weaken labor unions, and displace (either directly or indirectly) some domestic workers with skills and other attributes most similar to those of immigrants. There need be no direct job competition between immigrant and native born workers. Indeed the most significant effects are likely to be those of an indirect character, as when wages or working conditions are depressed below the levels attractive to native workers, or when employers come to prefer an all-immigrant work force as more compliant and less responsive to unionization efforts. Meanwhile, other U.S. workers not in competition with immigrants might experience somewhat higher wages and other benefits. In addition, the returns to capital might rise, and goods produced by cheaper labor might result in either higher profits or lower consumer prices depending upon market conditions.

While the conditions faced by some native workers might tend to deteriorate, those experienced by most immigrants would improve from what they would expect in their homelands (otherwise their migration would be irrational). Thus there might be substantial distributional effects (e.g., away from low-skill native and toward immigrant and high-skill native workers) while overall the aggregate economic effects might be of modest magnitude.

Long-term vs. Short-term Impacts at the Micro Level. When longer-term effects are considered, the picture becomes even more complex and murky. Certain industries requiring inexpensive and low-skill labor might be protected, and these would tend to recruit immigrant labor or, if feasible, to move their locus of operations to the regions to which immigrants are moving. Thus the garment industry might experience a gradual shift from Manhattan to East Los Angeles or to the border towns of Texas.

Meanwhile many industries would see the growth in labor costs restrained, and thereby experience reduced economic incentives favoring the investment needed to develop and manufacture more efficient production technologies. Of course, other important economic factors intervene here, such as the availability and real cost of capital for investment, the availability of such technologies, and the structure of government policies favoring or disfavoring such capital investment.

Productivity Impacts. To the extent immigrants enter the U.S. with higher average educational and skill levels than those of the indigenous population, as may have occurred during some periods in the past, immigration can be expected (other things being equal) to raise the average productivity of labor. The potential contribution of such capacities to the productivity and assimilability of immigrants underlies the educational and/or "needed skills" tests applied by most other countries to the majority of prospective immigrants.

If, on the other hand, immigrants' educational and skill levels are lower than those prevailing in the native labor force, immigration can be expected to lower the average productivity of labor. This could occur if there is a failure to control unlawful immigration by persons with low education and skill levels, and/or if education and skill criteria are essentially excluded from a substantial proportion of admissions decisions (e.g., current U.S. policy of relatively easy admission of recent immigrants' kin irrespective of their education or job skills). For both of the above reasons, it seems unlikely that recent U.S. immigration (legal and illegal combined) has contributed to improved labor productivity.

It also has been argued that immigrants as a class are more productive than would otherwise be indicated by their skill levels. The nonempirical form of this argument simply asserts *ex cathedra* that immigrants are a self-selected subset of the sending country's population who are especially hardworking, creative, ambitious, and/or entrepreneurial, and therefore do extremely well in the free enterprise economy of the United States. Some extreme proponents have gone so far as to argue that the more people there are (whether by immigration or by additional births), the greater the number of "geniuses," who thereby contribute to economic advance via their scientific and technological creativity. Such extreme arguments are not taken seriously by most experts.

There is also a significant empirical literature on the economic productivity of immigrants, and here there is a new and fascinating scientific debate. Following the pioneering work of the economist Barry Chiswick, analyses of cross sections of immigrant and native groups in successive censuses (e.g., for 1960, 1970, and 1980) suggest that most legal immigrant groups (excluding, for some reason, those from Mexico) experience substantial increases in income. So substantial are these gains that after ten to fifteen years these immigrant groups surpass the earnings of native born persons of equal educational attainment. Such findings lend support to the more subjective arguments that hardworking and creative immigrants contribute to productivity growth.

Such results have recently been challenged in a fundamental way by another economist, George Borjas. Using data from the 1970 and 1980 censuses, he analyzes earnings of the same immigrant groups both cross-sectionally and longitudinally. While his cross-sectional results parallel those of Chiswick, the longitudinal analyses of the same data give the very opposite results—only very slow earnings growth for immigrants, who never surpass natives of equal educational attainment. He offers two explanations for the cross-sectional findings that earlier immigrant cohorts earn significantly more than more recent immigrants: a fall in demand for immigrant labor, and an apparent decline in the "quality" (in labor-market terms) of more recent immigrants. Borjas concludes that findings of rapid immigrant advancement based upon cross-sectional data "provide useless and misleading insights into the process of immigrant assimilation into the labor market." It is fair to say that this is an area of immigration research that remains unresolved and demanding of further careful attention.

The above debate relates to the experience of legal immigrants, or at least to those who appear in the official census data. With regard to illegal immigrants, it is generally agreed that educational attainment is lower than for legal immigrants, and that average earnings are lower too. Whether the apparently large stocks of illegal immigrants who have accumulated during the past fifteen years will be successful economically depends heavily upon the importance of education for future economic productivity. Most economists believe that high skill levels will be essential for success in the postindustrial economy of the future, but some argue that automation will lead to a "de-skilling" of work into functions requiring little education. If the first view proves to be correct, illegal aliens likely will fare poorly; if the second view is right, they probably will do well. We shall have to wait and see which prognostication proves more accurate.

Adequacy of Labor Supply. There have been several predictions of future "labor shortages" in the United States, on the basis of which continued large-scale immigration has been recommended. It first must be said that most economists view with profound skepticism the very concept of "labor shortages" (other than short-term bottlenecks) in a flexible free enterprise economy. If real wages rise significantly in response to supply/demand imbalances, powerful economic incentives are thereby produced favoring additional labor force participation and capital investment in labor-saving technologies. Beyond this rather fundamental point, it is clear enough that the future demand for labor cannot be predicted with any real reliability. Demand for labor will be affected by quite unpredictable developments in economic expansion, technological advance, international trade, and other powerful forces. For this reason, most economists exercise great caution in predicting the size and composition of labor demand far into the future.

On the labor supply side, the evidence is clearer. The worries about labor shortages derive from the low fertility levels of the past decade, which mean that other things being equal the generations of the normal age of labor force entry in the 1990s will be much smaller than those "baby boom" generations maturing over the past decade or so. However, the most recent Bureau of Labor Statistics projections for the United States show continued substantial labor force growth right through the remainder of the century, e.g., increases from about 107 million in 1980 to between 130 and 150 million in 2000. Moreover, past projections have generally erred on the low side, due to overly conservative assumptions regarding female labor force participation and immigration. Current projections may also underestimate future labor force participation by more elderly workers, especially given trends toward elimination of compulsory retirement and reduction of very generous retirement benefits.

In short, it is hard to find empirical evidence to support predictions of "labor shortages" in the United States over the short to medium term, and long-term predictions of labor demand are highly suspect in a dynamic and technologically changing economy.

Education and Social Services

There has been a steady stream of argument concerning the effects of immigration upon education and social service programs. Much of this has spilled from the pens or mouths of committed advocates and, thus, has partaken of their penchant for exaggerated and selective use of evidence. As is universally the case, more is known about the impacts of legal immigrants and refugees, who appear in official data, than about the sub rosa population of illegal aliens. The debate on these subjects is lengthy and complicated, and cannot be reviewed in full here. A fair summary of what we know follows.

The use of education and social services by immigrants (including legal, illegal, and refugee) ranges from high to low, depending upon the benefit examined and the characteristics of the immigrant population. With respect to legal immigrants, those who are well educated tend to make little use of income transfer and unemployment benefits, although their children benefit from public educational provision. Elderly legal immigrants entering under the terms of family reunification can be expected to be heavy users of publicly supported health services for many years. (In some cases the availability of such health services is an important reason for the immigration in the first place.) Legally admitted refugees tend to make heavy use of welfare and other income transfer benefits in early years, but, depending upon their job skills and the availability of employment, tend eventually to move off the public rolls into the labor force.

With respect to illegal immigrants, those with low skills and earnings who are accompanied by their families probably make extensive use of publicly supported systems for health care, education, and income transfers; however, the ready availability of fraudulent documents and the unwillingness of many social service agencies to delve into their validity makes accurate assessment impossible. Other low-skill illegal aliens who are young and unaccompanied by families probably make little use of educational and health care services, but may be well represented in unemployment benefits. Measurement of such use by a clandestine population is difficult, but a study by the Illinois attorney general in 1982 showed that nearly half of unemployment compensation applications by aliens were based upon fraudulent immigration documents. In California many illegal aliens in the agricultural sector seem to make routine seasonal use of unemployment benefits.

The costs of providing such benefits to immigrants and refugees may be quite high for some services and quite low for others: health care, remedial education, and bilingual education are particular examples of services that are heavily used by some immigrant groups, while the use of retirement and Medicare benefits is likely to be quite low. For expenditures on education in general, the costs at the margin differ markedly: in school districts with rapid enrollment growth (e.g., Texas, California) costs may be quite high, while in those with excess capacity (e.g., New York City until recently) the costs for the same services may be quite low.

Legislative efforts to limit the entitlements of illegal aliens to government services have been modified substantially by judicial intervention over the past several years. In 1982 the Supreme Court ruled in a narrow five-to-four decision overturning a Texas state law that illegal alien children are guaranteed a free public education by the Fourteenth Amendment. In California a state court has ruled that illegal aliens are entitled to the subsidized "resident" tuition rates in state universities and colleges, rather than the much higher "nonresident" rates applied to U.S. citizens from other states and to lawfully admitted foreign students. A number of additional court cases challenging legislative and administrative limitations on illegal alien entitlements (such as Aid to Families with Dependent Children, Food Stamps, etc.) have been initiated by advocacy groups, and are now pending in various courts; thus, the costs of such benefits are subject to important changes that require periodic reassessment.

Political, Social, and Cultural Effects

Undue concentration upon economic costs and benefits obscures the noneconomic impacts that are perhaps the most important elements of immigration as they are perceived by the resident population and by many of the immigrants themselves. Although the economic effects are hard enough to assess, especially for illegal immigration, these noneconomic factors are essentially unapproachable via empirical evidence. They lie instead in the murky realms of the values inherent in political institutions and cultures, the question of societal cohesion and stability in the context of the historically contentious fissures of language and religion, and the perceptions and ambitions of political parties and politicians. Such matters are of central importance to the general well-being of all human societies, as is evident from the attention paid to them by political philosophers and practitioners throughout history. Moreover, noneconomic factors such as the nature, stability, and adaptability of political institutions and societal values form the essential framework within which economic growth proceeds or fails.

For all their murkiness, such matters are no less real or important than those we can measure with economic and demographic data, as is self-evident from the frequent references to the impressive successes of American cultural pluralism in contrast to the dismal failures in such countries as Lebanon and Northern Ireland. Indeed, there has been some discussion of the possibility that continued uncontrolled immigration to the United States might result in sectional problems such as those experienced elsewhere.

Leaving aside such nightmarish—and, we hope, exaggerated—scenarios, there are a series of weighty issues that have arisen in relation to immigration trends, issues that without exaggeration do go to the very heart of political rights and national unity. As has come to be considered normal in the United States, much of the action on these issues has occurred not in the executive and legislative branches, but in the federal courts.

One legal dispute in this arena would surprise most American political leaders and citizens. Put simply, the question is whether the large but uncountable numbers of illegal aliens in the country have a constitutional right to political representation in the United States Congress, notwithstanding their unlawful status. The legal basis of this dispute goes right back to the Constitutional Convention of 1787, though in a manner that almost surely was never contemplated by the Founding Fathers. In part due to the irresolvable issue of slavery that later was to nearly destroy the Republic, the so-called Great Compromise of the Constitution apportioned political representation on the basis of the number of "persons," but excluding 40 percent of the number of slaves, and all "Indians not taxed," all to be enumerated in a decennial census leading to reapportionment of the House of Representatives. Two centuries later, reportedly under heavy political pressure from activists in the Carter White House, the Census Bureau for the first time adopted special measures aimed at enumerating as many illegal aliens as possible in the 1980 census. This led promptly to a legal challenge arguing that because this illegal alien population was large and concentrated in a few states, their deliberate inclusion in apportionment calculations would deprive citizens and legal aliens in other states of their fair congressional representation. In defense of its actions, the Carter administration argued that illegal aliens must be treated as "persons" entitled to congressional representation. (It failed to note that many "persons" enumerated on census day are routinely excluded from apportionment calculations, such as visitors, diplomats, and others in a temporary status; a fair question might be whether, for purposes of political representation, illegal aliens resemble more closely visitors or citizens.) The Justice Department brief even went so far as to state that "nothing in the Constitution forbids a state from permitting even illegal aliens from voting for Representatives."

To date, the federal courts have avoided ruling on the matter on grounds that the plaintiffs did not have standing to sue. The effect is that the estimated 2 million illegal aliens who were enumerated in the 1980 census have been provided political representation by inclusion of their numbers in the reapportionment of the U.S. House of Representatives, with the apparent effect that California and New York each gained one seat, at the expense of Indiana and Georgia. In 1985 Senator Thad Cochran introduced legislation (S. 1734) that would prohibit the Census Bureau from continuing to include illegal aliens in reapportionment calculations.

A related set of issues has arisen from the question of whether children born to aliens illegally in the United States should be entitled to U.S. citizenship and the entitlements that go with it. This form of "birthright citizenship" is often assumed to be a fundamental element of the U.S. Constitution and its Fourteenth Amendment, but a recent legal study from the Yale Law School by Peter H. Schuck and Rogers M. Smith raises serious doubts as to the validity of this assumption. Thus the growth of illegal immigration has already resulted in the growth of both advocacy and scholarship on the very meaning of American citizenship.

Another source of conflict has been generated by the predictions of some Hispanic politicians that Hispanics will soon outnumber blacks as the largest minority group, and that therefore their political representatives warrant much greater influence. Unless these politicians are assuming much larger numbers of Hispanic illegal aliens than are most other observers, this "we will outnumber you soon" scenario could occur only if large-scale illegal immigration were allowed to continue or increase for the next twenty to thirty years. (See the discussion on projections below.) Since many of the politicians making such claims have been outspoken opponents of proposed measures to restrain illegal immigration, their claims have raised questions as to whether their opposition derives from professed fears about negative impacts of such measures upon Hispanic-Americans, or instead from political ambitions related to continued influxes of potential ethnic supporters. In any case, such claims to outnumber blacks have not been well received in the black community, thereby illustrating the potential divisiveness of immigration policies in a pluralistic and contentious society such as the United States.

Finally, there are the political frictions that have arisen regarding bilingualism in areas with large numbers of immigrants. Bilingual policies promulgated by federal courts and by federal, state, and local governments have led to organization of active opposition groups at national and local levels. In 1984 one such group in California collected over 600,000 signatures to force inclusion on the ballot of Proposition 38, entitled "Voting Materials in English Only." This proposition was adopted by a majority of 72 percent numbering some 6.4 million votes. An earlier referendum campaign in Dade County, Florida, led to prohibition of public expenditures on bilingual activities that had been promoted by the large Cuban immigrant population in that county.

Whatever may be the merit of any of these concerns and positions, the general proposition that immigration policy is relevant to issues of national cohesiveness is a compelling one, especially when immigration flows are large in relation to other sources of demographic change. One expression of such general concern was offered in 1980 in the pages of the influential journal *Foreign Affairs* by a moderate and respected foreign policy and business leader, George W. Ball. Commenting upon the Carter administration's actions leading to the boat lift of 125,000 Cubans from Mariel Harbor, Ball stated, "History has shown often enough that a nation's cultural and political integrity can be frittered away in a generation, and a politically squalid encouragement of indigestible voting blocs can destroy our national cohesiveness before we even realize what has happened to us."

Recent Responses to Immigration Trends: The Simpson-Rodino-Mazzoli Bills

Recommendations of commissions often fail to stimulate concerted legislative attention by the U.S. Congress. The Select Commission on Immigration and Refugee Policy, alluded to earlier, proved to be an exception. Its report received unusually prompt and serious attention and contributed significantly to important legislative proposals.

In part this was an accident. For the first time since 1954, the leadership of the Senate passed unexpectedly to the Republicans, who were thus obliged to appoint new chairpersons of committees and subcommittees from a group of senators almost none of whom had ever chaired a congressional committee. One of the four senatorial members of the select commission, Senator Alan K. Simpson, was appointed chairman of the Judiciary Committee's Subcommittee on Immigration and Refugee Policy. Thus was a direct link established between the select commission and the unexpected new chairman of the relevant Senate committee.

Senator Simpson, then a freshman, proved to be an effective and respected legislator. (In 1985 he was elected deputy majority leader of the Senate.) He established a close working relationship with his opposite number on the House side, Congressman Romano L. Mazzoli. Together they fashioned a set of proposals that drew heavily upon the recommendations of the select commission, which itself had embraced earlier proposals from Congressman Peter Rodino and Presidents Ford and Carter.

The principal provisions were threefold:

(1) delegalization of the knowing employment of illegal aliens (known by the shorthand "employer sanctions"), in effect reversing the explicit legalization of such employment embodied in the Texas Proviso of 1952;
(2) legalization of large numbers of resident illegal aliens who had established equities in the United States; and
(3) reforms to reduce the widespread use of fraudulent identification documents.

These proposals have received widespread public support, according to all available opinion polls on the subject, which typically show between 80 and 90 percent of Americans supporting measures to restrain illegal immigration (although there is substantial opposition to the proposals that would legalize illegal aliens). In addition, the Simpson-Mazzoli initiatives received remarkably strong and broad based editorial support from the press, including virtually every leading newspaper such as the *New York Times,* the *Washington Post,* the *Boston Globe,* the *Chicago Tribune,* the *Los Angeles Times,* the *Christian Science Monitor,* and so on. The only notable exception to this near-unanimous endorsement was the right-libertarian editorial stance of the *Wall Street Journal.*

Since their introduction in 1981, Simpson and Mazzoli's proposals have been variously modified and amended. Different versions have now been adopted by large majorities on three separate occasions by the U.S. Senate, and once by a narrow, five-vote margin in the House of Representatives. However, due to disagreements between the two houses and vigorous blocking tactics by advocacy groups opposed to one or another provision, Congress still has failed to produce a final compromise bill.

While the bedfellows of politics are notoriously odd, those involved in the immigration debate have been positively bizarre. The most outspoken opponents of the various bills so far debated have included:

(1) employers of illegal aliens (especially agricultural interests in the Southwest) who see their profits threatened if they are precluded from freely recruiting cheap and compliant illegal alien labor;
(2) some (though by no means all) Hispanic politicians and activists, who see the employers of illegal aliens as "exploiters," but who fear that the proposed measures might increase job discrimination and/or reduce the growth rate of their political constituency;
(3) some liberal activists who oppose improvements in identification procedures as a threat to civil liberties or who see immigrants as eventual political supporters;
(4) some conservative ideologists who oppose "employer sanctions" as government intervention in the marketplace, in some cases arguing that there should be wholly free movements of labor across international boundaries irrespective of the effects on the American labor force.

It is fair to say that this odd assemblage of mutually antagonistic allies has been able to block reforms proposed by three presidents, a blue-ribbon select commission, and the Judiciary Committees of the Senate and House of Representatives. By all accounts, the most effective lobbyists have been the growers' groups in the Southwest, which recently have invested millions of dollars in professional lobbying activities and have directed heavy political pressure upon members of Congress from their region. Other outspoken opponents have included certain liberal and ethnic lobby groups such as the American

Civil Liberties Union, the Mexican-American Legal Defense and Education Fund, and the League of United Latin American Citizens. Thus the immigration debate provides an illuminating case study of the oft-noted ascendancy of special interests in American politics over the past fifteen years or so.

At this writing, in early 1986, the matter hung firmly in limbo. The Senate had passed for the third time a bill sponsored by Senator Simpson. This time, in response to the effective lobbying effort of the western growers, the Senate adopted a new "temporary worker" amendment over the strenuous opposition of Senator Simpson. This amendment, sponsored by Senator Pete Wilson of California, would allow growers legally to import very large numbers of "temporary" workers from Mexico. Senator Simpson is joined in his opposition to this provision by most liberal and labor groups, including those that have strenuously opposed his own proposals. The Senate did show a certain ambivalence about Senator Wilson's amendment in further adopting, by a wider margin, a provision to terminate it after three years unless re-enacted by Congress.

It is interesting to note that many of the reforms recommended by the select commission and embodied in the Simpson-Rodino-Mazzoli proposals have long been urged by some of the nation's leading supporters of a liberal immigration policy. Their concern, based upon ample evidence of widespread public disenchantment with recent immigration trends, is that impatience with continued large-scale illegal immigration will reduce public support for the continuation of liberal admissions policies for legal immigrants and refugees. In introducing his companion legislative proposals in the House of Representatives in July 1985, the respected Democratic chairman of the House Judiciary Committee and long-time champion of liberal immigration policy, Congressman Peter Rodino, put the issues as follows:

> As Americans, we must ask ourselves how much longer we are willing to pay the moral, social, and economic price of avoiding our sovereign responsibilities to control our borders. Unless Congress acts to

address this problem now, the time may come when America is forced to close its door to everyone.

Immigration and Alternative Demographic Futures

International migration provides three important points of intersection between the industrialized and developing worlds, two of which are quite obvious and the third more subtle. The first obvious one is that high–population growth countries unable to provide employment and opportunity for their citizens generate large numbers of potential migrants. There are long delays or lags built into this process. For example, the rapid declines in Third World infant mortality during the 1950s and 1960s did not result in growth in the age groups seeking entry-level jobs until the 1970s and 1980s, and such growth should continue through the remainder of this century.

The second obvious point of intersection is that this large pool of underemployed labor may be attractive to some employers and policy makers in Western countries, if they experience rising wages, labor shortages, growing union power or declining population growth. Such interests formed the basis of the "guest worker" policy adopted by West Germany in the late 1950s and terminated in 1973.

The third and more subtle point of intersection has to do with the internal demographic effects of substantial immigration upon countries with low fertility. If domestic fertility in an industrialized country declines, as it has done in the United States and most other developed countries since the 1960s, then even a constant *number* of immigrants would account for an increasing *proportion* of population growth. (If domestic population increase approaches zero or negative growth rates, then *any* level of immigration would account for *all* of whatever population growth might occur; but caution must be exercised in such calculations, since at such low levels of domestic population increase even a very few immigrants could be said to account for all of population growth.) In the United States, for example, legal immigration twenty-five years ago accounted for about 15 percent of overall population growth. Recently legal immigration has represented 25 to 30 percent of U.S. population growth, and the percentage would be substantially higher (perhaps 40 percent?) if illegal immigration were considered.

Generally speaking, if absolute immigration numbers are substantial under conditions of slow or negative domestic increase, there can be quite rapid changes in the national, ethnic, racial, linguistic, and other social characteristics of the population. This is especially true if the immigrants come predominantly from higher-fertility countries, even if their postimmigration fertility levels tend to converge downward over the long term toward the levels prevailing in the receiving country. This phenomenon can be illustrated by alternative demographic projections that assume plausible levels of fertility and mortality along with different levels of immigration. It must be emphasized that such projections are *not* predictions or forecasts, but simply simulations of what would occur under the stated assumptions.

In one set of such alternative projections, demographers Leon Bouvier and Cary Davis assume constant fertility levels and gradually improving mortality conditions among resident population groups in the United States, that fertility and mortality levels among immigrants gradually converge to these same levels, and that the national composition of such immigrants approximates that experienced in recent years. They then adopt differing assumptions as to the magnitudes of net immigration (legal and illegal combined), and project out the implications of such alternative assumptions for population composition. For example, their projection that assumes net immigration of 1 million per year (which on historical experience might be seen as a plausible upper bound) results over the long term in a decline in the percentage of white/non-Hispanic residents from 80 percent in 1980 to about 50 percent in 2080. Under these assumptions, the Hispanic population would outnumber the black population by 2010. An alternate assumption of 500,000 immigrants per year (which might be a plausible lower bound) results in slower though still substantial population shifts. The white/non-Hispanic population declines from 80 percent to 60 percent, and Hispanics eventually outnumber blacks, though not until about 2075.

Several important caveats are in order in considering such projection data. First, these projections assume that recent low fertility levels continue, with immigrant fertility converging downward. Alternative assumptions are also plausible, e.g., increasing or declining domestic fertility, or quicker or slower fertility declines among immigrant groups. Especially if domestic fertility were to increase, the proportionate demographic effect of any assumed level of immigration could be reduced substantially. Hence these projections illustrate well the general point that the demographic significance of immigration is closely related to the levels of indigenous fertility.

Second, since immigration rates and characteristics have historically been subject to substantial shifts, projections such as these could be quite misleading if incorrectly interpreted as predictions or forecasts. Their value is illustrative only, given the fact that the implications of demographic rates can be seen only over extended time spans. It cannot be emphasized too much that population projections represent the logical playing out of sets of alternative assumptions about fertility, mortality, and migration. They do *not* tell us what *will* happen, but are a useful means of illustrating the logical implications of a specified set of alternative assumptions.

Third, such projections involve socially-defined categories of the 1980s such as "Hispanic," "white/non-Hispanic," the social meaning of which is likely to change over long time periods. Thus, the social significance of a distant population composition described in such current categories cannot be clearly perceived from today's perspective.

Fourth, one's reaction to these and other projections is fundamentally a matter of values. Some would find the projected trends highly desirable in political, cultural, or other terms, while others would react with neutrality, measured concern, or exaggerated alarm on similar grounds. In short, population projections on their own are of little policy significance. They provide only a quantitative framework for what are quintessentially value-laden judgments.

Although many alternative projections are possible, the general point remains that nations experiencing low fertility (as are most industrialized countries) and high levels of immigration from Third World countries can expect substantial compositional shifts over time in socially relevant categories such as nationality, ethnicity, race, religion and language. In the past, such shifts have generated strong public reactions contributing to xenophobic and jingoistic politics, such as occurred during the last major pulse of immigration to the United States around World War I. Loud echos of such concerns are now prominent in France, where many well-known figures (including the prime minister and leading presidential candidate, M. Jacques Chirac) have been expressing highly emotional and public alarms about the conjunction of low French fertility and high immigration rates from Arab countries. Similar though more muted worries have been voiced by prominent figures in West Germany, the United Kingdom, Canada, and elsewhere.

Conclusions

International migrations have emerged as a major point of intersection between the rapid demographic growth of the Third World and the slow increase in the industrialized West. Recent developments have led to fundamental transformations in the size, speed, and nature of international migrations, the bulk of which now originates in the rapidly growing populations of Asia, Latin America, and Africa. Much of this international movement has taken on an irregular and/or temporary form, often in contravention of relevant national laws. The issues involved have risen high on the public agendas of nations as diverse as the United States, West Germany, France, Great Britain, India, Venezuela, and Mexico.

International migration is of special significance for the United States, the one nation that is the destination of choice for the bulk of the world's immigrants, and the only Western nation sharing a long and unfortified border with a large developing region. The history of American immigration policy is complex and sometimes unsavory. Numerical limits have been in force for over sixty years, but there are serious defects of law and policy that have resulted in substantial and growing failure of such limitations. Recent proposals for legislative reform have been blocked successfully by interest groups that agree on little other than their opposition to proposed measures to limit illegal immigration. It remains to be seen whether, in the politics of the 1980s, the continuing opposition of such interest groups can continue to prevail over widespread public support for the proposed reforms.

6

Family Planning Programs

GEORGE B. SIMMONS

Introduction

Family planning programs are organized efforts to assure that couples who want to limit their family size or space their children have access to contraceptive information and services and are encouraged to use them as needed. At present, a majority of the governments of the world, both in the richer developed countries and in the poorer less developed countries, either directly support or indirectly encourage family planning programs. The widespread support for family planning has several grounds. First, by helping to reduce fertility and population growth, it is seen as making a major contribution to development objectives such as increasing per capita income. Second, family planning programs are viewed as an important component of national health programs. Since

---

GEORGE B. SIMMONS is professor of population and health planning at the School of Public Health at the University of Michigan, where his academic work includes a concentration on economics. He has done frequent field work in the Third World over the last twenty years, as well as extensive research, training, and consultation. Dr. Simmons has published widely, particularly on issues of fertility and family planning.

the health of both mothers and children is influenced by the number and spacing of births, access to birth control may be an important element of effective health programs. Finally, access to contraception is viewed as an important human right, allowing individuals to determine how reproduction affects their own welfare and to act accordingly. This view is particularly strong in developed countries, but it also influences the thinking of many Third World governments.

Family planning programs in less developed countries are closely connected with events in richer industrial countries. The contraceptive technologies currently used by national family planning programs of the developing countries were largely developed in the laboratories and clinics of the developed countries. Much of the original stimulus and political support for these programs as well as a significant share of the financial support also originated there. Some of the organizations that have been active in promoting family planning in the developed countries, such as the affiliates of the International Planned Parenthood Federation (IPPF), have been active participants in the international effort to make contraceptive services available in the Third World. In addition, the example from the industrial countries of public support for programs offering access to contraceptives to people of all financial statuses and geographical locations has done much to legitimate family planning programs in the Third World.

The United States has played a particularly important role in providing financial, political, and moral support to Third World family planning programs. It has given more financial assistance for family planning through both bilateral and multilateral channels than any other nation and has taken the political lead in support of family planning within the United Nations system and at international meetings. Private individuals and organizations based in the United States have done much to shape the climate of support for family planning. In large measure, political support for family planning has been bipartisan. Many leaders who oppose public support for abortion support U.S. efforts to encourage family planning programs in the Third World. Appropriations for family planning rose rapidly during the late 1960s and 1970s, and then plateaued in constant-dollar terms during the subsequent decade. What happens during the latter part of the 1980s undoubtedly will be influenced both by the climate of support for family planning programs and by the outcome of current debates about the overall nature of the federal budget.

The Scope of Family Planning Programs in the Third World

Family planning programs of the Third World differ in terms of financial and political support from the government, basic strategies that they have adopted for reaching the population, the contraceptive methods made available to potential users, and the number of acceptors served and the proportion of the population reached. There are significant variations within as well as between countries—between urban and rural areas and, especially in the larger countries such as India or Indonesia, among regions of a country.

Table 1 provides some basic indicators of the current use of contraception, the level of fertility, and the status of family planning in the major regions of the world. In developed countries, fertility tends to be low and contraceptive prevalence high. Governments support family planning more on the grounds of human rights and welfare than as efforts to reduce fertility. Services are relatively easily accessible. Developing countries vary much more. The poorer countries of Africa have high fertility, low levels of contraceptive accessibility and use, and little government effort to support family planning. The countries of Asia and Latin America tend to range across the entire spectrum from the African patterns to those of Europe or North America. This wide variation can be illustrated through brief descriptions of several well-known programs in large countries.

Illustrative Programs

India, the second most populous country in the world, has been concerned with the rate of growth of its population since the earliest period after independence. The first five-year

TABLE 1: Current Levels of Contraception, Fertility, and Family Planning Status for the Major Regions of the World

	Variable			
Region	Percentage of the population using contraception	Crude birth rate*	Accessibility of modern contraception	Government effort to encourage family planning
Africa	3–15	40–50	Low	Low
North Africa and the Middle East	15–40	33–45	Low-medium	Low-medium
Asia other than China	15–60	20–40	Medium	Medium-high
China	65	20	High	High
Western Europe	65	14	High	Medium
Eastern Europe and the USSR	60	15	Medium-high	Medium
Latin America and the Caribbean	25–60	15–40	Low-high	Low-high
United States and Canada	65	15	High	Medium

*Births per 1000 population

plans mention population control and family planning. Despite this early recognition of the problem, little was done to implement active programs until the 1960s when India began a campaign to reduce the rate of population growth. A health system based family planning program that gave primary emphasis to male and female sterilization was introduced. Exact estimates are difficult, but most observers would agree that the birthrate in India has dropped by about a third since the 1950–60 decade. The response has been somewhat uneven with a much greater drop taking place in the coastal and southern states than in the more traditional northern and central states. The gradual decrease in Indian fertility has come about in an environment of slow but fairly steady economic growth.

Mexico was, until the early 1970s, cited as a country where the persistence of tradition delayed any major decline in fertility. Mexican government leaders began to recognize, however, that the very high rate of natural increase was creating problems for development. Rapid increase in the labor force in the rural areas made it more difficult for workers to find employment; Mexico City was swelling to unmanageable size. In the early 1970s, the president of Mexico drew attention to problems attributed to rapid population growth in his country and called for efforts to reduce the rate of increase. Family planning programs were dramatically increased in scale and extended to most rural areas. Oral contraception (the pill) and intrauterine contraceptive devices (IUDs) were the most common methods used, although sterilization became increasingly popular. Mexican fertility fell by about 40 percent in fifteen years. This period of rapid fertility reduction was also characterized by rapid economic development.

Indonesia is often cited as one of the most successful national family planning efforts. The government of General Suharto decided that population control would be a key element in national development efforts and consistently gave high priority to family planning. A special agency was created to coordinate family planning, and government administrators at every level were informed that their degree of success in supporting family planning would be taken as an important criterion of performance. By the late 1970s reports suggested that nearly half of the married couples in Indonesia were using contraception. In Muslim Indonesia, where sterilization is discouraged, the methods most used were oral contraceptives and the IUD. Fertility fell by about 40 percent during this campaign, which, as in Mexico, coincided with a period of rapid development.

Egypt, with virtually all of its population living in the narrow confines of the Nile valley, has a classic population dilemma. Rapid development and urbanization taking place in a country with a limited and densely settled area of arable land have made population growth more visible here than in perhaps any other part of the world. Beginning during the administration of President Gamal Abdel Nasser, all modern Egyptian governments have given some support to efforts to reduce the rate of population growth. For many reasons, success has been quite limited. By refined measures, there has been a sustained but modest decline in fertility, but the rate of population growth has remained high. There is some evidence that private efforts are beginning to have some effect in the cities, but the system of government health clinics in the rural areas has not managed to generate extensive acceptance.

Kenya, at independence, was blessed with a favorable population-to-land ratio and a healthy economic base. It also had one of the highest population growth rates in the world (about 4 percent per year), and as its population increased, many of its development problems were exacerbated. The government instituted a national family planning program at a relatively early stage, but while there have been some local successes of a fairly small scale, by the mid-1980s there had been no measurable effect on the national birthrate.

These five examples cover the range of experience with national family planning efforts in the larger countries, with the exception of China. Because its major reduction in fertility was based in significant measure on its special administrative and political characteristics, China will not be discussed here. We will also omit discussion of the many small countries, especially in sub-Saharan Africa, which do not have government sponsored efforts in family planning. Most of these countries have relatively low population densities and have been preoccupied with other development problems. As a result they are just reaching a stage where they are treating family planning as a serious possible element in a national development program.

Family planning programs vary on a number of important dimensions: 1) the major constituency for the program—rural or urban, poor or middle class, spacers or limiters, young or old, etc.; 2) the contraceptive technologies offered to these different groups; 3) the effort made to generate demand for the services offered through the program and the extent to which these efforts are restricted to information alone or include attempts to persuade couples to adopt family planning; 4) the organization of services and the efforts at demand generation (e.g., what is the lead ministry or agency, and is there a role for the private sector?); 5) the budget of the family planning program; and 6) the assurance of support for the program from the political sector.

The Audience for Family Planning Programs

Countries have differed in the audiences which they have identified as the key targets for family planning. India has chosen to target rural couples who have already had several children including at least one son. This choice was made on the rather pragmatic grounds that nearly 80 percent of the population lives in rural areas, and most have little interest in using family planning until they have had at least two children. The program in Colombia has given much more emphasis to reaching the urban poor. Programs in Africa tend to stress the importance of encouraging mothers at all ages to space births. Programs in Thailand, where contraceptive prevalence has already reached fairly high levels, place emphasis on reaching younger couples. Most programs orient their services toward women, although in India and Bangladesh there has been a substantial effort to encourage men to use vasectomy, and most social marketing programs seek to attract men to the use of condoms.

The Choice of Contraceptive Technology

Despite the great progress in contraceptive technology during the past fifty years, there is still no single method that is appropriate for all couples. For couples that are sure they have had all the children they want, sterilization is an optimal method. Both vasectomy and laparoscopic tubal ligation can be carried out with relatively limited facilities, but require clinically trained personnel and special equipment. India has placed great emphasis on sterilization, since its target audience has been those couples who do not want more children. For those who want to space births or are unsure whether they want more children, there are several options, no one of which is appropriate for all. The IUD works well for some women, but in many countries infections and other complications affect between a third and a half of IUD users. IUD insertion and follow-up also require clinical facilities and special training. The pill has been well received in some countries. It can be distributed by village-level workers who are trained to screen potential users for contraindications or for side effects. Disadvantages include the need to take it regularly, and, in some countries, problems with storage and resupply. Condoms have the great advantage that they can be sold through commercial channels, but they are also subject to problems of supply and storage. In addition, there may be low use effectiveness. One of the major questions that the leaders of a national family planning program must address is which methods to offer and emphasize. Many observers have argued that programs should offer a range of methods; clearly, were there no resource constraints, that would be an optimal choice. Most programs, however, do not have the financial or human resources or the administrative capacity to provide high-quality offerings of all methods. Efforts to supply multiple methods can strain an already overloaded system.

Generation of Demand

National family planning programs have generally found that supplying clinical services is not enough. Many, therefore, have included efforts to increase demand for their services, although with varying prominence given to these activities. In India, it was found that many villagers were poorly informed about contraceptive services. Some had difficulty in reaching the clinics where services were located. Others had heard misleading rumors about negative side effects of family planning in general or of specific methods. For example, many Indian farmers, familiar with the use of draft animals in agriculture, confused vasectomy with castration. To offset these disadvantages policy makers in India and in many other countries have instituted elaborate outreach systems using village-level workers who help establish communications between the clinical centers where many services are offered and the intended client population in the surrounding villages. These village-level workers provide information and encouragement and a limited range of health and family planning services.

A second element in programs to generate demand is the use of various forms of mass media. Radio and television have proven to be effective tools in reinforcing messages concerning family planning and are used frequently, often in combination with advertisements in newspapers, posters, and special efforts at cultural events. Advertising family planning is a subject of considerable controversy in some countries because of objections by religious groups. In Egypt (and, one might add, in the United States) the media have been used much less extensively than one might expect on the basis of their perceived effectiveness in reaching the target audience.

Many observers feel that the family planning efforts can be strengthened if combined with complementary development efforts. In Korea, mothers' clubs, which are devoted primarily to promoting the health of children, are said to have played an important role in encouraging women to use family planning. In Egypt, efforts have been made to link income-generating projects with the family planning program in the hopes that if villagers feel more in control of their economic lives, they may make efforts to control their fertility.

Organizational Choices for Delivering Family Planning

Many programs have chosen to work primarily through the organizational structures of national health programs. Most Third World countries have national health programs with clinics and varying degrees of outreach activity throughout the country. These health systems are responsible for delivering basic health services, but their facilities tend to have small and sometimes inadequately trained staffs and few resources compared to the populations they are expected to serve. People who seek care from public health clinics usually are those who have no alternative. They must often be prepared to wait long hours, to be handled roughly, and to receive low-quality services. Moreover, staffs already overburdened by the demand for basic health care can rarely be expected to dispense high-quality contraceptive services. The health system is particularly poorly prepared to organize activities to generate demand for family planning.

To avoid these problems, some countries (Brazil and Colombia, for example), operate their national family planning programs through private voluntary organizations. Other nations have used commercial organizations to help distribute contraceptives such as condoms or pills. These special-purpose programs may add expensive infrastructure to government programs that are already greatly underfunded. Thus, not surprisingly, there are strong financial and organizational pressures to combine family planning with other programs such as health in the hope that substantial savings may be realized.

The Resources Devoted to Family Planning

Until the mid-1960s the resources devoted to family planning by governments and international agencies were relatively modest. They have expanded dramatically, but still constitute only a small fraction of the total resources available for development. Even governments that are making serious efforts to strengthen their programs seldom spend more than 1 percent of their development budgets on family planning. Compared with funds devoted to industrialization, agricultural development, or the military, the amounts are small. Generally, the level of expenditure on family planning is higher in Asia than in other parts of the world, but it is greatly influenced by the nature of local programs and by the cost of living. Since staff constitutes the major cost, richer countries with higher standards of living naturally tend to have higher family planning budgets, but poor countries, such as Bangladesh, may earmark larger proportions of the government budget for their programs.

Political Support for Family Planning

In some countries, family planning receives consistent support from the highest levels of government. Indonesia, China, and, more recently, Bangladesh are examples of countries where the national leadership has repeatedly emphasized the importance of family planning and population control as a part of national development. The smaller African and Middle Eastern countries are at the opposite end of the spectrum. There are signs that political leaders in the Middle East and Africa are beginning to recognize some of the disadvantages of very high rates of population growth, but few countries have translated that recognition into action.

The nations of the developing world vary enormously in terms of their degree of commitment to family planning. At one extreme, a few countries (Indonesia, China, and, more recently, Bangladesh are examples) have given family planning top priority and have organized programs that make or plan to make contraceptive services accessible in most parts of their country. At the other, there are countries (such as many smaller African and Middle Eastern nations) that have scarcely begun to recognize family planning as an effective tool for helping to resolve development or health problems and do not see it as part of human rights. In these countries, modern family planning services usually are provided only by local, private organizations (often with some assistance from international agencies) and rarely are offered in the rural areas. Between this set of extremes is a wide array of programs with different service orientations, budgets, and organizational approaches.

The Effects of Family Planning Programs

Family planning programs are designed to assist and encourage couples to reduce voluntarily the number of children they have and as a result to improve the standard of living and the health of the population. An examination of the empirical record provides some evidence on how well these programs have accomplished these ambitious objectives.

Background

Any attempt to measure the effectiveness of a public program is complicated, but the situation with regard to family planning is particularly complex. The immediate output of family planning programs is, in some sense, a set of nonevents, the nonbirth of children who would have been born in the absence of the program. Moreover, family planning programs are by no means the only influence on the level of fertility in a country. Fertility varies for many reasons, and the long-term trend is greatly influenced both by the pattern of national development and by other government programs (e.g., educational programs for girls). Often family planning programs are implemented during a period of rapid economic development, as in Mexico and Indonesia, and in such situations the respective influences of development and family planning on fertility are difficult to disentangle. Moreover, when family planning programs do influence fertility, the effects are likely to be long term and diffused in the population. They are not as obvious as those of, say, a dam-building project or a program to improve national transportation systems.

In general, one would expect family planning and other development programs to have mutually supportive effects on fertility. General development efforts may operate to create conditions in which many families wish to control their fertility, but in the absence of the availability of contraceptives, this desire may not be translated into effective action. Conversely, while family planning programs may always find at least some audience for their efforts, the magnitude of the response may be constrained unless general development is taking place. (It will be argued later, however, that the response to family planning programs organized without effective support from general development programs can sometimes be much larger than people suspect.) Like any other development effort, the impact of a family planning program is affected by the quality of the program itself. It can be inadequately supported or incompetently managed. Resources, whether adequate for the task or not, can be wasted. The target population can be confused or even alienated by a plethora of confusing messages, by the absence of contact with the program, or by services of unacceptably low quality. What does the record show?

The Effects of Family Planning Programs on Contraceptive Use and Fertility

The determinants of fertility are complex. To help sort out this complexity, demographers find it convenient first to define the "proximate determinants of fertility," which are discussed by Bongaarts in this volume. The proximate determinants of fertility are the variables (such as the proportion of the reproductive-age population that is currently married or the proportion of the currently married population that is using contraception) that define exposure to the chance of pregnancy or the birth of children. Other variables such as the level of per capita income or the existence of family planning programs influence fertility through their effects on the proximate determinants. Thus, increases in per capita income may be associated with a reduction in fertility, because the higher income leads to a lower proportion of the population being married or because more of the married population can afford contraceptives, but the influence is always indirect. Similarly, family planning programs work through the proximate determinants, since their primary purpose is to increase the proportion of the population that is using contraception, i.e., contraceptive prevalence.

Demographers are in agreement that variations in contraceptive prevalence are the major explanation for observed variations in fertility among nations. They differ, however, on the extent to which they believe that the observed variations in contraceptive prevalence are the result of the activities of national family planning programs, on the extent to which national family planning programs can be expected to bring about reductions in fertility that are consistent with development objectives, and on the extent to which these programs need to be complemented by other programmatic action, e.g., efforts to raise the age at marriage.

Evidence on the effectiveness of family planning programs takes several forms. First, and perhaps most superficially, it can be observed that the number of users of contraceptive services provided by programs is quite large. In India alone during 1983, 4.5 million couples accepted sterilization offered by the program, and a further 9.9 million accepted other contraceptive services. By comparison with India's very large population base these numbers appear more modest, but there is no doubt that the absolute number of couples reached is large. In other countries as well, the national family planning programs are offering services to very large numbers of couples. Moreover, in most countries in Asia and many in Latin America, they provide contraceptives to a significant proportion of the couples who are using any contraception at all. Thus there is considerable evidence that programs reach large numbers of people and that users of program services account for a large proportion of the contraceptive use in the country. What is less clear-cut is the extent to which the existence of the program is causally responsible for these gains. Would the same people have begun planning their families if no program were available?

People use contraception because they want to either limit or space their children. They believe that a change in their "natural" fertility will improve their health or economic status (or that of their children) or some other aspect of their lives. Knowledge of contraception and access to contraceptive services would also seem to be prerequisites for widespread use and have been the primary goals of family planning programs. These activities of informing people about contraception and making the services available are sometimes called the "supply" side of family planning. Other factors, such as changes in the economic situation or in the level of education, may be responsible for a change in desires concerning family size and spacing. These are frequently discussed as the "demand" aspect of family planning. Observed changes in contraceptive prevalence can be explained by changes in the supply of or demand for contraceptives or by some combination.

Controversy over Demand and Supply Factors

Debate about the relative importance of demand and supply factors in determining fertility levels has become quite heated on occasion. Both sides have demonstrated some tendency to oversimplify the issues. On the supply side, the oversimplification has generally taken the form of assuming that since the reductions in observed marital fertility are largely due to increases in contraceptive use, family planning programs are therefore responsible for such use. Such beliefs led some proponents of family planning to argue that simply supplying couples with pills or other contraceptives would lead to major reductions in fertility. On the demand side, the main oversimplification was to argue that there could be no reduction in fertility until "development" takes place. This view ignores the possibility that many couples may want to use contraception but do not have effective services available. Moreover, family planning education and services may constitute a form of development themselves, and, in some sense, programs may generate their own demand through diffusion from early users to others.

The question of whether it is development or family planning programs that explain the large increases in contraceptive use of the past twenty years has received a great deal of attention. Table 2, drawn from the work of Robert Lapham and Parker Mauldin, represents the most recent evidence on the subject. On the vertical axis, countries are classified by their development status. Across the top, they are classified on the basis of how much effort the national governments have put into family planning programs. Each cell in the table thus represents a combination of level of development and level of national effort in family planning. The numbers in the table represent the average level of contraceptive prevalence reached by the countries in each cell by the end of the period of observation.

TABLE 2: Contraceptive prevalence rates in 1977–83,* by 1970 socioeconomic setting index and 1982 program effort in 73 developing countries

	Program Effort								
	Very weak or none		Weak		Moderate		Strong		
Socio-economic setting	Country	Percent	Country	Percent	Country	Percent	Country	Percent	Percent mean
Low	Benin	18	Nepal	7	Bangladesh	19			
	Sudan	5	Tanzania	1					
	Sierra Leone	4							
	Ethiopia	2							
	Somalia	2							
	Yemen	1							
	Burundi	1							
	Chad	1							
	Guinea	1							
	Malawi	1							
	Mali	1							
	Niger	1							
	Burkina Faso	1							
	Mauritania	1							
		(3)		(4)		(19)			4
Lower middle	Bolivia	24	Haiti	19	India	32	Indonesia	48	

	Burma	7	Pakistan	6					
	Cameroon	2	Papua, New						
	Uganda	1	Guinea	5					
	Kampuchea	0	Senegal	4					
			Liberia	1					
		(6)		(8)		(27)		(48)	12
Upper Middle	Iran	23	Ecuador	40	Thailand	58	China	69	
	Syria	20	Turkey	40	Philippines	45	Sri Lanka	57	
	Ghana	10	Honduras	27	Dominican				
	Nicaragua	9	Egypt	24	Republic	43			
	Zaire	3	Morocco	19	Malaysia	42			
	Zambia	1	Guatemala	18	El Salvador	34			
			Algeria	7	Tunisia	31			
		(11)		(25)		(42)		(63)	30
High	Paraguay	36	Costa		Cuba	79	Hong Kong	80	
			Rica	66	Panama	63	Singapore	71	
			Brazil	50	Jamaica	55	Taiwan	70	
			Venezuela	49	Trinidad/		Korea	58	
			Peru	43	Tobago	54	Colombia	51	
			Chile	43	Fiji	38	Mauritius	51	
							Mexico	40	
		(36)		(50)		(58)		(60)	55
Mean		7		23		44		59	26

*Contraceptive prevalence is assessed at the latest available survey done in the country between 1977 and 1983. Mean prevalence, at each level of program effort and socioeconomic setting, is shown in parentheses.

Source: Robert J. Lapham and W. Parker Mauldin, "Contraceptive Prevalence: The Influence of Organized Programs," *Studies in Family Planning*, Vol. 16, No. 3, May–June 1985, pp. 117–37.

This table presents clear evidence that both family planning effort and the level of development influence contraceptive prevalence. At all development levels, the greater the effort governments have made in the area of family planning, the greater is the increase in the level of prevalence. Looking at the table the other way, for every level of family planning effort, the greater is the pace of development, the larger is the increase in the level of contraceptive prevalence. Thus both family planning effort and development are shown to influence contraceptive use. Similar results have been derived by the authors relating changes in fertility to development and family planning effort. Moreover, other authors have generally come to similar conclusions.

A different kind of evidence about the family planning programs is derived from research that deals with the variations within countries or in particular locations. Two kinds of result are salient. First, even when controls are established for the level of development, the use of increased resources for family planning seems to be associated with increased levels of contraceptive prevalence. Second, in many countries special projects have been introduced to experiment with new ways of introducing family planning. Often these efforts are intensive and involve higher levels of resources per unit of population than would be available in the regular national program, but in many cases they have also succeeded in achieving levels of contraceptive prevalence much higher than those attained in neighboring nonprogram areas with similar levels of socioeconomic development. One such program, in the Matlab district of rural Bangladesh, is serving as a model for endeavors to improve government family planning services.

In sum, there seems little doubt that family planning programs have played an important role in the fertility revolution that is taking place in many developing countries. But family planning is, by no means, the only factor involved. Development, in all of its various forms—education, increased income, changing economic roles, reduced child mortality, etc.—certainly plays an important role as well. Moreover, the mere existence of family planning programs is not by itself enough.

Family planning programs, like other development programs, vary in terms of their effectiveness. Some programs seem to have had a very large impact, while others have had only a modest degree of success or none at all.

While there is little doubt that family planning programs have had an independent effect on contraceptive use and fertility, there is still debate about whether these effects have been large enough, given the current balance between resources and population in many Third World countries. Some critics of family planning have been arguing that current programs are not extensive or strong enough to reduce population growth rates to acceptable levels. They point out that although birthrates have declined in many countries, in many others they have declined little if at all. Moreover, the declines have been concentrated in Latin America and East Asia, particularly in China. In other regions of the Third World, the number of new people added to the population each year is at or near historic levels.

Those who criticize family planning programs for not being sufficiently effective do not argue for their elimination. Rather they argue that current efforts need to be strengthened and supplemented by active efforts to encourage small families. They point to programs such as that of Singapore where preferences for housing and other benefits were given to parents with two or fewer children. They also point to the need to link population with programs in education, health, and community development, in the hopes that population control will become a national priority rather than an isolated effort. Such efforts are often described as "beyond family planning."

Social and Economic Effects of Family Planning

In addition to their effects on contraceptive use and fertility, family planning programs have other direct and indirect social and economic effects. Firm evidence on most of these corollaries is lacking, but there is little doubt about their potential importance.

Since family planning programs have existed for a relatively short time and there is a long lag between changes in fertility and the full range of economic consequences, it is unlikely that major changes in economic variables such as per capita income would be observed easily. Moreover, in trying to relate changes in income levels and population growth, cause and effect are difficult to distinguish. It is interesting to observe, however, that most countries that have been successful with family planning have also been relatively successful in assuring income growth. East Asian countries such as Korea or Taiwan have experienced very rapid economic growth during the period that fertility has been falling. The same can be observed of many countries in Latin America.

Family planning has more direct and immediate effects on health. Research has shown that child spacing and parity are important influences on both child mortality and on the health of mothers. Moreover, access to family planning gives women and couples more sense of control over their lives. This sense of control may be a first step toward control of the health and economic dimensions of their lives.

Reduced population growth through family planning diminishes the pressure on public services. With smaller cohorts, governments can afford either to offer educational and health services to a larger fraction of the population or to improve the quality of the services that are available. This effect of smaller birth cohorts and family planning programs is already making it easier for governments in Thailand and Mexico, for example, to provide schooling for their populations.

Although the effects are longer term, reduced rates of population growth will eventually lead to smaller numbers of young people entering the labor force. Since most developing countries suffer from severe underemployment, especially in the urban areas, this development will relieve the pressures to provide employment. These and other consequences of reduced fertility have been discussed in other chapters of this volume; as is characteristic of many topics of ongoing debate, the conclusions reached by different authors are not always the same.

The Determinants of Family Planning Effectiveness

In the previous section it was argued that national family planning programs can be effective, but that performance varies considerably. If public policy is to support effective programs, some of the factors that determine the effectiveness of family planning programs must be described in greater detail. Figure 1 describes in a simplified schematic manner the relationships among four major sets of variables which influence effectiveness (which, in this diagram, is defined by contraceptive prevalence):

1. *client transactions,* or the nature of the relationships that exist between the service providers and outreach workers of the program and the people whom they are expected to serve,
2. the *demand* that exists in the population for services,
3. the *management* of the program, and
4. *external factors* such as the level of budgetary support provided for the program or the degree of support from the political system.

Relationships between Providers and Clients

The people employed by a family planning program are expected to have many dealings with the general population. It may seem self-evident that family planning programs must assure the quality and quantity of those exchanges. But family planning programs are usually fairly large bureaucracies, and it is often difficult for people at different levels in the hierarchy to keep their focus on the importance of the exchanges taking place at the grass roots level.

It is easy to give some idea of what the ideal pattern of exchange might be. In the village, men and women would learn about the possibility of regulating their fertility from a combination of visits by village-level workers, supportive and noncoercive comments from village leaders and neighbors, and reinforcing messages from the mass media. At the clinic they would be given services in a prompt and friendly fashion by well-trained professionals who were truly knowledgeable about family planning methods as well as the nature of village life and who would take the time to learn enough about the individual's needs to give appropriate advice. Activities at the community and clinic level would be complemented by statements in the mass media and by public declarations of support by political leaders.

The reality is much more complex. The villager is often relatively poorly informed about modern medicine and trapped in a situation where any long-range planning is difficult. The village-level worker does not necessarily visit the village very often, and when she or he does come, it is often only to selected houses in the village. The worker may not be very effective in explaining family planning methods or suggesting the ways in which the use of contraception might help to improve the life of the family. At the clinic, there are often long lines, or key staff are absent, or the staff are abusive or cold in their manner with the villagers. There are well-documented stories from programs in all parts of the world of women waiting for hours for services only to be told that the service is not available, or that the clinic is closing and they must come back another day. Not all of the stories are so unfavorable, of course, but in some programs there are enough problems with poor relationships at the lowest levels in the program that few observers are surprised to find acceptance levels low.

In other words, even where many people would like to use family planning, they can be discouraged by poor field or clinic work. Lest one leave the impression that these problems originate with the village- and clinic-level staff, it should be recognized that the problems often begin by poor program design, inadequate staffing and resources, and other problems that might test the patience of even the best-intentioned staff.

FIGURE 1. The Determinants of Program Effectiveness

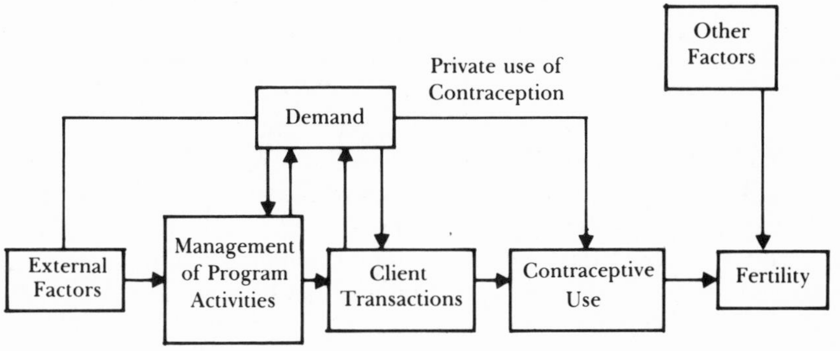

The Demand for Contraceptive Services

The demand for contraception is a function both of the desire people have for children and of the characteristics of the contraceptive services that are available and the way people react to those services. In societies where children have important economic or social roles and where high mortality makes their survival uncertain, it is likely that parents will want large families. Demand for contraception may exist only among parents who already have many children or who have special health problems. Among parents who want no more children, variations exist in the intensity of the desire. Some, such as those who risk their lives in village abortion, may be desperate to avoid more children. Others may be relatively indifferent. Decisions as to whether to use contraception will depend on many factors. Two of the most important are the quality of services offered and their cost.

The willingness of a couple or an individual woman to use contraception will be greatly affected by perceptions of the health risks associated with the method. In every program, visitors are told stories of women who have discontinued the use of a method because of side effects, or who have refused to begin using a method for fear of the possible negative health consequences. High-quality services and effective counseling can help to reduce this problem, but even in the best programs such concerns are of great importance. In some cases, such as the Indian experiment with the IUD in the early 1960s, rumors about the health implications of a method can have disastrous implications for the levels of acceptance.

Demand also depends upon the perceived cost of contraception. "Cost" in this case should be defined broadly to include factors such as the time required to get services and, perhaps, the psychological reservations people may have about the use of contraception. The demand for contraceptive services should, like other measures of demand, be defined as the amount of service that would be purchased or used by the population at different prices or costs. If the structure of demand remains constant, the actual amount of contraception used may vary as a result of changes in the cost to users. It is also possible that demand may shift over time due to changes in the economy or to the diffusion of new ideas about childbearing. These shifts in demand can be assessed by asking how much the demand has changed with the costs of contraception held constant.

Family planning programs can be thought of as organized efforts to lower the cost of contraception. From this perspective, it is then appropriate to ask whether observed changes in the level of contraceptive use are attributable to changes in the cost of contraception or to changes in the underlying structure of demand. There seem to be few situations where changes in the level of contraceptive prevalence can be attributed exclusively to one or the other. In countries such as Indonesia or India, contraceptive use increased rapidly during a period of substantial economic change. In countries such as Mexico, economic change may have led to substantial unmet demand before the national family planning program was introduced. Subnational projects, such as the Matlab project mentioned earlier, where contraceptive prevalence is high in a region otherwise little influenced by economic change, indicate what can be accomplished by family planning programs under ideal circumstances. Thus the evidence points to the conclusion that there may be substantial trade-offs between family planning and "development" as explanations for observed changes in the level of contraceptive prevalence or of fertility.

The demand for contraception is not static. Many observers feel that one of the major roles of family planning programs is to create or generate demand. This goal can be accomplished through outreach and mass media activities or, in the long run, by creating a process of diffusion in which the example of family planning "pioneers" convinces more conservative or reluctant members of the community that fertility control is a good idea or that it is acceptably safe.

In sum, the demand for contraception is an important factor limiting program effectiveness, but it should be recognized that low levels of prevalence are not automatically attributable to a desire on the part of potential parents for more children. Improvements in the quality of the services that a program makes available, reductions in the cost of contraceptives, and strengthening of outreach or demand generation activities can have a strong independent effect on couples' decisions about contraception.

Program Management

Management can be defined broadly as the leadership of the program and the set of procedures which are used to assure that goals of the program are achieved; it is both the set of individuals who have responsibility for organizing a program and the characteristics of this organizing process. As in any business endeavor, the quality of management is a major determinant of program effectiveness. The management system is responsible for assuring that the right types of services are offered by the program, and that the services are available in the right quantity and quality. It is also responsible for conducting effective demand generation activities where they are part of the strategy. In successful programs, managers seem to be effective both at finding resources and in assuring that resources are used to maximum impact. In unsuccessful programs, there is often a lack of purpose which diffuses the entire enterprise.

Two features of effective management deserve special mention: the system of accountability, and procedures that allow programs to detect and correct their mistakes.

Accountability. The family planning program depends upon its staff to carry out the complex, difficult, and arduous tasks inherent in accomplishing its goals. The staff is likely to undertake these tasks only to the extent that they believe that either rewards or sanctions will be associated with their job performance. The rewards may come in the form of pay associated with good performance, with the inherent satisfactions of the job (as might be the case for volunteer workers), or some combination of these and other incentives. The sanctions range from dismissal to lesser administrative sanctions for nonperformance.

All organizations face the problem of motivation among their staff. The difficulties in the field of family planning are particularly complex, however, because of the nature of the work. Family planning programs are intended to bring about changes in the behavior of people who may be reluctant or suspicious about any attempt to intrude into their lives. Family planning service staff often work under very difficult conditions. In the clinics, there may be a great many people clamoring for services in an environment of few resources. Clinic space may be limited, the supply of drugs may be much less than required, and the support staff may be poorly trained. In the field, distances between villages may be great, and there may be no alternative to moving on foot. Villagers may be indifferent or hostile, and workers may feel insufficiently trained or that they have little to offer. Under such conditions it is no wonder that the work of the staff often seems less effective than desired.

There are many things that program managers can do to help alleviate this situation. A prerequisite for making changes is recognizing that the problems of motivation involve a set of interrelated factors, all of which need attention. Working on just one part of the system is not likely to generate much change. Key elements in the system include the process of staff selection and training, the structure of rewards, the set of procedures for monitoring and evaluation of performance, and the provision of supervision for staff work.

Staff selection is a weakness of programs in many countries. Where unemployment is high it is not uncommon for the selection of workers to be based on political contacts rather than relevant work skills. If staff members are chosen initially because of their connections, managers may find it difficult to exercise control over their work. In the early 1970s, managers of the family planning program in one large north Indian state attempted to fire a considerable number of family planning workers who had performed poorly according to program records. Within a relatively short time a wave of political pressure was generated that was strong enough to force the administration to rescind the terminations. Political leaders proved more concerned about their constituents' jobs than about the success of the program. Similar examples can be cited for many other countries. In most Third World countries jobs with the government are permanent, and continuation is loosely, if at all, related to performance.

To avoid political interference, some programs have created rigid educational qualifications for family planning staff. Village-level workers may be required to have a high school or even a college education, when the appropriate personality for dealing with villagers and a willingness to work might have been more important qualifications.

Training is another weakness. In many countries staff members responsible for service delivery have a limited understanding of the methods they are delivering. It has been argued that the resulting problems are less than the users would have experienced if they had had unwanted pregnancies, but even if this assessment is correct, the individuals concerned may have an unpleasant experience with contraception, and their experience may discourage other couples from using contraceptives. Family planning staff members are often unskilled in establishing good relationships with their clients.

Training seldom gives them experience with realistic field conditions, and in most cases training is for relatively short periods of time.

The chief problem with the reward structure in most family planning programs is that the rewards are not sufficiently tied to performance. Salaries tend to be fixed. Promotions are difficult and sometimes based on connections or seniority rather than performance. Other rewards such as assignments in choice locations are similarly difficult to relate to performance. The situation, as seen in earlier examples, is no easier with regard to sanctions. In some countries, administrators have instituted special incentives for family planning work. In most South Asian countries, workers are rewarded for finding acceptors of sterilization and, in some cases, of IUDs. Physicians are also rewarded according to the number of sterilizations they perform. Although these incentives are intended to increase staff motivation, they may also be responsible for program distortions such as an excessive emphasis on sterilization.

Monitoring and evaluation are important components of family planning programs. By documenting both successes and problem areas they give managers the information base needed for decisions about program strategy and for the reward structure. Most monitoring and evaluation systems focus largely on new acceptors. As a result, there is little attention paid to helping users with side effects and otherwise encouraging continuous and effective use. Managers also tend to know little about the work patterns of the staff, and there is a strong incentive for false reporting of results.

It is often suggested that supervision is the answer to the problems of family planning programs. The problem is that good supervision is difficult to establish. Supervisors may be just as reluctant to go to the field or to put in long hours as the people they are supervising, and who will supervise the supervisors? The problems come full circle. Good supervision can make a big difference, but good supervision tends to come in systems that already have other features indicating high quality, such as careful selection of staff, meaningful rewards tied to job performance, and monitoring systems that can provide useful information to managers about performance. Those, in turn, require sufficient resources and political support.

Adaptability. A second dimension of effective management is adaptability. No activity works perfectly the first time it is tried, and many activities do not ever work very well even though they may have seemed promising when first suggested. Effective management systems learn from both their successes and their failures. Well-run programs in places like Taiwan or Thailand or Colombia have experimented with new ideas on a regular basis. They have established good evaluation systems and have learned how to adapt as new opportunities have developed.

Encouraging innovation and an orientation toward finding new solutions for problems is just as difficult as establishing accountability. Senior management and, to some extent, donors can help in the effort by giving special attention to problem solving. But in many cases the origins of the problem are systemic and require complex changes to remedy. In fact, it should be recognized that few of the problems described above are unique to family planning. Management problems of accountability and adaptability are common in development efforts of all kinds.

External Factors that Influence Performance

The performance of family planning programs is strongly influenced by factors that lie, in most respects, beyond their domain. One such factor is the level of demand. Two others are the budget of the program and the degree of political support that the program receives. While both of these conditions can be influenced by effective managers, they are strongly influenced by prevailing economic and political conditions, by the attitudes of political elites towards population and family planning, and by the programs of international donors.

The budget for family planning varies greatly from country to country, but seldom exceeds 2 percent of development expenditures. In a few countries, that may be as much money as the family planning program can effectively use, but there are countries where resource scarcity is a factor limiting performance. In many countries, for example, the ratio of rural outreach workers to population is quite low, with the result that workers cannot effectively reach all of the families in their area. In poor countries, governments may be unwilling to fund expanded efforts, special drives, or nongovernmental organizations working in family planning, on the grounds that their budgets are already fully committed. The World Bank, in a review of population programs and policies, has concluded that countries could effectively utilize a significantly expanded budget. Much of this additional funding could come from international agencies, but it is important that national governments contribute substantially.

Political support is key for the success of family planning programs. In countries such as Indonesia, Mexico, or India, the existence of a sustained positive stance toward family planning has greatly strengthened program performance. Political support may also have some direct effect. That is, if the national leadership says that contraceptive use is legitimate, couples may find it easier to make the decision to use contraception. More important, the positive attitude of the government manifests itself in the form of the appointment of more skilled and effective administrators for the program and greater budgetary support. Moreover, in a strongly favorable climate such as exists in Indonesia, other organizations may be more willing to cooperate with the family planning program. In short, political support can be translated into effective action.

Conclusions

Since 1950 there has been a dramatic expansion of family planning programs. This expansion has taken place in both the developed and the developing countries. In the developed countries, the presence of government efforts in family planning is a part of the general effort to assure that all citizens have access to basic services. In the developing countries, family planning programs are primarily supported because of a concern that very high rates of population growth may have negative effects on national development, measured primarily in economic terms.

Most of the larger developing countries have now organized substantial family planning programs. The exact approaches that are used vary according to local circumstances, but most systems include both the provision of clinic services to those who want them and outreach efforts to inform and encourage couples to plan their families.

Program success has varied considerably. While this variation is in some measure attributable to underlying demand for family limitation, the scale of program efforts and the skill of program implementation explain a significant part of the observed variation. Management capacity and political will are scarce commodities in many developing countries, and in all fields it is possible to document failures as well as successes. The examples of both the more successful of the national family planning efforts and the even more dramatic impact of some small-scale pilot or experimental efforts illustrate the potential for effectiveness. Conversely, the negligible impact of family planning in countries such as Egypt and Kenya suggests that the mere existence of programs is no guarantee of success.

Insufficient financial resources are an important element limiting program performance, but most observers agree that factors such as managerial skill or political support may be as influential as the size of the budget. Documentation on the exact role that these factors play and the corrective interventions that are possible is highly incomplete, however.

The extent to which family planning needs to be supplemented by "beyond family planning" efforts if national development objectives are to be achieved continues under debate. Basically, countries must resolve this issue for themselves in light of national goals and resources. Here also there is a need for further research and experimentation to establish the most effective programs and policies.

Developed countries can do a great deal to strengthen and

expand the efforts of developing countries to reduce rapid population growth. One important way to assist these programs is to continue and, if possible, expand the financial support that has been provided during the past two decades. To complement the financial support, developed countries should provide assistance with managerial skills necessary to improve program performance. More subtle, but equally important, is the intellectual backstopping that has been provided by many developed country institutions—universities and special assistance organizations, both public and private. This support has done much to document the progress and the problems associated with these programs and has encouraged leaders in developing countries to take the problem of population growth seriously and make serious efforts in family planning. Just as past efforts to document the characteristics of rapid population growth and its determinants and consequences have done much to increase the world's awareness of these problems, future efforts to document the nature of family planning programs and the factors that make them effective may do much to accelerate the reduction of fertility.

Ultimately, the responsibility for influencing population growth in the Third World is the responsibility of Third World governments and their peoples. Family planning programs, effectively designed and administered, can contribute to the decline in fertility and to wider development objectives. Developed countries such as the United States have played and, I hope, will continue to play a central role in furthering these important programs.

7

Population Policy: Choices for the United States

DAVID E. BELL

Introduction

The three elements that combine to bring about population change—births, deaths, and migration—historically have been treated quite differently in terms of public policy. Organized public efforts to reduce death rates have an ancient history, and over the past two or three centuries have had an increasingly powerful effect in reducing death rates in all parts of the world. Public policies toward international migration, which through most of history had to do with conquest, empire, slavery, and political exile, over the past century have become a prominent part of the legal framework of the nation-state.

DAVID E. BELL is Clarence J. Gamble Professor of Population Sciences and International Health, chairman of the Department of Population Sciences at the Harvard School of Public Health, and director of Harvard's Center for Population Studies. He was for many years vice president of the International Division of the Ford Foundation and served the federal government as administrator of USAID and director of the U.S. Bureau of the Budget. His research and writing interests concentrate on health and population in developing countries.

Deliberate, self-conscious public policies toward fertility, on the other hand, are quite recent, dating essentially, so far as the United States is concerned, from the eugenics movement in the early part of this century and the birth control movement in the 1920s. And only since the 1950s has it become acceptable in this country, and in most others, openly to discuss human fertility in all its aspects and to consider "population policies" in the full sense of examining simultaneously the causes and consequences of fertility, mortality, and migration.

One consequence of this late admission of human fertility to the public policy agenda is that no one, in government or out, can look back to lengthy experience with past policies as a guide to present policy making. This makes a discussion of population policy different from a discussion of policy toward, for example, agriculture or education, which have been the subjects of public policy and governmental action for two centuries or more. No public policies sought to affect fertility during the major demographic transitions in Europe and in North America, during which first death rates and later birthrates dropped, beginning around 1800. These enormous social changes, which brought annual death rates and birthrates in a century and a half from millennial levels on the order of 40 per 1000 of the population to current levels on the order of 10 per 1000, did not result from public policies and actions aimed explicitly at population objectives.

We are therefore largely on untrodden ground, and it is not surprising that we face uncertainty, confusion, and controversy when we seek to analyze population problems and decide what to do about them through governmental or other public policies. While a small number of scholars, beginning with Malthus, struggled to gather data and analyze what was happening, it is only since World War II that there has been major attention either by biological or social scientists. Moreover, we are dealing with issues that do not yield easily to cool rationality. Questions affecting human reproduction inevitably relate to the survival and success of families, communities, ethnic groups, and nations, and decisions touch deep roots in attitudes, beliefs, customs, and value systems.

In these circumstances, any short discussion of population policy is bound to be selective and incomplete. What is attempted in this chapter is deliberately limited. The chapter identifies a few elements of world population change that are of high importance to the United States, selects two policy issues for discussion (what should be the U.S. policy toward rapid population growth in the Third World, and what should be our policy toward slow population growth in the industrialized countries), and addresses for those issues questions of what our interests are, what our objectives ought to be, and how we might achieve them. Principal emphasis is placed on what appear to the author to be major areas of consensus among informed views of the subject. (Policies concerning immigration to the United States are not discussed here since they are treated in chapter 5.)

Population Changes as Seen from the United States

Four aspects of world population change stand out as background for considering U.S. policy choices.

Rising Total Population

Total population in the world is rising rapidly and will continue to do so for some decades to come. The world's population is estimated to have reached 1 billion persons about the year 1800, 2 billion about 1930, 3 billion about 1960, and 4 billion about 1975. Doubling from 1 to 2 billion took about 130 years; doubling from 2 to 4 billion took only 45 years.

It now appears that, after 200 years of accelerating growth, the rate of population increase crested in the 1960s and has begun to decelerate. The prospect of shifting to a stage of slower growth is clearly of great historical significance. But the deceleration will happen only slowly and the rate of growth will continue to be high for a long time yet. Projections of 6 billion persons by the end of the century or shortly thereafter seem very solid.

How long will the rise go on, and will the rate of growth

continue to fall steadily toward zero? Here we enter on uncertain ground. The only safe generalization about long-range demographic projections is that, so far, they have invariably been wrong. Therefore, a serious forecast much beyond the year 2000 is not possible. The evidence to date, however, does suggest that major declines in birthrates are occurring in many of the less developed countries, in many cases falling fast enough to close the gap with death rates that fell earlier. Since this is what happened in the nineteenth and twentieth centuries in the countries that are now industrialized, and since the processes of economic and social modernization are well launched in many developing countries, the inference seems strong that the fall in birthrates will continue and the deceleration in the rate of growth of world population will be sustained. If this occurs, a speculative projection—not a forecast —might be that around the middle of the next century total world population would be 8 or 9 billion persons and the rate of growth might be very low. Such an outcome would imply that the next doubling of world population would have taken seventy-five years. That would be an important slowing of the rate of growth, but in the light of world history it would still have been very rapid.

Uneven Population Growth

Population growth in the world today is extremely uneven. In general, the less developed countries are growing faster, the industrialized countries slower (some not at all). Approximately 90 percent of future additions to world population will be in the less developed countries.

But there are increasingly wide differences in rates of population growth among different developing countries. In some, while mortality rates have fallen, fertility rates have not. As a result, the highest population growth rates in history—around 4 percent per year—are being experienced in Kenya and other African countries. In most developing countries, mortality rates have fallen and, after a time lag, fertility rates have also fallen, but the amount by which fertility rates have fallen differs greatly among countries. From the early 1960s to the early 1980s, for example, birthrates in China fell by one-half, those in Thailand, the Philippines, and Costa Rica by one-third, those in Bangladesh, Malawi, and Liberia hardly at all.

An array of fertility rates shows, in general, a relationship with economic development such that the highest fertility rates are in the poorest countries (China and Sri Lanka are important exceptions). The same generalization holds within countries: higher fertility rates are generally found among lower-income groups. Deceleration of population growth over the next few decades, therefore, is likely to proceed very unevenly: future increases in numbers of persons will be concentrated in the poor countries, and, within countries, in the poorer communities—exactly in the places and among the groups least able to bear the resulting costs.

The Industrial Revolution Worldwide

In most less developed countries, large changes are underway in where people live, how they make a living, how well educated they are, and in other central characteristics of daily life. These changes are reflections of the steady spread around the world of the industrial and social revolution that began in Europe some 200 years ago—the application to human needs of steadily more sophisticated science and technology.

One of the results of these changes is that in most developing countries there is a large internal migration from rural areas to major cities. The cities are growing in population substantially more rapidly than the countries as a whole; to the natural rate of growth of people already in the cities is added the influx from the countryside. In Latin America, more than half the population already lives in urban areas, and throughout the Third World, cities of more than 10 million persons are becoming numerous. People flock to the cities because opportunities and incomes are relatively higher there and because new investment and new jobs are usually placed there. Their arrival in the cities adds to the heavy costs of water, sanitation, transportation, and other facilities for urban living. (In contrast to internal migration, international migration, while important for a variety of reasons, is sharply limited in scale in this age of extreme nationalism, and affects a very small fraction of the world's population.)

It is not only the lives of those who move that are being transformed. In industry, trade, transportation, services, the nature of work is steadily being altered. In agriculture, often mistakenly assumed to be stagnant and unchanging, the spread of science based production methods and modern marketing systems often brings radical changes to farm output and incomes in the space of a few years. Such changes are accompanied—and supported—by rapid increases in the numbers of children receiving formal education at the primary and higher levels.

These processes are highly dynamic and result in rapid differentiation in incomes and welfare between countries and within them. Countries like Malaysia and Brazil, relatively favored in natural endowments and with strong development policies, move ahead more rapidly, while others lag increasingly behind. Similar differentiations occur within countries; the people of Brazil's northeast, for example, with poorer agricultural resources and a legacy of social inequality, have a harder task in achieving modernization than the more fortunate in Brazil's center and south.

Population policy choices with respect to less developed countries must therefore be attuned to population growth occurring in highly varied settings of dynamic economic and social change. Overall, the data show average gains in per capita income, but slowly.

Little Population Growth in Industrialized Countries

In contrast to the situation in the Third World, population change in industrialized countries appears to be entering a new phase of incipient decline. Birth and death rates are extremely low by historical standards, and the average number of children being born per woman in virtually all the industrialized countries—the United States, Canada, Western and Eastern European countries, and Japan—is below replacement levels. Some countries are already showing actual declines in total populations, and if present trends continue this will be true of many industrialized countries within the next two decades. The population of the United States would be headed for the same pattern of decline, based on present trends in fertility, were it not for the continued inflow of immigrants, who add something on the order of 0.5 percent to the U.S. population each year.

No one knows whether these incipient declines in the population of industrialized countries will in fact occur, and, if they do, whether there will be some sort of self-corrective response. It is clear, however, that in these countries, low birthrates and increasing longevity are leading to rapid increases in the proportions of older people and to many new questions for individuals, families, and societies, ranging from very large unexpected demands on pension systems to huge new burdens for geriatric health care.

Major Policy Issues

These four elements of the world population outlook point toward two major population policy issues for the United States.

First, what policies should the United States follow with regard to rapid population growth in the Third World? The great majority of the next 4 billion persons added to the world's total population will live in the places that are the poorest, that are operating on the thinnest margin of resources, and that have the smallest array of skills and capital to provide jobs and income, health, and education for the onslaught of new children. This growth of population will, without question, contribute in a major way to the world's most serious problems of human welfare and survival over the next few decades.

Second, in contrast, population growth in the industrialized countries has slowed to virtually zero and may be approaching a period of decline. What policies should the United States follow with respect to slow or declining population growth in industrialized countries?

U.S. Policies Toward Rapid Population Growth in Less Developed Countries

The question of what policies the United States should adopt toward population growth in less developed countries begins with the question of what difference it makes to us. What interests of ours are involved in population changes in the Third World? There are a number of significant responses to these questions, here summarized for simplicity under two headings.

The Fear of Overpopulation

In the 1950s and 1960s, when awareness of the extraordinarily high rates of population growth in developing countries was spreading, there was much concern in the United States that world population growth would outrun the world's resources, leading to widespread famine, social disruption, and conflict. Cutting the rate of population growth was seen by many as an urgent necessity to prevent worldwide disaster.

In retrospect, these fears were greatly exaggerated. In fact, the record of the last three decades has been remarkably good: developing countries on the whole, by their own efforts and with much outside help, have not only kept up with population growth but gained in average per capita income. With respect to food, a central indicator of human welfare, over the period 1950–1980 food grain production in less developed countries rose, on the average, 2.9 percent per year. (This increase was larger than the rise in food grain production in industrialized countries over the same period, which was about 2.5 percent per year.) The rise in food grain production in less developed countries was larger than their growth in population, which was about 2.4 percent per year over the same period. Thus the growth in production of food grain has not only kept up with rising population, but has provided some margin for improving diets.

But what about population increases to come? Can the world feed the next 4 billion people? Most agricultural experts reply with a confident affirmative. They note that substantial margins of agricultural productivity already achieved in industrialized countries can be achieved in less developed countries. In industrialized countries, per acre production at the beginning of the 1980s was around 2.6 tons of grain, compared to 1.5 tons in less developed countries. And at 1.5 tons per acre, the less developed countries were already ahead of the average production in industrialized countries only thirty years earlier.

These are impressive bases for optimism. To translate them into enough food for the world's rapidly growing population, however, will be far from easy and will have to overcome a number of obstacles.

(1) Despite the sufficient overall growth rates in food production thus far, there have been periods of famine or near-famine in some places, notably in India, Bangladesh, Ethiopia, and the Sahel. Moreover, in one important area, sub-Saharan Africa, food production has not risen as fast as population.

(2) Future demand for food will rise not only to feed larger populations, but also to improve average diets; as incomes grow, people want more and better food. This poses sharp dilemmas when more meat is added to diets of higher-income groups. Since about five calories of grain are needed to produce one calorie of meat or poultry, there will be a continuing risk that better-off people will bid away limited food supplies.

(3) Future supplies of food will require a steady stream of new food production technologies, flowing from research on how to raise output in the many thousands of ecological areas, differing in soil, moisture, climate, pests, and many other characteristics, where food is grown. Fortunately, a system of international agricultural research centers has been established, which, working with national agricultural research systems in developing countries, has contributed much to raising productivity per acre. A strong emphasis on enlarging agricultural research will be needed over the years to come.

(4) Better food production technology does not automatically translate into larger food output. A framework of markets, prices, land tenure, and other conditions is necessary to give farmers incentives to adopt new technology and the supply lines and credit services they need. As is well known, many developing countries are following poor agricultural policies, and much improvement will be needed if future food needs are to be met.

(5) Larger food production will place heavy pressure on land and water resources, with marginal, high-cost supplies increasingly brought into use. In many Asian and African countries, cultivation is pushing up the mountainsides, leading both to higher production costs and to soil erosion. Wise policies and heavy investments, especially in irrigation facilities, will be necessary to achieve the required increases in food output without serious loss of the natural resource base.

(6) Finally, most developing countries have failed to deal effectively with hunger and malnutrition resulting not from overall food shortages but from poor distribution of the food that is available. Large groups in their populations are too poor to eat decently, and these groups in general are the groups with the highest birthrates.

It seems reasonable to conclude that it will require very strong efforts to keep pushing food supplies upward over the next two or three decades, and the slight slowing down that is anticipated in the rate of world population growth is not likely to ease this difficult outlook substantially. Severe problems of hunger and malnutrition will occur in the poorest countries and the poorest groups within countries.

At the same time, it seems evident that given wisdom and effort, the world can be fed, and the right way to look at the food outlook is not as an incipient dog-eat-dog struggle for survival, but as a major task in economic development. The work will be difficult, but the objectives are attainable.

What has been said about food can, in general, be said about other needs in developing countries—for employment and income, for social services like health and education. For the next two or three decades, at least, it will continue to be very difficult to achieve significant and widespread improvements in welfare for the world's rapidly growing population, especially for the poorer groups. At the same time, welfare improvements are clearly feasible, given good policies and strong efforts.

The view from the United States, therefore, should not be of a world undergoing a downward spiral of increasing conflict over inadequate resources, but of a world in which larger populations can be economic customers and competitors, collaborators in scientific and intellectual advance, potential cooperators toward peace. We can view rapid population growth not as an inexorable force pushing the world toward disaster, but simply as a major factor complicating and making more difficult the process of economic and social development. What then should follow about our interests and our policies?

The Opportunities of Development

U.S. interests in the development of low-income countries have been repeatedly challenged and debated, and repeatedly reaffirmed, under all presidents since World World II. The sustained consensus has been that several interests are served by development assistance.

(1) As one of the world's wealthiest nations, the United States has a humanitarian interest in assisting countries that face dire poverty.

(2) As the world's largest market economy, the United States has economic interests in the growth of developing countries as participants in a competitive, open, steadily larger international economy.

(3) As a world power, committed to the evolution of international security based on cooperative approaches to peace, the United States has security interests in the increasing strength of developing countries committed to a similar approach.

(4) As the world's largest open society, the United States has an interest in supporting the steady emergence of a world of independent nations, strong enough to stand on their own

feet, contributing to the common educational, scientific, and cultural advance of humankind.

All these interests are served by vigorous and imaginative U.S. assistance supporting the development of poor nations. Over the years, U.S. assistance has been properly subject to criticism for a variety of shortcomings. Nevertheless, it has had the virtue of continuing year after year to provide significant resources to a substantial number of developing countries.

U.S. development assistance has included support for agricultural and industrial development, for expansion of power and transportation, for increasing educational and health services. And since the middle 1960s, U.S. assistance for developing countries has included assistance in reducing rates of population growth.

Controversy over Support for Reduced Population Growth in the Third World

Two main reasons are usually cited why less developed countries, as part of their development efforts, should want to slow down population growth rates, and why the United States and other development assistance donors should help them do so.

First, from the viewpoint of the overall economy, rapid population growth hampers economic development. The faster the population is growing, the more the available resources for development must be used to provide jobs and services for the additional numbers, and the fewer are the resources available to raise living standards for all. Moreover, rapid population growth forces the use of marginal and less productive natural resources. In addition, rapid population growth tends to exacerbate inequalities in incomes by depressing wage rates and raising rates of return to land and capital.

Second, from the viewpoint of families, too many children, too closely spaced, make for the ill health of the children and their mothers and prevent the family from saving and investing either in economic assets or in the health and education of the children. These effects are the greater, the poorer the families concerned. These concerns for family health and welfare are the classic concerns that led to the family planning movement, first in industrialized countries and more recently in less developed countries.

These considerations—concern about resources and economic growth and concern about family health and welfare—as early as the 1950s led some less developed countries with high population growth rates, such as India, to adopt population policies aimed at reducing population growth, and led the United States in the 1960s to its position of providing assistance for population programs.

The U.S. decision to assist developing countries in slowing rates of population growth has been attacked vigorously over the years. One ground for attack was the argument that simply stopping population growth in a poor country would do little to alleviate poverty. That would be a valid argument if the only thing developing countries were trying to do, and the only objective of U.S. development assistance, was to slow down population growth. In fact, what developing countries are trying to do, and what the United States seeks to assist, is both to increase economic welfare and to reduce population growth, and the two policies clearly can be mutually reinforcing.

A second ground for criticism of U.S. population assistance was that it was forced on unwilling developing countries. There was some plausibility in this charge in the late 1960s and early 1970s when many developing countries had not adopted population programs, and the United States was promoting such programs vigorously. This was the situation at the time of the World Population Conference in Bucharest in 1974, when some developing countries argued that population programs were only a device of the rich countries to conceal their lack of generosity with respect to economic aid.

In the years after the Bucharest conference, however, the conviction spread rapidly through the developing world that rapid population growth does indeed hamper development. Major countries like Mexico and China, which had expressed skepticism at Bucharest, adopted programs to restrain population growth. By the mid-1980s, the great majority of less developed countries had adopted such programs, although several, particularly in sub-Saharan Africa, had not. Similarly, the great majority of analysts of population came to agree that population control programs are valuable, along with and complementary to programs to raise economic welfare, as part of a sensible development effort.

U.S. support for population restraint programs is therefore considered, by the great majority of those concerned both in the United States and in the Third World, to be an appropriate and important part of U.S. assistance to the development of Third World countries.

Ways and Means

It is one thing to agree that it is appropriate for developing countries to adopt, and for the United States to support, programs to restrain population growth. For several reasons, however, it is difficult in the present state of knowledge to establish effective programs to achieve specific targets of growth.

The natural starting point for a population program to begin is by providing family planning information and services to permit families to control the number and spacing of their children. It seems clear that when families learn how to use contraception to space their children, for the most part they also decide to limit numbers. But there is plainly no assurance that families' decisions on how many children they wish to have will result in totals exactly equal to what may be judged best for the society as a whole.

This has led to much research and debate on what motivates people to begin planning their families or to choose a particular family size and on how far these decisions can be influenced by public policy. Some important generalizations have resulted. It seems clear, for example, that as incomes rise and opportunities expand, most families want to limit the number of their children in order to be able to afford better education and health care for each child. As levels of education rise, especially among women, parents have fewer and healthier children. As opportunities for education and modern employment for women increase, women have fewer children.

These and other observations are consistent with the uniform experience of industrialized and developing countries alike: as economic and social modernization takes place, families reduce the number of children they have. However, such generalizations conceal wide variations in the timing and speed of decline in birthrates. They can give some general guidance for policy—speed up economic and social modernization, educate women, spread widely the benefits of economic growth—but they do not permit precise predictions of when and by how much birthrates will fall in response to particular program actions.

Beyond motivation, there are other major reasons for uncertainty in designing population programs. One is the question of what place incentives and even coercion should have in advancing family planning. Although the failure of Indira Gandhi's coercive family planning activities in India is often cited as evidence that coercion will not work—"it will bring down the government before it brings down the birthrate"—there are many kinds of encouragement short of coercion. Some of the more successful population programs, such as those in China and in Indonesia, have used different types of social pressure from peers in the community to encourage lower birthrates. Numerous programs rely on doctors and other medical personnel as authority figures to promote lower fertility. While it is easy to agree that outright coercion is not desirable and is unlikely to be effective, that leaves a set of choices that are more subtle and more uncertain and whose effects are difficult to predict.

Whatever may be the motivations and incentives, in most less developed countries family planning services—information, supplies, medical help when necessary—are not readily available to those who may wish to use them. There are persuasive arguments that contraception will be better accepted and longer continued if families see it in a health context, as part of a broader set of activities intended to make people, especially women and children, healthier and stronger. But in fact, in most rural villages and low-income urban areas in the developing world, neither health nor family planning services are available in any but rudimentary form.

Even if motivations and incentives are present, and family planning services provided, it is clear that the present array of contraceptives is not well adapted for use in developing countries, having a variety of defects ranging from inconvenience and discomfort to significant risk of dangerous side effects. The extensive worldwide use of sterilization and abortion testifies to the need for simpler and safer contraceptives, which have thus far eluded the medical research community.

Implications for U.S. Policy

How then should we sum up? At least two conclusions seem warranted with respect to U.S. policy toward rapid population growth in less developed countries.

In view of the effects of rapid population growth in developing countries—pressure on resources, obstacles to economic improvement, problems of family health and welfare—most such countries will want their efforts for economic and social development to include programs of family planning and other activities, such as accelerating female education, that can be expected to reduce rates of population growth. The strong interest of the United States in supporting economic and social improvement in less developed countries argues powerfully that U.S. development assistance should include support for population programs.

At the same time, it is necessary to recognize the novelty of this field as a subject for public policy, the limitations of knowledge about the impact of public programs, and the inadequacy of current technology to provide safe and effective contraception. This argues strongly for a nondogmatic, experimental approach to population assistance. It also argues strongly that U.S. development assistance should include substantial support to help build social science and biomedical research capacity in less developed countries to be concerned with population issues, and that resources in the United States should join vigorously in such research efforts.

U.S. Policy Toward Reduced Population Growth in Industrialized Nations

What interests and purposes of the United States are engaged by the slowdown in rates of population growth in industrialized countries? And what policy judgments do they suggest? A number of responses are here summarized under two headings.

Internal Adjustments in Slow-Growing Countries

In part, the agenda of population concerns in industrialized countries resembles those in developing countries. In the United States, for example, there is currently an "epidemic" of unwanted pregnancies among teenagers, more than a million per year, that we have so far been unable to deal with satisfactorily. In attempting to meet this problem we have encountered a combination of difficulties, including baffling questions of motivation, multiple social and family influences, and inability to provide effective and safe contraception, that are similar to those that are familiar in less developed countries.

In most respects, however, the agenda of population concerns in industrialized countries is quite different from that of less developed countries. The two principal elements that lead to a different agenda are the continued declines in fertility, now below replacement rates in Europe, Japan, Canada, and the United States, and the continued lengthening of average life spans, now well above seventy years in those countries. These changes have led to a variety of problems, of which four are cited here for illustration.

One is the problem of support for retired persons. In the United States this was thought to have been triumphantly solved at the end of the Great Depression by the introduction of Social Security. But as a result of the steady shift to a reduced proportion of younger persons and a higher proportion of older ones, the demographic assumptions on which the Social Security system was built have been deeply undercut. To retain the system's solvency has required, and will continue to require, facing alternatives, none of which is easy: to extend working years and delay the beginning of benefits, to impose larger taxes on younger workers, to reduce benefits for retired persons. The necessary modifications in the system will result in continuing readjustments in life styles, family relationships and expectations, and living standards, all to accommodate the largely unexpected changes in demographic characteristics. This points to the need to do two things: to improve our technical skill at projecting population changes and their consequences, and to learn to respond better through our political processes to the anticipated effects of demographic changes that are two decades or more in the future.

A second major problem of aging societies is the adjustment of social services, most conspicuously in health. In all the industrial societies the maternity beds are empty, the retirement and nursing homes are booming, and the problems of health and medical care for the aged are becoming ever larger and more costly.

These changes are raising hard and uncomfortable issues of policy—ethical and moral issues as well as economic issues. What is the right thing to do, for example, when life can be extended through the use of technical medical apparatus although the quality of the extended life is very limited? Throughout human history, the single, simple policy rule has been that any action to prolong life was desirable. Today that ancient guideline is being widely challenged, and the challenges are bound to increase as a result of the inexorable demographic changes that lie ahead. The numbers of persons in the U.S. population who are in their seventies, eighties, and nineties will increase greatly, as will the number of cases in which extreme medical measures may be able to preserve a form of life that may seem to be of doubtful quality. Questions of who decides on whether to prolong life and against what standards, questions of the role of the family and its medical, legal, and spiritual advisers and of the role of the state, all will require lengthy deliberation.

A third, less conspicuous problem that is now becoming more evident in the United States stems from the demographic fact of differential life expectancy between women and men. On average, women live several years longer than men, about seven years longer in the United States at present. Moreover, when older men, widowed or divorced, marry again, they tend to marry younger women. In consequence, the population contains growing numbers of elderly single women, many of whom lead lonely and unhappy lives. This is a social problem of much importance that has not yet received much attention. It is demographically inevitable that the numbers of single, older women will grow, as will the need for inventive, sensitive, and flexible methods for organizing living arrangements that will offer them richer opportunities.

A fourth concern, if present trends continue, is the prospect that a number of industrialized countries will enter a period in which their populations will decline in total numbers. While in earlier epochs of human history there were periods when total populations declined, this has not been true for the past several hundred years. The rise of the modern nation-state has coincided with a continuing increase in total populations. In recent decades, when population declines have become imminent in France and other European countries, the prospect has been viewed as something to be avoided if at all possible. Public policies, such as subsidies for larger families, have been instituted to try to raise birthrates. To date, such measures have not had much success. Thus it is apparent in industrialized countries, as in less developed countries, that the decisions by couples on the number and spacing of their children will not necessarily coincide with some larger public judgment about the desirable size for a community's or a nation's population.

Worldwide Adjustments

The policy issues presented by slow or declining population growth in industrialized countries are not limited to questions of internal adjustment. All the industrialized countries together are going through the same process, which is gradually shrinking their proportion of the world's population. Over the next few decades, the share of today's industrialized countries in total world population is likely to drop from around one-quarter to one-sixth or less.

Do we care? What difference might it make to the United States and the other nations that led the way in the industrial revolution and the demographic transition? Three concerns might be noted.

Third World Economic Capacity. First, we should note the steady rise of economic strength in the Third World. While we live in a world in which people are not permitted to migrate freely, capital is movable and so are science and technology. The assumption that modern economic growth is transferable is plainly valid, as witness the rise of Japan and the less complete but nevertheless impressive transitions underway in a dozen rapidly rising less developed countries.

Consequently, while different developing countries will of course advance at very different rates, we should anticipate a steady rise in economic capacity in more and more Third World countries. None will necessarily duplicate Japan, with its heavy concentration on industry and industrial exports: some may depend much more on agriculture and the export of agricultural products. But economic strength will surely rise in the Third World.

The central questions of policy raised by this likelihood are how to proceed, so far as our own policies are concerned, to keep our economy fresh, changing, and innovative and how to proceed internationally to keep the world economy open and competitive as it becomes larger and more interconnected.

The steady spread of science based agriculture, industry, communications, and services inevitably will mean a rapidly growing world economy with all the risks and opportunities that will bring. The United States does not need in any chauvinistic sense to be "Number One," but we do need to follow policies that will keep us up-to-date and on the frontier in introducing new technologies and in moving from old industries in which we have lost our competitive edge to new ones that offer better opportunities. The United States also needs to join vigorously in devising international policies and institutions calculated to promote the general advance of economic welfare for populations all around the world, ourselves included.

Intellectual Initiative and Innovation from the Third World. A second question worth attention is the effect of spreading education on the world's sources of innovation and new ideas. Modern knowledge of the natural and social sciences is being assimilated rapidly throughout the world. Moreover, the formal and informal networks of communication and collaboration that connect the world's leading specialists in various disciplines and professional fields increasingly include persons in developing countries.

It would seem permissible to anticipate that over the next few decades major sources of intellectual initiative and innovation are likely to come from what are now relatively poor countries. The numbers of young, well educated, creative persons in industrialized countries are likely to stabilize or decline; the numbers of such persons in developing countries will steadily rise.

As this happens, the condition of recent centuries during which "the West" has been intellectual leader and teacher of the world will be gradually transformed into a more polycentered whole. We have already seen this occurring with respect to Japan, whose skills in management, engineering, artistic design, and other fields have already contributed to the evolution of what is still called, inaccurately, "Western" civilization.

The outcome of all these changes should be a speeding-up of the rate of increase in human knowledge and in opportunities for gains in human welfare. The appropriate policy for the industrialized countries plainly should be to keep open international channels for educational and scientific interchange and to contribute to the international flow of ideas from which we stand increasingly to learn as well as to contribute.

The United States is in an especially favorable position to participate in and benefit from such a world. Our multiethnic society, with its long tradition of welcoming immigrants and refugees, has demonstrated on a national scale much of the lively and vigorous scientific and cultural life that could characterize an open international society. A number of our national policies, particularly those related to international education, health, and research, should clearly be strengthened to contribute more effectively than they now do to these potential benefits for ourselves as well as for the wider world.

The Concept of Progress. As a third and final point, it is interesting to note that the modern idea of progress as a historical and cultural imperative developed about two centuries ago. The concept of progress—of moving "onward and upward" in knowledge, in science, in economic welfare, in human advancement—grew and took hold precisely during the time when populations began to grow at accelerating rates, infant and child mortality began to drop, infectious diseases were reduced, and life spans were extended. How far were these physical evidences of improvement important to the idea of progress? And how far will that central concept of current civilization change if the world moves toward birth and death rates stabilized at low levels, population growth leveling off, life expectancies no longer rising, and a world population of around 8 or 9 billion people in the latter part of the next century?

Final Report of the Seventy-first American Assembly

At the close of their discussion, the participants in the Seventy-first American Assembly, on *International Population Policy: Issues and Choices for the United States,* at Arden House, Harriman, New York, April 17–20, 1986, reviewed as a group the following statement. This statement represents a general agreement; however, no one was asked to sign it. Furthermore, it should be understood that not everyone agreed with all of it.

Background and Introduction

Since 1963 the population of the developing world has more than doubled, to nearly 4 billion people today. The annual growth rate of the developing world stands today where it did in 1960, at around 2 percent. During the intervening period, however, as death rates declined, the growth rate actually increased, to over 2.5 percent per year during the late 1960s. A more recent decline in the birthrate has brought overall growth back to its current level. Barring wars or calamity, the prospects are that the population of the developing world will continue to grow rapidly well into the next century. The

United Nations Population Division, which has prepared "low," "medium," and "high" projections to 2025, shows in its low projection that the 1985 developing world population of 3.7 billion will at least double in forty-five years to 7.4 billion and could rise to 8.2 billion or even 9.1 billion people.

In 1963 the Twenty-third American Assembly published *The Population Dilemma*—one of the earliest attempts to place the issue of global population growth on the U.S. public policy agenda. That Assembly called attention to the rapid decline in death rates in the Third World since the end of World War II and the fact that birthrates were still quite high. Using U.N. projections, it foresaw that the population of the less developed countries (LDCs) would increase to around 3.7 billion in the mid-1980s—a remarkably accurate prediction.

Since the publication of *The Population Dilemma,* concerted public action has occurred, both in the industrialized and the nonindustrialized countries. The United States has played a leading role intellectually and financially in population assistance programs over a twenty-year period. Two international population conferences have called upon all countries to tackle the problem of rapid population growth, and most LDCs have adopted policies and programs aimed at reducing population growth. And, as we note below, considerable progress has been made. Both mortality and fertility have declined substantially, but the fact that growth rates in the developing world have not declined below where they were in 1963 demonstrates that the issue of rapid population growth remains a cause for continuing attention by the U.S. government and others.

During the 1960s and 1970s, nearly all of the many assessments of the world population situation found that continuing rapid population growth through maintenance of high fertility would be detrimental: the realization of the aspirations of the countries of the developing world for improvement of their social and economic status would be made not impossible, but more difficult. The United States responded to this situation by encouraging nations of the Third World to take steps to recognize that continuing high fertility and rapid population growth were major obstacles to development and to establish policies and programs intended to reduce fertility. Toward that end, it has also provided assistance for voluntary family planning programs in many parts of the world and has encouraged other nations to do the same. The policies of the United States rested upon a broad public consensus.

Recently, however, these positions have come under attack. The U.S. position in 1984 at the International Conference on Population sponsored by the United Nations departed in two major ways from the stance adopted by at least four previous administrations. It gave reduced significance to any effects of population increase on economic growth, saying that population growth was a "neutral" phenomenon, not necessarily positive or negative, but taking its character from a constellation of other factors that determine the situation in a particular country. The U.S. statement credited economic development, spurred by free market policies, as a principal force that leads to a voluntary lowering of fertility by individuals. In another vein, while voicing support for voluntary family planning programs, the new policy took a very strong stance against abortion, reiterating and extending the prohibition on the use of U.S. funds to pay for abortions performed for family planning reasons. Implementation of this policy has led to withdrawal of funding from the International Planned Parenthood Federation (IPPF). In view of these changes in U.S. international population policy, the Seventy-first American Assembly undertook a reevaluation of the world population situation and the U.S. response.

The Rationale for U.S. Policies Toward Reduction of High Fertility

There are two major bases for a U.S. government role in reducing high fertility. First, high fertility, over the long term, has negative effects on social and economic circumstances, such as those relating to education, health, and income, and on natural resources and the environment. Second, involuntary high fertility may infringe upon a person's human right to choose his or her family size.

Population growth is always slow in the sense that it moves

in small incremental steps, nearly invisible in the short term, yet compounding day by day. Numbers inching upward are hardly noticeable; yet they may lead to dramatic changes in the quality of life as populations double or triple. And these changes may well affect future generations. Even if fertility declines from high to replacement levels, it can take half a century for population growth to cease. It may take just as long for environmental degradation due to pressures on resources to become obvious. How one assesses the importance of the changes engendered by high fertility depends quite directly on individual attitudes and values, one's optimism about human adaptability to almost any situation, one's views on the role of women and the family, and one's personal "discount rate"—the extent to which the welfare of future generations is considered relevant to actions taken today.

Some of the factors affected by high fertility are discussed in the paragraphs that follow. Various international declarations have affirmed the fundamental human right of couples to choose the size of their families. For example, the United States has subscribed to the policy adopted at the U.N. International Conference on Population that "women and couples have the right to determine freely and responsibly the number and spacing of their children, and that they have the right to the means that would enable them to do so."

Health and Education

The participants in this Assembly concluded that reducing high fertility has important and unambiguous benefits for women and children. The health of mothers will be improved by reducing the numbers of unwanted pregnancies and encouraging women to have their children during optimal child-bearing years, neither too young nor too old. Equally important, if births are more widely spaced and reduced in number, the health and survival chances of newborns and older children are significantly improved.

Parents who have fewer children tend to invest more in the education of those they have, thus significantly improving their future prospects. By the same token, when fewer children are entering the school-age population more resources are available for improving the quality of education that is available.

It was concluded that access to family planning can, through reducing fertility, facilitate a diversity of family, social, and political roles for women. These opportunities include increased education and increased employment options.

Economic Development

The consensus of the participants in the Seventy-first American Assembly differed from the views expressed by the U.S. government at the 1984 International Population Conference in Mexico City in its assessment of the impact of population growth on the well-being of people and the development prospects of most of today's LDCs. The participants concluded that rapid population growth in the least developed countries (acting primarily through the effects of high fertility) has substantial and generally negative economic and social effects and that fertility reduction in those cases can bring about corresponding benefits.

While the participants were careful to state their position that fertility reduction policies are not alternatives for sound economic and social policies and institutions, fertility reduction, particularly in the poorer developing countries, can relax constraints on human capital formation, help countries create enough jobs to accommodate the labor force, reduce the stress on social and political institutions, and lessen the problems of maldistribution of income and opportunity. Reduction of fertility in and of itself will not cause poor nations to become rich. But it can provide time and relieve pressure on societies to direct resources toward satisfying the minimum needs of a rapidly growing and economically dependent population. Furthermore, since high fertility tends to affect the poor disproportionately because it depresses wage rates, it can contribute to a significant worsening of income distribution and concomitant social and political tensions.

The participants reviewed the arguments in favor of high fertility, including the argument that high fertility induces technological innovation and infrastructure development. They concluded that on balance, in most LDCs, such benefits, to the extent to which they exist, are likely to be overwhelmed by the negative effects outlined above.

Resources and the Environment

The relationships between population growth and depletion of natural resources and degradation of the environment are usually complex, but they are basic to development and human well-being. While population growth cannot always be considered the primary cause of environmental problems, it is often a contributing factor, as in the case of desertification. Under conditions of high fertility and rapid population growth, renewable resources must be shared by increasing numbers of people, possibly outstripping regenerative capacities and leading to degradation of the resources. Degradation of such resources as clean water, topsoil, and vegetative cover in LDCs undermines economic development by constraining improvements in health, agricultural production, and infrastructure. Rapid exploitation of natural resources attributable to increasing population densities can also lead to irreversible changes such as species loss. Those countries with very high growth rates may be least able to intervene to protect their own environments; slower population growth may give them greater opportunity to acquire the economic or political capacity to do so before the resource is exhausted.

Other Effects

Some participants noted that reductions in fertility will bring about lower rates of urban growth, reduce the hardships involved in urban overcrowding, and thereby possibly reduce some of the socio-political problems that such rapid growth can engender. It was noted that political leaders in many countries are concerned about the social, economic, and political burdens associated with rapid urban growth.

U.S. Policy Approaches to Altering Global Demographic Trends

Any national population policy must take into account the possibly diverse attitudes and values of citizens as well as an understanding of the objective effects of population growth on a country's long-term development. U.S. policies toward family planning should reflect this diversity.

Family Planning

In 1965 the U.S. government decided to establish within its overall foreign aid program a new program to support family planning in developing nations. At the outset, the U.S. Congress embraced the fundamental policy that U.S. funds would be used to support population programs on a strictly voluntary basis.

Provision of voluntary family planning services has become a principal policy approach endorsed by the U.S. government for promoting individual choice in the area of human reproduction and for altering national and global demographic trends. Over two decades of foreign aid by the United States devoted to this purpose have contributed to the development of family planning programs in many of the developing countries of the world.

Today, not only the United States but most of the other developed Organization for Economic Cooperation and Development (OECD) countries provide foreign aid for family planning, together devoting about $500 million annually for this purpose. While this represents only 2 percent of all official development assistance, developing country recipients of this aid have dramatically increased their own national expenditures in support of their family planning programs to a total now in the range of $1.5 billion annually.

Extensive evaluations of the efficacy of these foreign aid and local government expenditures in promoting access to and use of contraception in the Third World have demonstrated impressive successes. Large increases in the use of contraception have resulted as a direct consequence of these programs in many parts of the developing world. There have been substantial declines in national fertility levels and substantial increases in the ability of couples to choose freely the size and spacing of their families.

Participants recognize that family planning programs vary in terms of their scale and content and their effectiveness with which they have been implemented. Continuing efforts are being made as part of U.S. support for family planning to increase our understanding of these variations and of the factors which determine program effectiveness.

Contraceptive Research

As experience accumulated with these programs, the basic policy approach was expanded to other areas. In the early 1970s it was recognized that currently available methods of fertility control fell short of people's family planning needs and that the traditional private sector sources of new contraceptive technology were not investing substantially in research and development leading to improved methods. The U.S. government, along with a number of other developed countries and the World Health Organization, established special funding programs that are contributing to the search for safer and more effective contraceptives having fewer undesirable side effects. Recently, liability suits in the United States, coupled with widespread terminations of insurance coverage, have had the effect of deterring contraceptive testing and research, particularly by the private sector. As a result, there are significant shortfalls in funding by the private sector for research, both basic and clinical, in this area.

Status of Women

Another policy approach adopted in the 1970s emerged in recognition of the difficulty many women in developing countries have in gaining access to contraceptive information, supplies, and services because of severe restrictions on women's rights and roles in many societies. Many Third World governments, with assistance from UN agencies and the United States and other developed country foreign aid programs, began special programs to improve the education, status, and opportunities of women in their countries. The commitment to policies and programs to promote the rights of women and improve their roles and status in their families and communities has grown enormously throughout the world in the intervening decade.

Health

Another basic policy approach, the promotion of primary health care in the Third World countries, which is related to both individual rights and well-being and to national development efforts, has also had profound effects on demographic trends. Maternal and child health care programs have been components of many family planning programs since their inception, and all governments have seen health and family planning as closely linked, mutually reinforcing parts of national development efforts.

Education and Development Policies

Education, especially for women, has also come to be recognized as an important determinant, not only of national development and individual advancement, but of lower demand for large families in many countries. Other broader development policies and programs, including those promoting agricultural development, rural development, and industrialization, all combine their much larger impacts on individual welfare and national development with indirect effects on fertility. While these larger development programs should in no way be conceived of as policies to alter demographic trends, the particular way in which aspects of these are implemented can exert powerful fertility impacts—for example, by causing increases in the age of marriage and by shifting the balance of the economic costs and benefits of children.

Beyond Family Planning

In recent years, some Third World governments have sought to further stimulate the use of family planning by people in their countries through the adoption of policies that go beyond actively promoting smaller families and facilitating access to contraceptive information and services. These policies introduce the concept of inducements to individuals to adopt contraception or to limit their family size, or, in other cases, the concept of disincentives or penalties to discourage individuals from bearing more children.

It is evident that there is a continuum of measures, beginning with information and education and extending through various types of encouragement and inducement all the way to physical coercion, that might be considered by governments as possible means to achieve such social change. At one end of that continuum, there is almost universal acceptance of information and education as appropriate means to encourage family planning; at the other end, there is universal condemnation of physical coercion for such purposes. Exactly where to draw the line between appropriate inducements and improper compulsion is very difficult to decide in the abstract, and, moreover, the line may be drawn differently in various nations because of differences in cultural traditions and value systems.

During the last two years, both Congress and the administration have strongly reaffirmed support for voluntarism in U.S. family planning assistance programs and opposition to policies that are not consistent with internationally accepted human rights.

Abortion

An area of controversy in the United States has been policies regarding the availability and use of abortion. Millions of abortions are now performed annually throughout the world. Many of these are performed in developing countries where abortion is illegal, and extensive documentation indicates that such abortions are a leading cause of maternal mortality in most of these countries. Provision of family planning services has been shown to reduce abortions, both in countries where it is legal and especially in countries where it is illegal. However, because of deep controversies over the acceptability of the use of abortion, in 1973 the U.S. government prohibited the use of any of its foreign aid funds for abortion services and, in 1984, it further prohibited the provision of any of these funds to nongovernmental organizations that are in any way involved with abortion using their own monies.

Immigration into the United States

The United States continues to be the prime receiving nation of the world and historically has benefitted from the contributions immigrants have made to our society. A main impetus for migration to the United States has been the differences in economic and social opportunity between this and other countries. Rapid population growth in developing countries since World War II has increased the size of the population that would like to migrate. Fertility declines in high-fertility countries would serve to reduce additional pressures fifteen to twenty years hence. Moreover, over the long range, the contributions of fertility declines to economic development could lessen the economic differentials favoring emigration.

However, development assistance is no substitute for immigration policy, concerning which numerous issues are being debated in the United States. The participants in the Assembly concurred that U.S. immigration policy needs to be reformulated, but they could neither explore nor resolve the complex questions raised. Among these are the following: What levels of legal immigration are desirable? What criteria should determine admittance: family reunification, U.S. unemployment, U.S. needs for skilled workers, immigrants' potential economic contributions, or humanitarian concerns about refugees? To what extent should worries about the future size and composition of the U.S. population shape immigration policy? How can basic rights of immigrants and refugees be respected? What are the magnitudes and impacts of undocumented migration?

Recommendations

The foregoing assessments of international population trends and policy approaches led participants in the Seventy-first Assembly to the following recommendations for U.S. foreign policy concerning population in the years ahead:

1. The participants strongly recommend that U.S. assistance for population programs be maintained at least at its current share of overall U.S. development assistance.

2. The participants fully endorse both the voluntary basis for U.S. family planning assistance and its goal to provide people with a full understanding of the family planning options open to them, including the benefits and drawbacks of those alternatives, along with full access to contraceptive services.

3. There was a strong consensus that the United States should not permit its foreign aid funds to be used for activities that entail abridgement of human rights. The participants recognize that different countries hold different views and perspectives concerning what constitutes appropriate means of encouraging and assisting people to use family planning. For this reason the participants recommend that the U.S. government should respect the sovereignty of other countries and should not impose sanctions on other countries or organizations working in those countries that carry out programs that cannot be supported directly with U.S. assistance funds, provided that these programs are consistent with internationally recognized human rights.

Consistent with such policy, the participants believe the U.S. government should maintain its full support for the U.N. Fund for Population Activities.

4. The participants reached a consensus that the U.S. government should not withhold its funds from countries or organizations that engage in abortion activities where abortion is legal. The participants specifically recommend that this policy be applied to restore funding to the International Planned Parenthood Federation.

5. The participants agreed that reproductive freedom is a fundamental human right. A majority felt that this right should include access to contraception and abortion and recommends that U.S. policy should not frustrate the exercise of this right.
6. Efforts should be undertaken to improve the education, economic opportunities, and health of women. Women's issues, needs, and organizations should receive much greater attention and financial support from the U.S. foreign aid program.
7. The Assembly participants agreed that the current policies and laws related to immigration into the United States are inadequate and that reevaluation and reformulation are required.
8. The participants recognized the need for increased efforts in research, development, and education related to improvement of voluntary fertility control. They recommend:

- improvement of the technical, managerial, and other capacities required within developing countries to enable them to develop and carry out appropriate population policies and programs;
- increased efforts to ensure that family planning programs are designed and managed effectively and efficiently and offer high quality client care;
- the provision of education programs to increase the individual person's knowledge of reproductive physiology and other aspects of reproduction to enhance his or her own ability to determine the number and spacing of children and improve health and well-being;
- increased research to expand contraceptive options, including basic research in reproductive biology and continuing work on development and testing of new methods;
- and the consideration of measures to reduce current legal and liability barriers in the United States to contraceptive research, testing, and availability without reducing current standards of quality and safety.

Participants
The Seventy-first American Assembly

PHYLLIS ALBRITTON
Legislative Assistant
Office of Representative John E. Porter
Washington, D.C.

GEORGE V. ALLEN, JR.
Shaw, Pittman, Potts & Trowbridge
Washington, D.C.

JODIE ALLEN
National Issues Coordinator
Office of the Chairman
Chrysler Corporation
Washington, D.C.

DAVID E. BELL
Professor and Chairman
Department of Population Sciences
Harvard School of Public Health
Boston, Massachusetts

†THE HON. DANNY J. BOGGS
U.S. Sixth Circuit Court of Appeals
Cincinnati, Ohio

JOHN BONGAARTS
Senior Associate
Center for Policy Studies
The Population Council
New York, New York

*Discussion Leader
**Rapporteur
†Delivered Formal Address
‡Participated in Panel Discussion

**SALLY K. BRANDEL
Central Intelligence Agency
Washington, D.C.

JOHN C. BURTON
Dean and Arthur Young Professor
Columbia Business School
New York, New York

ANSLEY J. COALE
Associate Director
Office of Population Research
Princeton University
Princeton, New Jersey

JOEL E. COHEN
Professor of Populations
The Rockefeller University
New York, New York

ALLAN H. DECHERNEY
Professor of Gynecology & Obstetrics
School of Medicine
Yale University
New Haven, Connecticut

PAUL DEMENY
Vice President & Director
Center for Policy Studies
The Population Council
New York, New York

JOAN B. DUNLOP
President
International Women's Health Coalition
New York, New York

**V. JEFFERY EVANS
Health Scientist Administrator
Demographic & Behavioral Sciences Branch
Center for Population Research
National Institute of Child Health & Human Development
Department of Health & Human Services
Bethesda, Maryland

DAVID FEIN
Harriman Scholar
Office of Population Research
Princeton University
Princeton, New Jersey

KATHARINE FERGUSON
Producer and Reporter, U.S. Foreign Policy
National Public Radio
Washington, D.C.

H. BERNARD GLAZER
Chief
Economic Development Division
Office of International Development Assistance
Bureau of International Organization Affairs
U.S. Department of State
Washington, D.C.

MARGARET G. GOODMAN
Staff Consultant
Committee on Foreign Affairs
U.S. House of Representatives
Washington, D.C.

MARSHALL GREEN
Population Crisis Committee
Washington, D.C.

CHARLES HAMMERSLOUGH
Harriman Scholar
Office of Population Research
Princeton University
Princeton, New Jersey

OSCAR HARKAVY
Chief Program Officer
Population/Urban Poverty
The Ford Foundation
New York, New York

WILLIAM S. HOFFMAN
Director
UAW Social Security Department
Solidarity House
Detroit, Michigan

‡SANDRA MOSTAFA KABIR
Executive Director
Bangladesh Women's Health Coalition
Dhaka, Bangladesh

SIOMA KAGAN
Professor of International Business
School of Business Administration
University of Missouri-St. Louis
St. Louis, Missouri

**MARY M. KRITZ
Associate Director
Population Sciences
The Rockefeller Foundation
New York, New York

‡ADRIAN LAJOUS
Fundacion Mexicana de Planificacion Familiar de Mexico
Mexico City, Mexico

JUDITH L. LICHTMAN
Executive Director
Women's Legal Defense Fund, Inc.
Washington, D.C.

*MARY D. LINDSAY
New York, New York

DOUGLAS W. MARSHALL
Corporate Strategic Planning
General Motors Corporation
Detroit, Michigan

PHYLLIS McCARTHY
Director
Quo Vadis Family Center
Torrance, California

W. HENRY MOSLEY
Professor and Chairman
Department of Population Dynamics
School of Hygiene & Public Health
The Johns Hopkins University
Baltimore, Maryland

ANNE FIRTH MURRAY
Program Officer
The William & Flora Hewlett Foundation
Menlo Park, California

LILLIAN PUBILLONES NOLAN
Staff Consultant
Subcommittee on Western Hemisphere Affairs
Committee on Foreign Affairs
U.S. House of Representatives
Washington, D.C.

MARK PERLMAN
The University Professor of Economics
Department of Economics
Faculty of Arts and Science
University of Pittsburgh
Pittsburgh, Pennsylvania

HARRIET F. PILPEL
Counsel
Weil, Gotshal & Manges
New York, New York

SAMUEL H. PRESTON
Director
Population Studies Center
University of Pennsylvania
Philadelphia, Pennsylvania

MARKLEY ROBERTS
Economist
Department of Economic Research
AFL-CIO
Washington, D.C.

ROBERT RODALE
Publisher
Rodale Press
Emmaus, Pennsylvania

ALLAN G. ROSENFIELD
Dean
School of Public Health
Columbia University
New York, New York

‡FREDERICK SAI
from Ghana
Senior Population Adviser
Population, Health & Nutrition Department
World Bank
Washington, D.C.

*S. BRUCE SCHEARER
President
Population Resource Center
New York, New York

JURGEN SCHMANDT
Director
The Woodlands Center for Growth Studies
The Woodlands, Texas

SHELDON J. SEGAL
Director for Population Sciences
The Rockefeller Foundation
New York, New York

FRANCES SEYMOUR
Harriman Scholar
The Woodrow Wilson School
Princeton University
Princeton, New Jersey

ELEANOR BERNERT SHELDON
New York, New York

CECIL G. SHEPS
Taylor Grandy Distinguished Professor of Social Medicine and Professor of Epidemiology
University of North Carolina
Chapel Hill, North Carolina

GEORGE B. SIMMONS
Professor
Population & Health Planning
School of Public Health
University of Michigan
Ann Arbor, Michigan

*STEVEN W. SINDING
Director
Office of Population
Agency for International Development
Washington, D.C.

HUMPHREY TAYLOR
President
Louis Harris & Associates
New York, New York

MICHAEL S. TEITELBAUM
Program Officer
The Alfred P. Sloan Foundation
New York, New York

†THE HON. JOSEPH W. TYDINGS, JR.
Finley, Kumble, Wagner
Washington, D.C.

DONALD E. VERMEER
Professor
Department of Geography & Anthropology
Louisiana State University
Baton Rouge, Louisiana

ROBERT WARREN
Chief
Statistical Analysis Branch
Immigration & Naturalization Service
Washington, D.C.

ALAN RUFUS WATERS
Professor of Management
The Babcock Graduate School of Management
Wake Forest University
Winston-Salem, North Carolina

‡WU JIANMIN
Counselor
Permanent Mission of the People's Republic of China to the United Nations
New York, New York

VICKI L. WILDE
Women's Issues
Office of Representative
Olympia J. Snowe
Washington, D.C.

JANICE WILSON
National Executive Board
Coalition of Labor Union
Women
Hartford, Connecticut

GEORGE ZEIDENSTEIN
President
The Population Council
New York, New York

KARL ZINSMEISTER
The American Enterprise
Institute
Washington, D.C.

About The American Assembly

The American Assembly was established by Dwight D. Eisenhower at Columbia University in 1950. It holds nonpartisan meetings and publishes authoritative books to illuminate issues of United States policy.

An affiliate of Columbia, with offices at Barnard College, the Assembly is a national, educational institution incorporated in the state of New York.

The Assembly seeks to provide information, stimulate discussion, and evoke independent conclusions on matters of vital public interest.

American Assembly Sessions

At least two national programs are initiated each year. Authorities are retained to write background papers presenting essential data and defining the main issues of each subject.

A group of men and women representing a broad range of experience, competence, and American leadership meet for several days to discuss the Assembly topic and consider alternatives for national policy.

All Assemblies follow the same procedure. The background papers are sent to participants in advance of the Assembly. The Assembly meets in small groups for four or five lengthy periods. All groups use the same agenda. At the close of these informal sessions participants adopt in plenary session a final report of findings and recommendations.

Regional, state, and local Assemblies are held following the national session at Arden House. Assemblies have also been held in England, Switzerland, Malaysia, Canada, the Caribbean, South America, Central America, the Philippines, and Japan. Over one hundred forty institutions have cosponsored one or more Assemblies.

The American Assembly
Columbia University

Index

abortion:
fertility transition and, 125
National Academy of Sciences 1971 report on, 18–19
1984 U.S. policy statement on, 12–13
Seventy-first American Assembly report on, 238–39, 240
spontaneous, 107
abstinence from sexual relations, 108, 118
age distribution (age structure), death rates and, 42–43
aged, the, in industrialized countries, 224–25
Agency for International Development, U.S. (USAID), 14
agriculture, labor force in, 103
American Assembly:
nature and function of, 246
sessions of, 246–47
Seventy-first. *See* Seventy-first American Assembly
trustees and officers of, 247–48
Twenty-third, 3, 230

Ball, George W., 166
Bangladesh, 20, 73, 103
Bell, David, 26
bilingualism, 165–66
birthrate, demographic transition and, 40–42
Bongaarts, John, 25
Borjas, George, 158–59
Bos, Eduard, 151
Bouvier, Leon, 171
Bracero program, 143–45
breastfeeding, 108, 118
Brokaw, Thomas, 69
Brownell, Herbert, 145
Bulatao, Rudolpho, 93

capital/labor ratios, 71, 72
capital supply, 20–21, 71
Carter, Jimmy (Carter administration), 164, 166
childbearing decisions:
cultural and institutional context of, 92, 93
externalities and, 78–87
common property resources, 82–87

childbearing decisions (*continued*)
subsidized schooling and other social programs for children, 80–81
intergenerational relations and, 87–89, 91
programs that go beyond family planning and, 89–92
purposeful control of individuals over, 92–93
child mortality, 88, 112. *See also* infant mortality
China, 39, 47, 70
Chiswick, Barry, 158, 159
Coale, Ansley, 25, 71
Coale-Hoover study (or model), 14–15, 17, 20, 71–72, 96–97
Cochran, Thad, 164
common property resources, externalities from childbearing and, 82–87
contraception, 105. *See also* family planning programs
Seventy-first American Assembly report on, 236
transition in reproductive behavior and, 117–18, 122–31
effectiveness of contraception and, 128–29
future fertility trends, 129–31
initial phase of fertility decline, 117–18
midtransitional societies, 122–25
Crosson, Pierre, 84

Davis, Cary, 171
death rates:
age distribution and, 42–43
demographic transition and, 40–42
deforestation, 84–86
Demeny, Paul, 8, 24–25, 75
demographic situation, global. *See* world demographics situation
demographic transition, 40–42
developing countries. *See* less developed countries (LDCs)
divorce, 109

Eastland, James O., 146
economic effects:
of family planning programs, 193–94
of immigration into the United States, 155–60
economic growth (or development), 67–75, 96–104, 226–27
aggregate indicators of, 74–75
Coale-Hoover study on, 14–15, 17
demographic-economic models and, 71–74
National Academy of Sciences 1971 report on, 16
natural resources and, 69–71
1984 U.S. policy statement on, 10–12
Seventy-first American Assembly report on, 233–34
education (schooling), 21, 22, 100–101, 218
as externality from childbearing, 80–82
immigration and, 160–62
Seventy-first American Assembly report on, 232–33, 237
Egypt, 179–80, 183
employment, 22–23
productive, 101–3
environment, the:
National Academy of Sciences 1986 report on, 20
Seventy-first American Assembly report on, 234
estimates, demographic, 29
Evenson, Robert, 74, 78
expectation of life at birth, 43–44
externalities:
from childbearing, 78–87
common property resources, 82–87

subsidized schooling and other social programs for children, 80–81
concept of, 77–78

family planning programs, 7–8, 68, 175–206, 220–22
assistance by developed countries for, 205–6
audience for, 181
choice of contraceptive technology in, 181–82
contraceptive prevalence and, 187–93
demand and supply factors in, 188–93, 197–99
generation of demand, 182–83
determinants of effectiveness of, 195–204
budget of the program, 203–4
demand for contraceptive services, 197–99
management, 199–203
political support, 205
relationships between providers and clients, 195–96
fertility and, 186–89
illustrative programs, 177–81
measurement of effectiveness of, 186
organizational choices for delivering, 183–84
political support for, 185, 204
programs that go beyond, 89–92
Seventy-first American Assembly report on, 238
resources devoted to, 184
Seventy-first American Assembly report on, 235–36, 238, 241
social and economic effects of, 193–94
United States support for, 176
welfare economics and, 76, 88–92, 95
widespread support for, 175–77

family size:
average desired, 127
child mortality and, 88
failure to achieve desired, in traditional societies, 110–12
fertility, 41–42, 48–53. *See also* total fertility rate
family planning programs's effects on, 186–89
mortality and, 114–17
natural, 106–9
projections of demographic changes and, 61–62, 66
transition in levels of, 105. *See also* reproductive behavior, transition in
future trends in, 125–32
midtransitional societies, 121–25
onset of, 114–21
pretransitional (traditional) societies, 106–14
food production, 214–16
foreign aid. *See* population assistance, U.S.

Gray, Ron, 113
growth rate. *See* population growth rate

Hadley, Eleanor, 144, 145
health, 218–19
family planning programs and, 194
poor, fecundity and, 112–14
Seventy-first American Assembly report on, 232, 237
Hispanics, in the United States, 165, 171–72
Hobcraft, John, 88
Hoover, Edgar, 71. *See also* Coale-Hoover study (or model)
Hutterites, 109

illegal immigrants in the United States, 143–47

illegal immigrants (*continued*)
citizenship for children of, 165
education and social services and, 161–62
estimates of numbers of, 150–54
political representation for, 163–64
Simpson-Rodino-Mazzoli bills and, 167–69
Immigration and Refugee Act of 1952 (McCarran-Walter Act), 144–47
immigration to the United States, 138, 173
alternative demographic projections and, 170–72
bracero program, 143–45
fertility and, 149–50
illegal. *See* illegal immigrants in the United States
impacts of recent, 153–66
economic impacts, 155–60
education and social services, 160–62
labor supply, 155–57, 159–60
political, social, and cultural effects, 162–66
productivity, 156–59
numerical trends in, 147–53
phases of, 138–47
1790 to 1875, 138–40
1875 to 1921, 140–42
1921 to 1968, 142–45
1968 to present, 145–47
refugees, 146–47
Seventy-first American Assembly report on, 239–40, 241
Simpson-Rodino-Mazzoli bills and, 167–69
incentive schemes for reducing fertility, 89–91
income inequality, 22, 79
income, per capita. *See* per capita income
India, 15, 74, 96, 97, 100, 182–83
individual welfare, 74, 75. *See also* welfare economics
Indonesia, 179
industrialized countries. *See* more developed countries (MDCs)
Industrial Revolution, 211–12
infant mortality, 47. *See also* child mortality
innovation, 21
intrauterine contraceptive devices (IUDs), 179, 182
investment, 99–100

Japan, 70

Kenya, 119, 180
Khan, A. R., 73

labor supply, immigration and, 155–57, 159–60
Lapham, Robert, 189
Lee, Ronald, 74, 78
less developed countries (LDCs; developing countries; Third World). *See also* world demographics situation; *and specific topics*
death rates in, 43
economic capacity of, 226–27
expectation of life at birth in, 44–45
intellectual initiative and innovation from, 227–28
mortality trends in, 44–47
urbanization in, 56–58

McCarran-Walter Act (Immigration and Refugee Act of 1952), 144, 147
1965 amendments to, 145–46
malnutrition, fecundity and, 112–14
marriage, delayed, 108–9, 118
Mauldin, Parker, 189
Mazzoli, Romano L., 167
menarche, malnutrition and, 113
Menken, Jane, 5
Mexico, 96, 97, 100–3, 178–79
immigration to the United States from, 143–45

migration, international, 60, 133–38. *See also* immigration to the United States
  alternative demographic projections and, 170–73
more developed countries (MDCs), 212–14
  population growth in, 37–38
  United States policy toward reduced population growth in, 223–28
mortality, 41–48. *See also* infant mortality
  age distribution and, 42–43
  expectation of life at birth as measure of, 43–44
  fertility and, 114–17
  improvements in, 43–47
  projections of demographic changes and, 50, 61, 64–65

National Academy of Sciences (NAS), 72, 80, 87
  1971 report of, 16–19
  1986 report of, 19–24
    on capital supply, productivity, and per capita income, 20–21
    on human capital, 21–22
    on income inequality and employment issues, 22–23
    on individual childbearing decisions, 23
    on innovation, 21
    on resources and the environment, 19–20
nation-state system, international migration and, 135
natural increase, rate of, 39–40, 53–55
natural resources, 69–71
  common property, 82–83
  National Academy of Sciences 1986 report on, 19–20
  Seventy-first American Assembly report on, 234

oral contraception (the pill), 179, 182

Pebley, Anne, 88
per capita income, 15, 17, 20–21, 68–75, 97–99
political consequences of population growth, National Academy of Sciences 1971 report on, 17–18
political representation, for illegal aliens, 163–64
population assistance, U.S., 14, 218–19. *See also* United States population policy
  1984 U.S. policy statement on, 12
  Seventy-first American Assembly report on, 240
Population Dilemma, The (American Assembly), 3–4, 230
population growth. *See also* world demographic situation; *and specific topics*
  Coale-Hoover study on, 14–15, 17
  immigration and, 170–71
  1984 U.S. policy statement on, 9–11
  per capita income and, 68–75
population growth rate:
  in developing countries, 6, 7
  global, 31–34, 36–37, 209–11
    projections beyond 1985, 34–36, 62
  in less developed countries, 37–39
  in more developed countries, 37–38
population policy, 207–9. *See also* United States population policy
  aggregate indicators of, 74–75
  welfare economics and, 75
Preston, Samuel, 23, 25
productivity, immigration and, 156–59

progress, concept of, 228
property rights to land, 84–85
public policy. *See* population policy

refugees, 137, 146–47
reproductive behavior, transition in, 105–32
  future trends, 125–32
  in midtransitional societies, 121–25
  onset of, 114–21
    initial phase of fertility decline, 117–21
    mortality and fertility declines, relationship between, 114–17
    types of transition, 119–21
  in pretransitional (traditional societies), 106–14
reproductive rights, 91–92
resources:
  common property, 86–87
  National Academy of Sciences 1971 report on, 16
retired persons, in industrialized countries, 223–24
Rodgers, Gerry, 88, 90
Rodino, Peter, 146, 167, 169–70
Rosenzweig, Mark, 88

schooling. *See* education
Schuck, Peter H., 165
Schultz, T. Paul, 81
Seventy-first American Assembly, 5
  final report of, 229–41
    abortion, 238–39
    background and introduction, 229–31
    contraceptive research, 236
    economic development, 233–34
    education, 232–33, 237
    family planning, 235–36, 241
    health, 232, 237
    immigration into the United States, 239–40, 241
    programs that go beyond family planning, 238
    recommendations, 240–41
    reduction of high fertility, U.S. policy toward, 231–34
    resources and the environment, 234
  participants in, 242–46
siltation of water resources, 83–86
Simmons, George, 25–26
Simon, Julian, 71, 86
Simpson, Alan K., 166–67
Simpson-Rodino-Mazzoli bills, 167–69
Smith, Rogers M., 165
socialist countries, externalities from childbearing in, 81–82
social services:
  family planning programs and, 194
  immigration and, 160–62
Sprinkel, Beryl, 155
sterility, 107, 113–14
sterilization, 122–23, 181
subfertility, 111

Taeuber, Irene, 70
technological advance, international migration and, 136
Teitelbaum, Michael, 26
Texas Proviso, 144, 167
total fertility rate (TFR):
  definition of, 48
  world trends in, 48–53
traditional societies, reproductive behavior and fertility patterns in, 106–14
  desired family size, failure to achieve, 110–12
  malnutrition and poor health, 112–14
  natural fertility, determinants of, 106–9
transportation systems, 86–87
Trussell, James, 88

unemployment, 23, 80, 101
United Nations, 29, 61, 130

United States:
immigration to the. *See* immigration to the United States
population changes as seen from the, 209–13
United States population policy, 68. *See also* Seventy-first American Assembly, final report of
current debate on, 24–25
major issues in, 213–14
in the 1960s and 1970s, 7
1984 policy statement, 9–13
population assistance, 12
previous policy statements compared, 13–14
toward rapid population growth in less developed countries, 214–23
design and establishment of programs, 220–22
development assistance, 217–18
fear of overpopulation, 214–17
reduced population growth, controversy over support for, 218–20
toward reduced population growth in industrialized nations, 223–28
unwanted pregnancies, 128–29
urbanization, 22–23, 55–58

van de Walle, Etienne, 23

wages:
externalities and, 78–80
real, 73–74
water siltation, 83–86
welfare economics, 68, 75–77
externalities and. *See* externalities
family planning programs and, 88–92, 95
intergenerational relations and, 87–89, 91
widowhood, 109, 117, 118
Willcox, Walter F., 27–28
Wilson, Pete, 169
women:
differential life expectancy between men and, 225
Seventy-first American Assembly report on status of, 236–7
World Bank, 15–16, 61
world demographic situation, 27–66
demographic transition, 40–42
estimation of, 29, 30
fertility and, 41–42, 48–53
future of, 58–66
fertility, 61–62, 66
mortality, 59, 61, 64–65
population size and regional composition, 63–64
rate of population growth, 62
young adult population, changes in, 59–60
mortality and, 41–48
population growth, 27–40, 209–11
less developed countries, 37–39
natural increase, 39–40, 53–55
projections beyond 1985, 34–36
rate of, 31–34, 36–37
urbanization and, 55–58

young adult population, projections of changes in the size of, 59–60

Zaire, 70
Zimbabwe, 121